Island Compliance Risk and the Protocol of Global Finance

T0270793

Kirk Harrison Taitt examines the threat money laundering and terrorist financing pose to Caribbean island nations involved in international financial services, the role of compliance regimes in averting sanctions and the future of these nations at the table of global capital. He addresses and, indeed, positions island nations in a strategic space outside the global clamour, unceasing debate and severe criticism over their bona fides/qualifications to engage in the trillion-dollar industry of offshore finance, alongside their G20 nemeses. He asserts a high ground (ethical) approach as essential to counteracting potential reputational harm.

Throughout the book, Taitt weaves a governance, risk and compliance (GRC) thread in order to speak directly to practitioners and to demonstrate how a strong GRC paradigm at the jurisdictional and institutional levels could be leveraged for competitive advantage.

Among the key recommendations outlined in his *IRIE Mitigation Matrix* are: effective regulatory governance of the jurisdiction's financial system by ensuring conformance with international standards, the deployment of sufficient resources to adequately supervise financial institutions and the promotion of values-based decision-making amongst corporate financial managers and leaders. He also recommends ongoing engagement of the wider civil society to ensure present and future generations of the Caribbean island financial centre (IFC) workforce appreciate the value of personal moral excellence in business and its inextricable link to sustainable development of the IFC sector.

Kirk Harrison Taitt is a senior GRC practitioner who currently serves as the Head of Compliance in a small financial services firm in Barbados. A founding member and past President of the Barbados Association of Compliance Professionals, Kirk is the architect of several training courses in regulatory compliance for the credit union industry. In addition to professional accreditations with the International Federation of Compliance Associations and the Australian GRC Institute, Kirk holds a BSc. in Management and a Master of Philosophy degree in Governance and Public Policy, both from the University of the West Indies. He is married to Juliana and together they are the parents of three "MusTaitteers".

Island Compliance Risk and the Protocol of Global Finance

Governing Evil Money

Kirk Harrison Taitt

Routledge
Taylor & Francis Group

LONDON AND NEW YORK

First published 2019
by Routledge

2 Park Square, Milton Park, Abingdon, Oxfordshire OX14 4RN
52 Vanderbilt Avenue, New York, NY 10017

Routledge is an imprint of the Taylor & Francis Group, an informa business

First issued in paperback 2020

British Library Cataloguing in Publication Data
A catalogue record for this book is available from the British Library

Library of Congress Cataloging-in-Publication Data
A catalog record has been requested for this book

ISBN: 978-1-4724-8335-5 (hbk)
ISBN: 978-0-367-66979-9 (pbk)

Typeset in Bembo
by Taylor & Francis Books

To Claudine

You wrote my first essay
I won the prize
A chance to ride
In the saddle of life
Part of me you will always be
Champion of your legacy

Contents

Illustrations

Figures

Tables

Box

Foreword

As Kirk Taitt, the learned author of this very well written book, has cogently established, the subject of regulation is old, current and multifaceted. It may therefore be a useful point of departure to consider this text within that theme and against that tenor.

In essence, the present day regulatory ethos embodying the capital markets, inclusive of national and international business does not conceptually differ from the regulation of ancient early Egyptian, Greek, Indian and Roman civilisations. Indeed, it is a truism that it did not previously require the realms of paper, sections and subsections of our present regulatory arches. However, in the past, and from time to time in varying forms, it is safe to recognise that norms, privileges and customs, and a commitment to honour, have all served as informal codes of regulation and in broad terms also of supervision.

No doubt this all-pervasive element of regulation, captured so admirably by the author in its contemporary context, is reinforced because the reasons for regulation while variable from time to time, are often generic and to a large degree the same. For not only does it seek to contain the conduct of the professional actors within the system, but at the core, it always attempts to influence both behaviour and beliefs of those amateur and professional players who are in the game, seeking fortune and success – a metaphor mixed but carefully chosen! This all-pervasive view of regulation particularly as it relates to the more complex contemporary economies and societies results in some measure with the use of a regular restatement of the cliché, but also of the reality whereby regulation is often referred to as a "double edged sword" or a "necessary evil".

Even if, lazily, one is not prepared to approach this book's extraordinarily well researched subject matter within a holistic framework, yet its text remains one of immense value, particularly as one navigates the wide range of contemporary regulation. For written with an effective economy of language and beauty of prose, the author has delivered a large basket of goods, regulated carefully by a good sense of fairness, detailed analysis and finely honed accuracy.

Sir Trevor Carmichael, Q.C.

Preface

This is the first of what I hope will be many books. My reason for penning it in the first place was to enhance my work as a compliance operative and to ensure that when I stood up to train expectant staff I would have something to say beyond the norm. What I did not bargain for was the transformation I would experience along the way. I had heard about what might happen, but cannot tell you when the change actually came about. Suffice that it did.

I found myself pausing as I considered those who have gone before me, their toil within their own research space and their efforts at uncovering and explaining reality as they saw it. In the wee hours of the morning I would laugh aloud and occasionally call out to a sleeping wife to listen to what a particular writer said. She cared enough to hear, but never heard.

I fell in love with reading and writing all over again. Like a child I looked forward to receiving the gift (which I bought myself) of a specific writer in book or tablet form. I preferred the book form, but now there is no more space and so I have had to leverage modern-day technology to my advantage; and that is great!

My heart would pound as I sat to write because I knew it was the creative process uncoiling from within, calling for its egress. That same heart would grow quiet when I picked up and pored through an author's endeavour as if out of reverence of his or her effort and completion of a work of art.

As a part-time student at the time, I struggled with the demands of work, family and above all applying the unique mind-set of enquiry, reflection and interpretation. Understanding research jargon took considerable time. Moreover, it took humility to sit at the feet of Dr. Don Marshall and after an hour of engagement leave his office not understanding a word he said. But then to go back …

Strangely enough, what never waned was my motivation to complete the thesis underlying this work. You see, I grew up in the professional regulatory environment of the Central Bank of Barbados. It was there I cultivated a passion for learning and a desire to contribute; inevitable outcomes of working at an institution which is scholarly in orientation and concerned with bettering lives.

Many of my former mentors have since moved on (as have I), retired or, at the time of this book, hold senior roles within the Bank. In some way, I hope this book makes them as proud of me as much as I am thankful to them and their contribution to my development.

P.S. Although some of them have long passed on, I hope one day to meet and talk with those eminent persons who remain alive today, whose work I read, whose thoughts I imagined and whose breath I breathed throughout this exciting journey.

Now that would be something!

Acknowledgement

Is the book done yet? Goodness, how much longer?

Valid questions from the three "MusTaitteers", Johari, Zindzelé and Kaiross.

What's the hold up? How much longer do we have to wait?

Valid questions from family, friends and colleagues. Well … here it is guys!

Much obliged E.J.

Thank you Juliana. Ours is a story in motion.

Island compliance risk

The risk of marginalisation and reputational harm island financial centres encounter as a result of blacklisting, media derision and disempowering social relations; for failure to comply with transnational laws, protocols and other fluctuating expectations of 'G' numerated countries and agenda-driven non-state actors.

... and the dare of the islands to assert their destiny, despite it all!

K. H. Taitt

Introduction: Connecting the dots

"Extraordinarily evil", declared Manhattan Judge Denny Chin describing Bernie Madoff's $65 billion swindle of thousands of trusting investors in a reign of financial trickery spanning several decades. Some of the fraudulent proceeds have been traced to offshore hedge funds located in island nations. Back in 1990 when the insidious global deception perpetrated by the Bank of Credit and Commerce International (BCCI) and its top management began to unfold, there was little indication these two financial tragedies would intersect at the crossroads of offshore finance. As it turned out, BCCI had established legal structures from the outset in multiple offshore jurisdictions, amongst them, spinoffs of Luxembourg entity BCCI SA Ltd, a Netherland Antilles company – Credit and Commerce American Holdings NV and a Cayman Islands enterprise – BCCI Overseas Ltd.

Not only does the prescient connection of these extraordinary events beckon our attention, but when put alongside new-fangled efforts at global taxonomies through base erosion and profit shifting (BEPS) mitigation[1] and the great commotion triggered by the leaked client files known respectively as the Panama and Paradise Papers,[2],[3] they together evoke fresh emotions concerning offshore financial centres (OFCs) and their role in the deployment of global capital.[4]

No doubt, the spiriting away of the proceeds of crime to offshore jurisdictions is amongst the plethora of means by which illicit funds may be concealed or laundered. After all, the more complex the paper trail, the harder it is to identify the true, illegal source of funds. But does this necessarily signify money laundering as being endemic to these centres or, is it just a perception?

In this book, I fuse my experience as a compliance operative in the financial services industry, with my interest in research. I do so to examine how non–compliance with standards governing the prevention and control of money laundering and terrorist financing ("evil money") can conceivably harm the social, economic and political well–being of island nations engaged in the business of offshore finance. I explore whether the harm is real or perceived, and pinpoint whether regulatory governance measures alone, are the answer. Also pondered is the future of these nations at the table of global capital.

The perspectives girding the book coalesce around my belief that sovereignty claims are flattened the moment espying raconteurs of global governance determine that independent shores are being corrupted by evil money. Through the lens of international political economy, I illuminate how the strain of competition, fomented by an insatiable drive to accumulate wealth, ignites risqué behaviours disruptive to the regulatory order. Thus, in order to offset intervention risk it is critical that incumbent governing officials continue to nurture a resonant culture of jurisdictional oversight. Concomitant with this posture is a need for behaviour modification on the part of institutional agents and their retreat to values-based decisions and actions. This stance is borne out in the results of a mixed methods research strategy rooted in functionalist theory.

Mission possible

In the course of this exercise, I felt obliged to address the underlying and extant tensions between onshore and offshore spaces. What is the source of these tensions and is it possible, I asked myself, that these tensions could somehow be resolved? Other (t)issues flowed: to begin with, is money laundering and the factors which give rise to its proliferation really understood? What about the link between money laundering and organised crime and, further, its association with corruption? Also, even if one were to discover evil money as a veritable threat, would it be exclusive to island financial centres (IFCs)? At this point I needed to be certain of what constituted an IFC. I determined that in light of their innovative product and service offering and consistent with their own outlook as catering to a global clientele, as well as to maintain an all-important perspective, I would refer, in this book, to OFCs located in island nations as international financial centres, or alternatively island financial centres (both IFCs).[5]

Another concern of mine was how the business of banking has been impacted by compliance regimes. How have clients fared in the daily scheme of things? Is it realistic to insist on privacy in an age of transnational crime? What of state sovereignty? Is there still such a thing as the state? Or are we in a new era of statehood? What does that look like?

The roguish behaviour of some professionals in the financial world is concerning to most. So too are the apparent lapses in the policies and procedures of financial institutions. Yet even with incarcerations, unprecedented fines and other sanctions, there is more of the same. Is this simply an issue of poor risk management; lax board oversight even? Or might it have something to do with the capitalist system itself?

With a perpetual spotlight on OFCs, what is the role of regulation and regulatory officials in these spaces? Is this role any different to similar roles in onshore localities? How do impacted island nations view rule adherence in the first place? In other words, what is their motivation for compliance?

Cut and thrust of competition

In the post-Bretton Woods[6] era and certainly within the last three decades (1988–2018), Caribbean and other IFCs have risen to prominence as key providers of international financial services. However, despite a demonstrated ability to bench-press beyond their business weight so to speak, and a clear contribution to international business fare, the fidelity of island states is often called into question. An embedded negative perception of these locales has made an already uphill battle even more strenuous and the prize of respect more elusive. On top of that, as a country's most viable asset in a competitive business environment, reputation can quickly be turned into a potent liability, rendering it both difficult to manage and defend against an apparatus of global finance operating at discursive levels.

Amongst the weapons of slow destruction – and these ones assuredly do exist – are well choreographed, authoritative reports of standard-setters, editorials, articles and otherwise widely-read assertive journalistic disquisitions; extra-regional television commentaries and spirited debates on globally watched networks; and the list goes on. Ensconced in this discourse is the systematic "tax haven" branding, which makes ripe fodder for a sometimes partisan news media whose coverage is careful to focus on the sensational – tax evasion, money laundering, bank failures, organised crime and corruption. Countervailing voices which seek to promote the value and contribution of these centres to global finance are easily undermined against this intransigent system of concentrated power (Hampton and Christensen, 2002).

So convincing can the vitriol be that the non-discerning could forget these centres are sovereign nations in their own right and at a fundamental level possess, as with larger nations, a right of self-determination. Even though the extent to which state autonomy in the traditional sense can be held onto in a connected world is debatable, surely the ability to chart one's *fiscal* course – essentially deciding how money may be legitimately derived and best applied – is the responsibility of duly elected officials. We can argue though that retention of state autonomy in the present dispensation may correlate somewhat to the size of a nation's economy and magnitude of its surplus/deficit; the depth of its natural resources, level of investment in science and technology; the street smarts of its intelligence agencies and political influence amongst the global community of nations. Oh and how could we forget the extent of its nuclear capability! All these traits when combined help to tilt the idea of sovereignty and the retention thereof in favour of powerful, industrial nations. Be that as it may, let us revisit this notion a bit later in the book.

How is it possible?

For now, it suffices to wink at the idea of controls within international financial services – not considering the specific location from which these services are delivered – and the role these checks and balances are generally observed to play in offsetting various risks.

I say this because the focus on IFCs could also blur the significant control lapses occurring in the backyard of the very proponents of global regulatory compliance. To wit, that Madoff's deception, though copping a meritorious 150 years in the slammer thereby "translating society's rage into a number",[7] could have transpired in a modern-day environment of tight regulation raises serious questions. Furthermore, that a top oversight agency such as the Securities and Exchange Commission (SEC), legislatively empowered to maintain the integrity of the US stock market, could have missed the underlying suspicious activity, is also worrying. Stepping back, the BCCI fiasco occurred, admittedly, in far less stringent circumstances. Yet it is almost forgivable on a comparative basis in light of the nascence of consolidated banking supervision at the time. Nonetheless, it still leaves you wondering if regulation *by itself* may be overrated as a control mechanism. Surely, the frequency and scale of sanctions that continue to be meted out across the financial industry point in that direction.

Tarnish and feather: the movie

Legislative and regulatory reform played out across the political screens of Caribbean island states in the years spanning 1995–2005. During this period, state arms were twisted into effecting material changes to their national financial framework to account for the prevention and control of money laundering. Also simultaneously arising during this time was extensive discourse around so-called harmful tax practices by small island states.

The harmful here being an offered lower tax regime aimed at attracting business on a competitive basis. Of note is that revision to legislation aligning with what were, in fact, unprecedented conformance expectations, was carried out under threat of sanction. Countries which did not respond to the mass diffusion of these new policies by making the necessary adjustments were promptly disclosed to a global public in a list of non-co-operative countries and territories (on the money laundering side) and "blacklist" on the tax side; all blacklists nonetheless. Thus was ushered in a new era of global compliance risk management with the unholstered side-arm of intimidation used to elicit sovereign state surrender.

Unmistakably, fallout from the negative impact on the name and reputation of the maligned jurisdiction was too high a cost to bear especially for small island nations. Thus, with the international community looking on, there appeared to have been little choice these nations felt they had, but to comply.

It was a master stroke by a newly deputised sheriff in the Financial Action Task Force (FATF), an arm of the Organisation for Economic Co-operation and Development (OECD) which at the time comprised a subset of the now G20 countries.[8] Although having neither input from nor the backing of small island states at the time of roll out, the assent of ranking nations proved enough to set in train the task of getting the rest of the world (at least 170 additional countries) on board. An empowered FATF could now roll out its policy instrument, that is to say, Forty Recommendations (40 Recs.) to guide nations on how they should go about protecting their financial systems against money laundering.[9]

Since that time (on the tax side) there have been other lists of similar and different hues (grey, white) which have emerged. Although their timing is unpredictable the objective is the same: to draw attention to sovereign practices deemed inconsistent with acceptable standards as prescribed by a handful of countries. Once recalcitrant states engage the necessary reforms or express a commitment to do so and still, within agreed timelines, sinus rhythm obtains. As it stands, the notion of unfair tax competition appears to have been mollified with the implementation of information exchange protocols between and among agreeing countries. At least until the goal post moves again. And so it did in June 2016 with the establishment of the OECD's professed Inclusive Frame-work, the foremost aim of which is to put an end to tax revenue risk deemed to be occurring through the actions of BEPS.

No doubt, the effect of blacklisting over time has yielded outcomes sufficient to encourage divergent states on the US mainland to join the fray, amongst them Chicago, Connecticut and Montana. Their 2015 declarations of intent to tax foreign sourced income acquired in *state designated* tax havens is, presumably, to address unsubstantiated claims of tax base erosion according to Frieden and Hogroian (2016). On observation though and as far as we can tell, no change appears to be required on the part of branded nations. Helpful is the absence of any bilateral diplomatic relations between sovereign island nations and particular non-sovereign US municipalities. This is sufficiently off-setting for the moment. Rather, the effort seems aimed at alerting foreign subsidiaries of US companies of some form of tax liabilities outside federal double taxation arrange-ments. In terms of the apparent lack of concern of the use of the negative "haven" label, it is not inconsistent with disaffected jurisdictions when it comes to dealing with tax matters in general. However, by choosing to overlook formalised tax information exchange agreements established between island offshore spaces and the US federal government, in my view, this undermines the spirit of international relations. This ill-considered action merits federal intervention and correction. That said, we should not hold our breath. What these unilateral actions highlight, though, is the arbitrary and self-serving manner in which blacklisting can be applied. While the threat in this instance seems aimed at disincentivising the US taxpayer from leveraging offshore financial services, there remains the subtlety of disquiet and suspicion projected onto smaller states that their products are illegitimate, their services fishy and hence should be avoided completely.

The advent of blacklisting of self-governing nations by individual states of the United States follows on the heels of another threat; this time in the form of a potential 30% withholding sanction on US-sourced income for countries and their financial institutions' non-compliance with the Foreign Account Tax Compliance Act (FATCA). Avoidance of sanction under FATCA is only possible through sovereign sign up to an inter-governmental agreement (IGA) with the Internal Revenue Service (IRS). The IGA allows for the upload of financial statistics on qualifying US persons either directly to national tax authorities or alternatively to the IRS itself.

Operating external to the traditional state machinery and parallel to this expedition of blacklisting and sanction is an organised system of institutional expertise and interpretation delivered through financial operatives and rating agencies. The emergence of these see-mingly expert voices schooled in the science of high finance reflects an unprecedented congeries of non-state actors whose soothsaying must now be integrated within the island state's daily governance activities. These voices execute their mission within a self-defining aural space with prophetic utterances capable of influencing global investment consciences irrespective of sovereignty claims or proven political processes. Against such overwhelming discourse and unproven competence, an unsure trust is induced from a jargon weary cli-entele. For IFCs, most of which lack retaliatory power, the impact of non-state actors should not be underestimated, but rather factored into national threat matrices.

Here or there?

Imperceptibly, the idea of *onshore* and *offshore* has been both defined *by* and *in relation to* traditional banking centres. Caribbean and other islands doing business in the realm of international financial services are deemed "off the shores" of a larger geographic main-land. Although within proximity, they remain operationally distinct organisms despite the retention of crown dependency in some cases. The mainland itself plays host to myriad international financial services to wide-ranging clientele across the resident and non-resident spectra. But even before the association of finance with offshore, the idea that radio signals could be refracted across borders, penetrating the airwaves of sovereign countries thereby allowing for external entrepreneurial broadcasts to new markets at competitive prices, was a prototype of a new international business model which required a re-scripting of the idea of statehood (Palan, 2003).

The notion of "offshoring" is also linked to deregulating activities of larger economies in the 1980s–1990s when the limitations of doing business were eased and external doors opened to support international expansion. Over time, the offshore rhetoric has been consistent enough to become embedded in the culture of global finance. Still, the sen-sitivity of these so-labelled spaces to the slightest of criticism has made rebranding efforts as bona fide providers of international financial services tough.

However, to better appreciate the challenges faced by OFCs it would be useful to understand what traditionally obtained in the operating zone of their nemesis, the *onshore* financial centre. Immediately, dominant centres such as London, New York and Tokyo come to mind. As the older, more experienced hubs involved in the business of financial capital acquisition, conversion, disbursement and exchange (World Bank and IMF, 2005) over considerable time, they have had the opportunity to develop a tried and trusted business brand. As such, until the emanation of new offshore alternatives, these particular onshore arenas have been the theatres of choice for a patronage not constrained by residence status. Indeed, it is within this domain that the wealthy or otherwise surplussed investor put up for sale his or her capital surfeit to institutional lenders, cash-seeking governments, business enterprise of all types or their intermediaries. Within this competitive context and in the spirit of true capitalism it was inevitable that new competition would emerge to take advantage of interstices. Obvious to the small island state and ripe for exploitation was the tax rate.

Size does not matter

Innovation and expansion are elements built into capitalist economies irrespective of size and represent a natural outworking of the nature of business. Objectives to increase market share, augment one's client base and explore new business opportunities all form an intrinsic part of a company's success. On an aggregate basis, the resulting creation of jobs has the potential to stimulate new output levels, influencing national productivity measures and, in the end, positively impact a country's gross domestic product. The prospect of lower corporate levies means potentially more funds available for investment and thus profit by any measurement. And this is how island jurisdictions, small in size though they may be, have been able to mount a serious challenge for global capital. Competing mostly on the basis of lower taxes has been instrumental in attracting finance away from traditional banking domains. And since the natural response of a competitor is to at least match its arch rival, installing tax friendly sites onshore would be a competitive strategy aimed at neutralising a rising offshore class. This, however, is irrelevant given the anteceding presence of onshore tax enclaves long before those in the islands ever emerged.

So, in the absence of an effective countervailing tactic, it was at this juncture that the marriage of money laundering and tax evasion took place in the absence of witnesses – that is to say, proof. Related discourse began to unfold, promoting the notion that preferential tax regimes were not only unfairly competitive, but where unsupported by an appropriate regulatory environment, could facilitate the concealment of criminally derived monies alongside legitimate business. In this sense, the publication of the FATF's list of non-co-operative countries and territories may, in some quarters, appear to have been justified. In fact, if you look at it purely from the standpoint of potential investors wishing to make good business decisions, then it is reasonable they be afforded access to appropriate information. At the same time, however, the harshness of the action put island jurisdictions on the back-foot, with little or no corrective recourse, except of course, to fall in line. The damage was already done. An embedding of perception that illicit activity was intrinsic to island offshore finance was formed in an ethereal space, so that although:

a   the last maligned nation state was removed from the FATF's list of non-co-operative countries and territories since June 2003 having engaged the necessary regulatory reforms;

b the majority of Caribbean nations have been, as at the moment of writing, deemed largely compliant by the OECD's Global Forum on Transparency and Exchange of Information for tax purposes;

c FATCA reporting mechanisms under formal IGAs have been activated by a substantial number of Caribbean governments; and

d there is an espoused commitment on the region's part to implement the OECD's common reporting standards framework,

the initial stigma, coupled with the historical uncertainty of what so-called offshore finance actually involves, is still haunting.

Fiscal choices

Furthermore, such ignominy could be stirred up again by an overzealous international media keen to exploit the slightest hints of jurisdictional non-compliance. Even beyond compliance, external media power can also be co-opted to negatively portray sovereign states where these states make choices in their own national interest, for example, to charge or not to charge taxes on offshore type business activities. In fact, the attention accorded the reformation of tax havens by Britain's former Prime Minister Gordon Brown and his then G20 colleagues at an April 2009 summit[10] when juxtaposed with the 2017 reintroduction of legislation in the US Congress to restrict the use of tax havens to minimise tax obligations,[11] although several years apart, goes to show the ongoing, high level debates that abound on the matter.

In April 2016, another former British Minister – David Cameron – while promulgating strong views against so-called tax havens, lost his voice when the leaked Panama Papers disclosed he was a beneficiary of the sale proceeds of shares held in an offshore trust, set up years before, by his late father.[12] Within a broader context of ongoing global debate on the merits of OFCs, the Panama Papers themselves reflect a type of archetypal role these centres play: on the upside as a means of deploying the generally accepted wealth management tool of tax minimisation; but on the downside, as an often unwitting participant in tax evasion activities and the stashing of illicit wealth.

Moreover, the $780 million fine slapped on the Swiss banking giant UBS by the IRS in February 2009 for assisting close to 20,000 American clients in hiding their assets to avoid Uncle Sam's levies did not augur well for an already sullied image of OFCs. Most notably, this sanction followed closely on the heels of the exposure of two billion-dollar Ponzi schemes with links to island nations. As a matter of fact, in the context of the Sir Allen Stanford $8 billion fraud, a *Forbes* editor[13] insisted on the untrustworthiness of Caribbean finance, citing the laundering of criminal proceeds, secrecy, and weak regulation and supervision. This, alongside alluring, but dishonest marketing of high interest-yielding financial products, was deemed responsible for steering apparently gullible US investors away from the reliability of their own trusted onshore space.

It is incendiary comments such as these which seek to typecast IFCs as wild and financially deceitful by promoting money laundering dogma, to be exact: stolen, hidden loot, admixed with ultra secrecy, questionable standards and, by implication, a weak political will to change (Marshall, 2007). In poetic contrast, the United States is overtly portrayed as a haven of financial safety and protection. Of course, the 2007 sub-prime mortgage crisis which transuded the "safe haven" of US shores and which, incidentally, threw most of the modern world's economies into recession, proved otherwise.

Derisking

Marginalization has projected even deeper into island livelihood with the unexpected severing/reduction of correspondent banking ties. Under pressure from homeland regulators to address their risk profile, US financial institutions – which have provided mutually beneficial intermediation for over a century – have determined the potential sanctions and reputational risk they have to face in doing business with a designated high risk region as exceeding the financial benefit of retaining its business. Apparently, therefore, for strictly risk management purposes these entities have chosen to cut off or, in some instances, restrict a vital life-giving service to regional economies.

By present-day risk measurement standards the correspondent banking arrangement would have been denoted a concentration risk in the first place, for which mitigants (chief among them diversification) should have been implemented to offset its latent reality. But that is easier said than done, given the dollar's dominance in international trade. And while it is certainly not within the purview of correspondent banks to neither support the development nor indeed the sustainability of island (Caribbean) societies – much like it is not the responsibility of island nations to consider the well-being of onshore nations when it comes to deciding at what rate, in what form and upon whom of its citizenry taxes should be levied – it is important to understand the implication of their unanticipated actions.

The bulk of commercial trade in products and services has historically been conducted with US/North American companies. How will payment for goods and services be rendered to a US supplier in the circumstances? How are international investment flows expected to be received? How will foreign debts be serviced; profits, royalties and dividend payments effected; transfers of remittances engaged? What about educational costs for children studying in US colleges? Of course, an easy way out is also the potentially more costly: replacement correspondent financial institutions in recognising the dependency factor may opt to increase the price of doing business to marginalised countries. But then, would concentration risk be eliminated or merely relocated?

Setting the field of play

This initial exposé of issues creates our *mise en scène*: those emerging island nations of the English speaking Caribbean which provide financial services to external institutional and personal clientele (non-residents). According to mainstream thought, the base from which these services are delivered is the OFC.

Over 40% of offshore banks are located in island nations of the Caribbean region. The remaining 60% are flung across Europe, Asia and the Pacific, and Africa and the Middle East, respectively (Errico & Musalem, 1999). In terms of their global impact it is the Bahamas, Bermuda, the British Virgin Islands (BVI) and the Cayman Islands that are the more renowned jurisdictions. In fact, as non-G20 countries, these centres' prominence is underscored in the March 2018 Global Financial Centres Index. Out of the 110 nations assessed, the Cayman Islands ranked at number 22, Bermuda at number 36, the Bahamas at number 59 and the BVI at number 60.

Drawing from their experience in conducting financial sector assessments, the World Bank and the IMF conclude that in general OFCs are locations "where the bulk of financial sector activity is offshore on both sides of the balance sheet" (World Bank and IMF, 2005, p. 51). In short, the source of funds is externally derived and applied to the primary benefit of *non-resident* counterparties. In respect of the services provided, these are specialist in orientation and range from regular banking activities to asset management, trust and estate planning, insurance services and the use of special purpose vehicles. These services are undergirded by a discretionary strategy mindfully leveraged to appeal to investors. OFCs in turn derive benefit from this type of business activity by way of revenue yields from annual licence fees, corporation taxes, employment opportunities for locals and the attendant transfer of knowledge. Traditionally and transactionally speaking, OFCs are neither regarded as capital sources nor investment reservoirs, but strictly as intermediation vehicles facilitating the movement of funds (Lane and Milesi-Ferretti, 2010).

So, what next?

Having laid the foundation, I move to further distil the initial concerns highlighted in an extended discussion in Chapter 1. Next, I do a bit more digging across Chapters 2–4 as I attempt to forge a path out of the darkness, as it were, that allowed for some measure of contribution to both knowledge and practice. Thereafter, I followed my instincts to develop, in Chapter 5, a frame of reference within which I believed the issues raised could best be solved. Here I also explained how I went about securing the necessary information for further analysis. The real tinkering, though, happens throughout Chapters 6–8. This is where I present and work through extensive insight gleaned from multiple sources. Concluding comments naturally follow in Chapter 9. Lastly, in order to address the challenge IFCs encounter in maintaining pace with ever moving compliance targets and associated sanctions risks, I include a bonus Chapter 10 where I introduce the *Island Risk Exposure (IRIE) Mitigation Matrix*.

So, with our cross-checks complete and seatbelts fastened, we are now ready for take-off!

Notes

1 The base erosion and profit shifting (BEPS) project is an initiative of the Organisation for Economic Co-operation and Development (OECD) and G20 countries aimed at developing measures to align taxation with the location of primary economic activity and value creation. A global consensus-based set of tax rules are also under development. Further information may be found at https://www.oecd-ilibrary.org/taxation/oecd-g20-base-erosion-and-profit-shifting-project_23132612.
2 The "Panama Papers" refer to a set of leaked files of specialist offshore financial services provider, Panamanian Law firm Mossack Fonseca. The documents have been a centre of controversy since their exposure in 2016, and shed light on the offshore holdings of various individuals including politicians and their families, as well as celebrities and global conglomerates.
3 Similar in origination to its Panamanian equivalent, the "Paradise Papers" are a trove of documents relating to the confidential offshore investments of numerous high profile individual and corporate clients, held (mostly) on the books of Bermuda offshore law firm Appleby. The information was leaked to the German press in 2017 and is the subject of ongoing analysis and investigation by journalists worldwide.
4 The term "offshore financial centre" (OFC) is used interchangeably with the terms "international financial centre" and "island financial centre" (both IFC). This is also true of the terms "international finance" and "offshore finance". The retention of both terms is useful for ongoing discussion and ultimate reconciliation.
5 The use of the "offshore" nomenclature is still necessary throughout the book and for various purposes (e.g. to accurately reflect referenced literature, prevailing thought, etc.).
6 In July 1944, a total of 44 nations assembled at a United Nations Monetary and Financial Conference in Bretton Woods, New Hampshire. Coming immediately following the end of

the Second World War, the objective was to put in place the framework for a new international monetary system. The conference gave birth to the International Monetary Fund (IMF) and the International Bank for Reconstruction and Development. See the US Department of State archives at https://2001-2009.state.gov/r/pa/ho/time/wwii/98681.htm

7 See B. Weiser, Judge explains 150 year sentence for Madoff. *New York Times*, 28 June 2011.

8 The original Group of Nations comprised seven countries: Canada, France, Germany, Italy, Japan, the United Kingdom and the United States of America.

9 Following the terrorist attack on New York's World Trade Center on 11 September 2001, an additional nine special recommendations were introduced specifically dealing with controls around terrorist financing. In February 2012, those special recommendations were absorbed into an expanded 40 Recommendations. The updated Recs. of February 2018 include measures aimed at mitigating the proliferation of weapons of mass destruction.

10 See L. Elliott, Brown plans global scrutiny of tax havens. *The Guardian*, 23 March 2009.

11 Stop Tax Haven Abuse Act. Available at: https://www.congress.gov/bill/115th-congress/house-bill/1932

12 See R. Booth, H. Watt & D. Pegg, David Cameron admits he profited from father's offshore trust. *The Guardian*, 7 April 2016.

13 See R. Lenzner, Lessons from the big scams. *Forbes*, 2 July 2009.

References

Errico, L. & Musalem, J., 1999. Offshore banking: An analysis of micro and macro prudential issues. *IMF Working Papers 99/5*.

Frieden, K. & Hogroian, F., 2016. State tax haven legislation: A misguided approach to a global issue [Online]. Available at: https://www.cost.org/globalassets/cost/stri/studies-and-reports/tax-haven-study-final-3-14-16.pdf [accessed 30 July 2017].

Hampton, M. & Christensen, J., 2002. Offshore pariahs? Small island economies, tax havens, and the re-configuration of global finance. *World Development*, 30(9), pp. 1657–1673.

Lane, P. & Milesi-Ferretti, G., 2010. Cross-border investment in small international financial centers. *IMF Working Paper 10/38*.

Marshall, D., 2007. The new international financial architecture and Caribbean OFCs: Confronting financial stability discourse. *Third World Quarterly*, 28(5), pp. 917–938.

Palan, R., 2003. *The offshore world: Sovereign markets, virtual places and nomad milllionaires*. New York: Cornell University Press.

World Bank & IMF, 2005. *Financial sector assessment: A handbook*. Washington DC: World Bank.

1 Relieving congestion one tissue at a time

Prologue

Modern-day variations notwithstanding, banks of yore were traditionally the rallying point for borrowers and lenders. It is no wonder then that these money moving trustees have found themselves at the navel of the work involved in procedurally distilling evil money from good.

Onshore and offshore obstipations

Due to a deficit of funds for commercial or other purposes, borrowers would seek out financing opportunities to assist with closure of operational gaps. Lenders, on the other hand, were willing to supply excess funds to a responsible repository mostly for safe-keeping purposes as long as they were able to access them again given reasonable notice (Whitehead, 1969). These dual needs were mathematically satisfied by way of an inter-mediation process which allowed for disbursement of funds over the period required, but at a cost to the borrower. Simultaneously, the lender was rewarded for temporarily parting with funds. The broking entity also developed a capacity to facilitate commercial related payments, a vital need for traders of the day. This early intermediation principle would later be reflected in a central banking model, the major differences being in cli-entele and economic influence. A central bank's clients are those institutions it is legally required to regulate and whose operations it is required to supervise. Most importantly, through its open market operations in the banking system a central bank is able to influence the supply of money throughout an economy, and in so doing enable the monetary policy of presiding governments.

As with other types of business, successful banking is built in part on reputation. This intangible commodity is of critical importance to clients as they would want assurance their money is safe and accessible to them on demand. Indeed, where depositors have a sense – even if that sense is unfounded – that their money is not, in fact, safe it can trigger the rapid withdrawal of funds or, in cases of severe reputational loss, a run on the bank. By extension, an international institutional lender may also consider that its dis-bursed funds may be at risk of non-repayment. In such instances, demand clauses may be invoked and appended security leveraged. Worst yet, there is always the option to refuse to engage in future transactions with a country due to the perceived high risk involved.

The erosion of depositor and/or lender confidence as a result of the money laundering stigma can therefore potentially affect a country's or a bank's ability to attract and retain legitimate capital (Masciandaro, 2004). Bank solvency may also be impacted where large amounts of illicit funds are suddenly transferred outwards. This is particularly so in the case of the Caribbean due to the open and dependent nature of their economies. It would therefore suggest that a single market environment could itself attract several risks: the movement of criminal elements and their enterprise across market territories; financial company mergers or acquisitions where the bona fides of inherited clients are not known; or the appended institution may, itself, be a criminal operation. There may also be regulatory failings where the absence of effective oversight and ongoing due diligence on shareholders and directors could result in impropriety at the highest level of governance.

The overarching point to be made here is that given the plight of small island nations to find alternative means of earning foreign exchange, they are by now fully aware of the importance of engaging a robust regulatory framework if national reputations are to be maintained. What is therefore left to be assessed is the extent to which national motivations to comply are linked to the desire to protect jurisdictional reputation.

Commercial evolution

If we understand this original configuration of banking, the importance of legislation in guiding behaviour and the reputational pillar on which the tradition is built, we could perhaps glean a better understanding of its offshore derivative and the exponential evolution of commerce as a result of financial globalisation or "financialisation".

While offshore banking is essentially a financial service, it does have its own distinctions. For example, although regulated, offshore financial institutions are not used as a conduit for government monetary policy. Their activities are also more extensive in scope. Generally, there is no restriction around reserve requirements or interest rate charges and since clientele are non-residents of the jurisdiction in which their assets are located, transactions are mostly conducted in foreign-denominated currency (Blum et al., 1998). The implication here is that although there may be a regulatory reporting requirement, there is in fact less sovereign influence over offshore financing activities.

The globalisation component of the equation, according to dominant discourse refers to the unprecedented level of cross-border engagement and interaction between and among people, business and countries. This is made possible – chiefly – by the lowering of trade barriers and the development of faster and more efficient means of transportation whose capacity allow for the movement of greater volumes of goods and people. Of course, all of this is underpinned by extraordinary technological innovation.

However, when we think of financialisation, we transverse the heart of global markets and the resonant, fiscal ingenuity and agility to engineer spin-off products masterminded in a virtual framework of risk and return (Beck, 2002; Langley, 2004, Blackburn, 2006). The c(overt) strategic intention is to maximise shareholder value (Marshall, 2008, pp. 357–358). This type of innovation, while made possible in the free market system of capitalism is premised on equations purporting to predict the future in such a way as to engender present-day confidence. It is also this type of innovation which adds to the complexity and perplexity of neo-finance and the tendency of ordinary folk to yield its control to third parties (Marshall, 2008, p. 362).

Hedge funds, futures, financial haggling and speculation by finance experts (aka "quants") on what the markets may or may not do lead one to agree with the characterisation of the workings and operations of the contemporary international financial system as "casino capitalism" (Strange, 1997). Contributions by Neal in 1990, Germaine in 1997 and de Goede in 2005 as cited in Marshall (2008, p. 364) note the linkage of high finance to gambling as being consistent with historical norms. Risk-oriented models of the day were applied to offset unknown future impacts. With this apparent ability to quantify financial risk taking and therefore provide greater tangibility to outcomes, the door was opened to the technical validation of a new subdivision of finance (Marshall, 2008, p. 364).

Onshore and offshore disputations also resonate in philosophical outlook. The advent of the latter represents a fundamental change; a shift describes Wallerstein (1974) of financial capital away from the "core" (industrial nations) to the "periphery" (weaker and therefore non-comparable) smaller nations. Following this assertion, if say half of offshore capital is "housed" in or simply passes through island financial centres (periphery nations), it could create a sense of powerlessness, that is to say, a perceived loss of control over what might otherwise be taxable income for onshore nations. Competitively speaking, therefore, some kind of tension is likely to emerge. And in the spirit of capitalist competition for one's share of the proverbial pie, it is expected that firms (countries in this case) and/or their representative cartels would engage actions deemed appropriate for the achievement of market objectives. Typically, competition on price, product and place undergirded by a spirited marketing strategy would be a good starting point to attract business away from one's rivals. But then, up come the politics of compliance and suddenly governing actors shift back to being frightened competitors. How could lost business be regained through a traditional marketing strategy except the marketing instrument is tinged with the psychology of distrust and doubt? For, once issues of integrity are raised and indeed formed in public minds, the bona fides – that is to say state character in the form of qualifications, reputation, ability, facility and skills – are immediately brought into question. In fact the very notion of a "harmful tax competitor"[1] immediately demarcates and alienates the one said to be doing the apparent harm. Thus with the seed of scepticism sown, a would-be investor is now forced to examine the trade-off between doing business with a country of questionable repute and one which is untainted. Depending on the option taken there is the risk of losing one's own access to the bounty of international business and the important relationships that characterise the trading community.

Noting the Harmful Tax Competition Initiative as essentially a means of economic domination which undermines international rules and practice, Sanders makes the point that Caribbean IFCs in particular were in fact encouraged by their former colonists to engage other options, specifically financial services, to support building out their small economies and "maintaining democracy and civil order in their societies" (Sanders, 2002, p. 326). Evidently, OECD countries could not portend the fiscal impact of their then innocent suggestions on their own economies and the formidable threat that would emerge from previously subjugated nations as regards the redistribution of the wealth of nations.

Now let me be clear: as a compliance officer myself, I believe accountability mechanisms are necessary to curb unwanted behaviours. In fact, while not always fully compliant themselves, I note the bent of onshore nations is to promote compliance as a minimum standard for players in globalised markets. Standards are benchmarks against which conformance is measured to promote order in our various contexts.

However, in my view a blurring emerges when competitors assume a structural position of oversight, insisting and indeed creating, unilaterally, a rule-based framework aimed at "levelling the playing field". Now pray tell, how can a playing field be levelled without engagement of players on the field? Really? The conflict of interest reeks and the abuse of power leaps out when your primary opponents are deliberately excluded from the rule and decision-making process. What ever became of good, old fashioned, independent oversight?

In order to quell potential opportunistic conduct of state actors in circumstances of this nature, Masciandaro (2004) speaks of deliberately embedding offsetting measures in a broadened financial policy-making agenda. Outside addressing the problem of bias, this posture is felt to better support the efficiency of global financial flows and resource allocation. It is also the kind of thinking consistent with the macro-level regulatory oversight strategy of Keohane (2001) and Scholte (2002), as well as standard setting bodies (e.g. the World Bank and the IMF).

Self governance vs. selfishness

Whereas limited natural resources can place offshore nations at a comparative economic disadvantage, the importance of self-governance does not suddenly dissipate because of physical resource limitations. Instead, what is required to advance beyond such strictures is state analysis, social engagement, a legal framework and, above all, political will. This process of seeking and fostering alternatives quite rightly falls within the decision-making capacity and domain of an autonomous state (Antoine, 2001; Hartman, 2002; Rahn, 2002). Traditionally, there is no consulting between and among countries regarding in-state taxation frameworks. And neither should there need to be. From whence therefore, comes the apparent tension?

Arguing that EU member states of the OECD are the highest and most widely taxed, such that people are "quite literally taxed from the cradle to the grave and beyond",[2] Sanders (2002, p. 330) notes that high income tax yields tend to be used up in national defence projects and ever increasing social liabilities of these nations. The latter is compounded by longer life expectancy against shrinking contributions by eligible (some of whom are unemployed) members of the work force. The hunt for additional revenue sources is therefore constant and in the absence of creative economic options, the first port of call is ordinarily state cash, namely more taxes. Yet, notes Sanders, there is a limit if incumbent governments want to survive upcoming election cycles (Sanders, 2002, p. 330).

This erosion of an administration's revenue stream may be considered a factor of both political opportunity and consumer choice in a competitive environment. That said, how can it be mistaken as a failure of offshore finance providers to assist industrial nations in maintaining their tax base? It is uncertain if the shoe was on the other foot so to speak and onshore nations had adopted low tax regimes from the get go whether there would be an issue of harmful tax competition; likely not. True capitalist competition is incomplete without venturing into the area of taxation for advantage and this may have been an oversight on the part of industrial nations (Sanders, 2002). Understandably, though, taxation, even as a competitive strategy may have been far from the governing minds of OECD countries. The more immediate of concerns was finding an avenue for excess productive capacity as this had so outsized benchmark levels required for social sustenance that exploring new markets was the next economical and indeed logical step.

In short, a place to sell one's goods at higher prices for greater corporate yield was too alluring to look the other way. With hindsight, this trade-based response to solving the ultimate problem of tax competition – in essence, a kind of economic self-de-regulation – could conceivably have been a strategic error on the part of OECD (onshore) nations, exacerbated not merely by failure to address the fundamentals of their own tax regime, but also the high-handed manner in which wholesale change was sought (Sanders, 2002, p. 331).

In contrast, the virtue of small islands in clinging to a low tax regime in its international financial services space as a primary drawing card is rooted more in livelihood than anything else. It is, indeed, more of a competitive advantage and thus a strength which should be exploited for maximum benefit. There is, after all, neither moral nor legal obligation for IFCs to assist onshore states in their fiscal revenue-generation processes (Antoine, 2001).

At the same time, little argument can be made against the need for operative rules which not only set a framework conducive to good business, but also promote fairness. This seems to be the underlying premise for the OECD's BEPS project. Consumer protection and deterring the abuse of the financial system by the criminally minded must remain high agenda items. It is this felonious leveraging of the global payments and conversion network that is of particular import to our debate and to which we now turn.

Anti-money laundering policy diffusion

Paradoxically, the lifting of currency controls under neo-trade liberalism also creates the need for regulatory management over transactions (Levi-Faur, 2008; Alldridge, 2001; Vogel, 1996). In the same way, international rule making is deemed necessary to curb money laundering in light of relatively easier access to world markets than before (Alldridge, 2003). The fact is that huge volumes of capital are transacted in this vast, virtual space, and provide the criminal minded with ample, parallel opportunity to launder or hide ill-gotten gains, thereby concealing their true source – crime. Once funds are successfully concealed in the banking system criminals may access them again to further finance more illicit or illegal activity including the trafficking of drugs and terrorism, considered by many as two of the most powerful forces against human development in the new millennium.

It would not be uncommon for reasonable persons to wish to contribute to the stemming of evil money flows particularly if there is ultimate common societal value to uncovering financial crime. However, far from volunteering to be part of the army drawn up to fight what is supposed to be a common foe, there is the unfortunate situation where western institutional powers perceived coercion to have been the only option available to them to rally an all-important global support. Could it be that the underlying premise for "going to war" in the first place was faulty and therefore to avoid the inevitable challenge to the decision, force was deemed the most effective option? Or could it simply be the exercise of a perceived entitlement by a few, to make decisions for the many, even if such decisions were effected without wider and appropriate consultation with the latter?

Coercion or not, the vast majority of sovereign states have adopted similar anti-money laundering (AML) regimes and this despite their geography, economic power or social makeup (Sharman, 2008). The cost of reform includes a new line item in national budgets to account for disbursements to specialised agents responsible for maintaining performance standards and similar corporate expenditure to attract and maintain personnel skilled in compliance architecture and the manning of compliance stations. A third, though unquantifiable cost, is the forced price paid by the financial services client in the loss of personal privacy. What would make such heavy investment in AML worth it would be confirmation of their efficacy in the risk mitigation process (Sharman, 2008, pp. 651–653).

Discourse of course

The significant question is how could a handful of nations as represented, in this case, by the OECD's FATF so successfully influence the adoption of AML policy standards on a global scale? The answer, we have come to realise, sits snugly and subtly within a power dynamic aimed and shot across multiple bows to signal the dual intention of moving in a self-considered direction whilst also warning of escalation potential where a compliant response is not forthcoming. In the interim, the shaping of reality, essentially what is perceived by external observers to be true, is undertaken to strengthen the position of the self-referencing protagonist. We see these actions fleshed out in the work of certain supranational institutions, the recurring rhetoric of ministerial and senatorial surrogates, widely read literature, imagery and organised systems of expertise which give further voice and meaning to the intended change (Hulsse, 2007; Sharman, 2008). These forces provided tandem support to the idea that a composite, global, rule-based framework is essential for the sustainability of an increasingly integrated banking and financial market. In this way, discourse is strategically and systematically constructed with the latent aim of building a bridge between what is and is not intended.

We appreciate that within a democratic context, the business of governance involves taking multi-level policy decisions. The decision to move in a particular policy direction comes about through a combination of research, debate and other forms of engagement between and among relevant actors. Potential outcomes, whether positive or negative, are also considered by these vesting parties. Not so, however, when it comes to the adoption of global AML policies in the developing world. Rather, notes Sharman (2008, p. 636), this occurred in part through forces of change extrinsic to these nations and exercised through "discursively mediated processes" in the form of "direct coercion, mimicry and competition".

Direct coercion was exerted through a tarnish and feather approach and its attendant power to create the impression that as a result of recalcitrant behaviour, whether true or not, rogue nation exposure was merited. The notion of mimicry, though, had its own pheromone, emitting from a social dynamic akin to peer pressure and the desire of national regulators to remain socially in sync with fellow island financial centres and by extension the broader community of nations (Sharman, 2008, p. 636). As the other compliance stimulant, the influence of competition could not be overlooked. In short, by not following, willy-nilly, what other (competitor) states were doing by adopting AML standards, divergents actually made themselves stand out, even if for the wrong reason; casting aspersions on their own character, implying they were not interested in aligning to a purpose and cause bigger than themselves (Sharman, 2008, pp. 649–650). This effect was immediately eliminated once compliance was forthcoming.

In terms of the criminalisation of money laundering itself, this was only regularised in 1986 when the United States first identified it to be so in a context of that nation's war on drugs (Hulsse, 2007). Since that time, approaches and debates in the literature were largely rooted in an economics confab. These arguments were formulated by global architects of policy diffusion such as the IMF, the World Bank and FATF. Generally, this perspective considers money laundering from the slant of its negative impact on financial markets, national banking systems and jurisdictional reputation. Some scepticism, though, is cast by Alldridge (2001) on the primacy of economics in giving shape and life to money laundering's nascent life. Also, at the fundamental level the idea that the *source* of funds should represent the essence of the money laundering definition is considered inadequate by Casella (2003). We discuss these contrary views in upcoming chapters.

Unlocking the paradoxes

Indeed, one of the paradoxes of the so-called globalisation phenomenon is the reality that criminal money is able to be moved alongside legitimately derived wealth (All-dridge, 2001; Taitt, 2006). A criminal's expectation is not unlike the ordinary, honest person who wishes to derive maximum value and benefit from hard earned money. In fact, to the criminally minded there is no distinction between ill-gotten gains and legitimate funds.

Technological innovation may be both engaged and accessed by the honest and corrupt. While relaxed trade barriers encourage comparative advantage, promote greater exchange of goods and services and naturally spawn networks and alliances, they also simultaneously enable criminals to pursue new and similar relationships amongst themselves. Access to information particularly via the internet and improvements in education, while producing a more knowledgeable and sophisticated client, have concomitantly produced an equally adept criminal. Cross-border movement of people while allowing for the exchange of skills and the shoring up of national economies, has also facilitated the exportation of new types of villains and by extension new forms of crime (Taitt, 2006, pp. 21–22).

Friman and Andreas (1999, pp. 1–2) speak of a side of the global economy which merits attention, dark though it may be. That side has to do with purely illicit trade by much the same actors as on the licit fence (that is, state and non-state). By applying a standard business model of strategic planning and sophisticated operational execution, their work is organised, systematic and generational. But this is where similarities with the good guys end. Threats of bodily harm, example killings, revenge killings, promised killings, bribery and corruption are all enshrined as tools of intimidation to exact not merely compliance, but also loyalty to an unwritten code of practice and retain discretion at all cost. With such scary consequences, what kind of clientele could these entities possibly have? The hard fact remains that outlawed or not, there remains a demand for illegal drugs, weapons, forced immigrant labour, child slaves and the like, all of which yield "revenue" for and on behalf of its perpetrators. A methodical, business-like concealment of these earnings naturally follows: the further these nettings are distanced from the illegal acquisition point the better. This makes it all the more difficult to reassemble the various pieces of the puzzle necessary to lay bare the evil source. And because of the need to keep secret the evil source, no taxes will be paid. Moreover, rapid and material outflows will ensue if only to emphasise this reality (Naylor, 1994).

Professional devils

Not only do criminals take advantage of the high tech platforms for personal or organisational benefit, but also the non-criminal high achieving types, in an effort to maximise personal returns, attract higher income levels, gain rapid promotion or purely for the fun of it, may themselves fall prey to the lure of promised financial gains. In doing so, they can either act illegally or in ways which contradict personal, organisational or societal values/norms. In short, high performance cultures, propelled by competition among business actors, while potentially stimulating optimal employee productivity may also create the opportunity for the rogue-trader, risk-taking type of individuals whose unchecked behaviour could have long-term injurious effects on the organisation.

Numerous examples over the years constitute reference points for this assertion. A good place to start is in the 1990s with Nick Leeson, the young trader convicted for his single-handed role in the failure of the reputable UK Barings Bank (Stevenson, 1995). An equally young professional, Kweku Adoboli, was caught in a similar fraud whilst a trader at UBS (Scott, 2012). The losses caused to their former employers as a result of their separate actions was comfortably over $1 billion each, with Leeson's fraud in particular costing Barings its very existence. In its final days, the United Kingdom's oldest merchant bank at the time was auctioned off to Dutch bank ING for a mere £1.

The former Enron corporation's misdeeds are classic in the fraud literature and aptly convey how corporate culture as set by the board and its executive management can shape a company's future, positively or negatively. The concealment of millions of dollars was accomplished with the assent and engagement of powerful senior executives. Closer to the offshore finance domain and occurring in the same year as the Madoff scam was another Ponzi scheme, this time of $8 billion and perpetrated by a former Knight of his own *wrong* table, Sir Allen Stanford. These larger than life famously rich characters stood at the apex of leadership of their transcendent organisations, overseeing (well, not really) other people's money and no doubt enjoying significant prominence, respect and admiration. While their actions reflect a special type of greed, one cannot help but wonder the extent to which the pressures of capitalism contributed to their universal financial misbehaviour.

However, it does not stop there. Who could forget the despicable rigging of the London Interbank Offered Rate (LIBOR), the global benchmark for interest rates by a handful of UK banks and their representatives also in 2012? LIBOR is the global benchmark against which interest rates are determined for banking products. The rate influences the price of lending right down to households, and therefore impacts trillions upon trillions of credit dollars and tens of millions of consumers alike. Evidently, not even LIBOR at the time was off limits to the vagaries of capitalist competition.

Fast forward to 2016 and behold the fallout from the actions of Wells Fargo bankers. Apparently, under performance pressures, up to 2 million accounts were created and tagged to actual clients, unknown to them. To date, this has cost senior executives their jobs and the potential claw back of an estimated $75 million in personal emoluments. The bank itself was fined $185 million by federal regulators. On the heels of this unbelievable in-house caper comes another dizzying (July 2017) discovery, again on Wells Fargo's front line. It appears that tens of thousands of clients were sold auto insurance coverage (outside the regular car insurance) to shore up the bank's potential losses due to standard depreciation accounting. This arrangement allowed the bank to remain in the money where the underlying loan became seriously impaired and the vehicle repossessed to recover owed funds. While the individual credit rating of affected clients took a hit in these cases, their non-refunded insurance premiums made a client's debt situation look worse that it really was. The bank's failure to refund premiums also came to light in thousands of cases of early loan redemption even though the need for insurance was now nullified (Morgenson, 2017). For failing to properly administer this insurance offering under US law, the bank was assessed a hefty fine of $1 billion in April 2018, split evenly between the Consumer Financial Protection Bureau[3] and the Office of the Comptroller of the Currency (OCC).[4] Outside the natural difficulty in managing such a widely dispersed corporation, the entity's culture or the way things are done, might have a lot to do with the noted failings.

Later on, as part my research design, I examine more closely a few of the cases identified here and others not mentioned. The intention is to unearth common threads and/ or themes if any, with a view towards understanding the application of rules and their potential limitation in curbing deviant behaviour.

Banking outcomes and the (in) sufficiency of compliance systems

By making banks legally culpable for failure to report activity considered suspicious on the part of a client, the traditional fortress of client secrecy/confidentiality is penetrated, thereby providing law enforcement with the kind of insight into a client's affairs which it considers necessary to get its job done. The benefits to state actors are thus clear. Unfortunately, the activities of the ordinary citizen desirous of benefiting from financial enhancement and asset protection vehicles are also subsumed into this process. At the micro-level therefore there is the risk that in fulfilling reporting obligations under FATF rules, a misunderstanding of a client's activities could result in the release of otherwise private information and the unwarranted besmirching of financial character.

Not only is the veil of banking privacy now countermanded, but also the early notions of bankers as merely custodians, lenders and facilitators of payments, as noted earlier, have all but disappeared. A new investigative tone of engagement beyond yet coincidental with the sales pitch must be exercised by these service providers to detect and deter nefarious activity, while promoting themselves as the solution to the client's financial problems. These regulatory requirements have a knock-on effect, which, in the end re-distribute part of the burden of accountability for corralling criminals to the business side of civil society, namely the banking system.

Such a burden has a premium attached to its implementation and will − although originating from external regulatory sources − be indirectly yet ultimately (at least in part) funded out of the client's pocket, whether that client is honest or corrupt. Furthermore, as ongoing criminal innovations result in the devolution of new regulatory requirements, the cost of compliance could continue on an upward trend. Unfortunately, a correlating improvement in client service delivery may not ensue where the objective basis for rules become prized above clients' reasonable expectation to have their needs met given the plethora of choices afforded by competing financial institutions. In this regard, reconciliation between conformance and the execution of client service must occur in order for both sides − regulation and business − to win.

Lastly, the various pressures to conform when combined with the competitive financial services environment as noted earlier, put the question as to whether there is a foreseeable future for IFCs in the Caribbean region. Also, to the extent that a single market and economy does emerge, would the trading space be commercially viable?

For all the examples before us, we need to ask ourselves whether purely regulatory controls can correct future misgivings. To that end, we have not yet explored in full the reality of principal-agent collusion and the idea that the workings of systems and procedures are subject to human control and will. Also, whether or not one appreciates that national sovereignty in the present global environment is more complex than in the past, regulatory adherence sends the right signals and could help to preserve the reputation of financial institutions and, by extension, the jurisdictions in which they reside.

Notes

1 From the OECD's Harmful Tax Competition Initiative. Further information may be found at https://www.oecd-ilibrary.org/commonwealth/taxation/international-tax-competition/the-oecd-harmful-tax-competition-initiative_9781848597587-10-en
2 Inheritance taxes are also levied!
3 See https://www.consumerfinance.gov/about-us/newsroom/bureau-consumer-financial-protection-announces-settlement-wells-fargo-auto-loan-administration-and-mortgage-practices/
4 See https://www.occ.gov/news-issuances/news-releases/2018/nr-occ-2018-41.html

References

Alldridge, P., 2001. The moral limits of the crime of money laundering. *Buffalo Criminal Review Law*, 5(1), pp. 279–319.

Alldridge, P., 2003. *Money laundering law: Forfeiture, confiscation, civil recovery, criminal laundering, and taxation of the proceeds of crime*. Hart: Oxford.

Antoine, R., 2001. The offshore financial services sector: Legal policy issues on the path to development: A legal defense. *Journal of Eastern Caribbean Studies*, 26(4), pp. 1–27.

Beck, U., 2002. The terrorist threat: World risk society revisited. *Theory, Culture and Society*, 19(4), pp. 39–55.

Blackburn, R., 2006. Finance and the fourth dimension. *New Left Review*, 39, pp. 39–70.

Blum, J. A., Levi, M., Naylor, R. T. & Williams, P., 1998. Financial havens, banking secrecy and money laundering. *Criminal Justice Newsletter, United Nations*, 8(34 and 35), pp. 1–72.

Casella, D., 2003. Reverse money laundering. *Journal of Money Laundering Control*, 7(1), pp. 92–94.

Friman, H. & Andreas, P., 1999. Introduction. In: H. Friman & P. Andreas, eds. *The illicit global economy and state power*. Maryland: Rowman & Littlefield Publishers Inc., pp. 1–17.

Hartman, B., 2002. Coercing cooperation from offshore financial centers: Identity and coincidence of international obligations against money laundering and harmful tax competition. *International & Comparative Law Review*, 25(2), pp. 253–290.

Hulsse, R., 2007. Creating demand for global governance: The making of a global money laundering problem. *Global Society*, 21(2), pp. 155–178.

Keohane, R., 2001. Governance in a partially globalized world. *American Political Science Review*, 95(1), pp. 1–13.

Langley, P., 2004. In the eye of the "perfect storm": The final salary pensions crisis and financialization of Anglo-American capitalism. *New Political Economy*, 9(4), pp. 539–558.

Levi-Faur, D., 2008. Foreword. In: J. Brathwaite, ed. *Regulatory capitalism: How it works, ideas for making it work better*. Massachusetts: Edward Elgar Publishing Inc.

Marshall, D., 2008. Gaining fluency in finance: Globalization/financialization and offshore financial centers. *Contemporary Politics*, 14(3), pp. 357–373.

Masciandaro, D. ed., 2004. *Global financial crime: Terrorism and organized crime, money laundering and offshore centers*. Farnham: Ashgate Publishing.

Morgenson, G., 2017. Wells Fargo, awash in scandal, faces violations over car insurance refunds [Online]. Available at: https://nyti.ms/2uARoTI [accessed 12 September 2017].

Naylor, R., 1994. *Hot money and the politics of debt*. Montreal: Black Rose Books.

Rahn, R., 2002. Taxation, money laundering and liberty. *Journal of Financial Crime*, 9(4), pp. 341–346.

Sanders, R., 2002. The fight against fiscal colonialism: The OECD and small jurisdictions. *The Round Table*, 91(365), pp. 325–348.

Scholte, J., 2002. Civil society and the governance of global finance. In: J. Scholte & A. Schnabel, eds. *Civil society and global finance*. New York: Routledge, pp. 11–32.

Scott, M., 2012. Ex-UBS trader is accused of gambling in a big loss [Online]. Available at: https://dealbook.nytimes.com/2012/09/14/as-his-fraud-trial-opens-ex-ubs-trader-is-accused-of-brazen-gambling/ [accessed 11 September 2017].

Sharman, J., 2008. Power and discourse in policy diffusion: Anti-money laundering in developing states. *International Studies Quarterly*, 52(3), pp. 635–656.

Stevenson, R., 1995. Breaking the bank – a special report. Big gambles, lost bets sank a venerable firm [Online]. Available at: http://www.nytimes.com/1995/03/03/business/breaking-the-bank-a-special-report-big-gambles-lost-bets-sank-a-venerable-firm.html?pagewanted=1 [accessed 11 September 2017].

Strange, S., 1997. *Casino Capitalism*. Manchester: Manchester University Press.

Taitt, K., 2006. Regulation and the burden on banks and client services. *Offshore Investment*, February, pp. 21–22.

Vogel, S., 1996. *Freer markets, more rules: Regulatory reform in advanced industrial countries*. New York: Cornell University Press.

Wallerstein, I., 1974. *The modern world system I: Capitalist agriculture and the origins of the European world-economy in the sixteenth century*. New York: Academic Press.

Whitehead, G., 1969. *Commerce made simple*. Oxford: Butterworth-Heinemann Ltd.

2 Borderless money and high sovereign stakes

Prologue

So, we have established offshore finance as, essentially, the lodgement and administration of monetary resources in a location outside the asset owner's home country. Let us take a moment and retrace our steps a bit to look at the genealogy and path towards the current pre-eminence of this global controversy.

The original planting

The geography of island nations and their assumption of ownership by colonialists also hold significant sway in the historical development of these spaces as offshore centres. We know that in early Caribbean societies, the means of production was slavery. Slaves owned nothing, but were themselves objects of ownership. This imperial reality did not suddenly change at emancipation. In fact, there was no deliberate transition strategy in place at any level (legal, political, social, economic or otherwise) to support the elevation of the previously downtrodden to a point of equality with former masters. Neither did there exist a similar plan to support the former slave owner, in the movement away from his comprehensive domination of a certain human sect to a now shared one with his former property.

Thus, the freed slaves found themselves with little or no means – financial or otherwise – to change their erstwhile situation. There was also the deep psychological scarring reverberating down several generations which could simply not be erased through the mere enactment of laws. It was therefore inevitable that a new kind of dependency would emerge. And this, when coupled with the importance of money (credit) in enhancing one's standard of living, would further empower, and indeed entrench, already empowered and entrenched owners of capital as forces potent in the shaping of a new social, political and economic space for Caribbean post-colonial states.

It was within this context that the role of merchants emerged as the primary reference point for credit at that time. It was also within this context that the colonial elite (plantation owners and their offspring) opted, as it were, to retain their tried, tested and – yes – profitable business fare of commercial trading over creating an environment for industrial self-sufficiency (Marshall, 2008). This deep branding into the heart and soul of early Caribbean societies would be later fleshed out into a contemporary business model whose platform was based on the delivery of financial services as an undisputed regional commodity (Marshall, 2008).

Words and power

Beneath the layer of financial seeds was a foundation of natural beauty gifted to the islands at birth, so to speak, and which would further enhance their appeal. Indeed, the movement to and from the region via ships brought the seamless exchange of culture and experience through the picture(s) painted by aristocrats, bourgeoisie and other travellers apparently enamoured by the region's stunning charm and sublime character. The effect no doubt was a "visual aesthetic of a welcoming society" (Barrow, 2004).

Documenting travels was also a part of the mechanics of and therefore a critical tool of colonialisation (Pratt, 2007). This had a two-fold purpose: first, of communication, and, second, of reinforcement. By communicating, business and political powers in the metropolis were kept abreast of the state of their financial and administrative interests in the annexed territory. As for the stay-at-home citizen, distant lands were brought into pictorial proximity thereby enabling the individual to vicariously experience the empire-building process, ultimately sharing in its adventure and excitement. The outcome was to reinforce the *dominus* mentality consistent with empire (Pratt, 2007).

Subsequent portrayals of Caribbean societies (and later, OFCs) in the post-emancipation era involved the applied images of romance and "piratical adventure" (Marshall, 2008, p. 365). What also did not help much was the lack of understanding of what was actually involved in the offshore business (Blum et al., 1998). Folklore, therefore, had its way for a time even as the sector expanded throughout the decades with the effect of only reinforcing what was already believed to be a mystery. Of course, with mystery comes suspicion, and with suspicion, blame. Still, these elements remain part of the rigging of offshore finance's sails despite greater clarity of the services they provide and their role in modern business.

Mirror formations

Taken together, these visual portrayals were, in fact, the prophetic contours of touristic societies which would long resonate in the annals of European cultural liturgy (Marshall, 2008, p. 365). Of course, sown seeds that are properly watered can potentially grow into trees. And for Caribbean societies the traded winds of a colonial legacy would leave an unmistakable footprint in island sands, marking them as "geographies to be conquered and (simultaneously) temptations to be resisted" (Marshall, 2007, p. 930). This picture, cites Marshall, is recast in the new international financial architecture whose main actors are the "rational, western (male) form" – as represented by onshore financial nations replete with the protective armour of regulatory guidance, financial rationality and prudence. This starring figure is "at variance with the exotic and sexualized 'Other'" – meaning the Caribbean and Pacific IFCs. Therefore, although the apparent actions of tax evasion by this "Other" are executed severally, the relationship is negatively and prejudicially impacted. In short, discredit and insult is brought upon the male (onshore nation) while accentuating the IFC as a "temptress" and instigator of the breakdown in the relationship in the first place (Marshall, 2007, pp. 930–931). A little further and this might very well be Adam blaming Eve to make himself look good; except there is no evidence to suggest an intention by the former to repress his helpmeet and consign her to a position outside her rightful place alongside him. There is historical evidence, though, that mirrors a residual gender stereotype in which patriarchal societies sought to keep women in their so-called rightful place. Any serious challenge to male authority was met with sanction and usually with inconsequential recourse.

That there could conceivably be an application of gender bias to state social interactions, while indeed disconcerting, unearths a recurring predilection to abuse power where protective frameworks to mitigate such are not in place. Arbitrational oversight, legal enforcement and other checks and balances are immediate examples. The issue of directives against threats to shame is in keeping with imperialist tendencies to intervene for the purpose of shaping conduct. To Marshall, it is action which epitomises outdated modes of gender engagement and thus does not bode well for mature international relations (Marshall, 2007, pp. 932–935).

From a business perspective, discourse from outside in points to the de-regulation of traditional financial markets as triggering the move offshore. Leading up to this transition, however, there was a corporate simmering taking place as organisations had grown weary of high business costs, the burden of regulation and the impact on profits. In particular, these inhibitors created a hunger for new markets amongst financial institutions most notably for long-term capital, a domain which was dominated at the time by corporations and sovereign governments (Blum et al., 1998, pp. 32–33). Parallel to this corporate lust was an escalation in worldwide demand for funding to support infrastructural and other types of development and at varying levels of sophistication. Equally important was satisfying the requirements of highly mobile and knowledgeable clients of all stripes for enhanced tax planning options to maximise their wealth (Roper et al., 2003).

What followed was the migration of large conglomerates outside their "discomfort" zone in search of a better corporate life: new capital, low costs of production, less red tape, less taxes, greater privacy and enhanced profitability – the corporation's dream. In addition to financial services companies, whole industries such as car manufacturers and telecommunication service entities seized the opportunity to launch into new territories (Maurer, 2001; Roper et al., 2003).

The push offshore by the financially astute, strategically nimble businesses coincided nicely with seismic technological shifts at the time. This enabled responding entities to leverage emerging computer technology to their advantage. In this way, the traditional notion of physical and static geographical space deemed necessary for the delivery of commerce gave way to the contemporary reality of virtual business and, indeed, a capacity for corporations to operate as effectively, albeit from an external location. Thus, differentiated service models and financial products could now be developed to meet clients' expectations on a competitive basis (Roper et al., 2003). To sum this all up, there was a clear correlation between capitalist expansion and the maturing of the offshore industry (Palan, 2003).

But why island nations specifically? What was their primary drawing card, so to speak, in this global reinvention of business?

Since the interests of commerce and society are best served and, indeed, protected within an appropriate legal framework, one clear contributing factor which should be acknowledged is the colonial legacy of a common law judicial system. This made transition to island jurisdictions relatively easy. In particular, the textualist approach to legal interpretation germane to the British legal system better supported the needs of business in terms of the clarity and transparency required to quickly set up legal structures (Atiyah & Summers, 1987). In short, the question of the intended meaning of a law, the purpose of its original enactment and related ambiguities – all elements of American jurisprudence – were actually part of the burden companies wished to avoid. The more literal, defined legal system of the islands was a better fit for purpose (Atiyah & Summers, 1987, pp. 100–101). Hence the discretion and other incentives previously noted, when allied with these nations' own efforts at: (a) economic diversification; (b) attempts to create new job opportunities for its citizenry; and (c) the potential for knowledge transfer, created a perfect context of mutual beneficence.

Not to be ignored is the "unintended consequence" of the development of techno-logical infrastructure brought to offshore island markets (BVI, Bermuda, Turks and Caicos, etc.) by multinational enterprises such as the UK-registered Cable and Wireless PLC (Maurer, 2001). This, literally, opened up a global telecommunications portal allowing for real time financial exchange and an ability to seamlessly manage time zone differences to the advantage of relocating corporations (Maurer, 2001, p. 469).

This outside in perspective is consistent with a 2000 Report of the Working Group on Offshore Financial Centres, in which the Financial Stability Forum identified the chief trigger of IFC growth as the imposition of tighter regulations in the financial sectors of industrial nations in the 1960s to the 1970s. Increased regulations took the form of higher reserve requirements, interest rate caps and restrictions on the range of financial products; capital controls, financial disclosure requirements and high effective tax rates (Financial Stability Forum, 2000, p. 8). The effect of such impositions was to restrict funds available for lending and thus limit potential profits whilst increasing the regulatory burden – all ingredients for engaging a deliberate search for new business-friendly locales.

But is that it, that offshore was externally driven and island spaces were dealt a hand (out) from capitalism which they have since passively played, even if with good results? The correlation is, after all, evident over at least 150 years notes Palan (2003, p. 8). That said, capitalism's momentum, whilst certainly stimulating innovation, could have hardly, on its own, flung open acquiescent island doors. Instead, the delineation or "bifurca-tion" of the "sovereign space into heavily and lightly regulated realms" for competitive purposes indicates more of a hands-on engagement of marauding capitalist forces than anything else (Palan, 2003, p. 8). Island offshore centres, therefore, should consider themselves as proactively, and maybe unwittingly, redrawing the traditional boundaries of state and hence what sovereignty means. I revert to this notion towards the chapter's end. In the meantime, the value of the offshore market to global business beckons attention, even if traditionally this has not been strong enough to offset prevailing criticism.

Pressure points to OFCs

It is well known that Fortune 500 companies benefit from tax breaks afforded them by holding profits in subsidiary companies incorporated in offshore jurisdictions. Were Apple, Microsoft and Google among others, made to repatriate their worldwide profits, it would result in their paying a 35–40% tax levy. Against the billions in profits held by these entities externally, such a levy would yield significant tax revenue for Uncle Sam, but simultaneously cut deep into corporate treasuries.

In light of the above, outside the money laundering and tax evasion brouhaha, are we seeing another (potential) source of motivation for the negative barrage of offshore rhetoric? Is there something here? Antoine (2001) thinks there is. Asserting the legiti-macy of the offshore concept and hailing it as "important for the economic survival" of small nation states, she contends that the perception of money laundering and other undesirable financial activities as being exclusive or concentrated in the offshore sector is "misguided" (Antoine, 2001, p. 6). Hers is a plausible assertion: the products and services offered by IFCs are not dissimilar to those promoted by US banking cities/states such as

Manhattan, Delaware and New Jersey; key European domiciles such as Switzerland, and historical financial kingdoms such as London. In fact, during a presentation on harmful tax competition at a meeting of the International Tax Planning Association in New Orleans (20 November 2000), Marshall Langer noted that non-resident aliens and foreign corporations domiciled in Manhattan do not attract taxes on interest earned on bank deposits. In this respect, hundreds of billions are believed to be held by these persons. He asserted that this has been the case for nearly eighty years and any attempt to impose taxes would result in the relocation of these deposits somewhere else. Of note however is that, within the dominant discourse, these US locales are neither regarded as tax havens nor considered vulnerable to money laundering, even though the United States itself is considered a country of primary laundering concern. Indeed, questions were raised as to why the OECD's premier issue of a global tax haven list (2001) did not identify onshore nations already steeped in the international financial services business, including the said United States, Switzerland, the United Kingdom, Luxembourg as well as Hong Kong and Singapore (Rogers, 2002).

The double standard has never been more evident as even the State Department, CIA and IRS have determined through their own assessments that so-called high tax nations are more than likely to attract illicit funds than so-called tax havens (Mitchell 2003, p. 127). Outside the economics behind regaining lost revenue, politics may also be at play (Antoine 2001, p. 7). There is also the view that the leading voices of tax harmonisation are surfing the benevolent activity of the fight against drugs and terrorists as a means of casting doubt on the character of OFCs for their own purposes (Sanders, 2002; Mitchell, 2003; Hampton and Levi, 1999). Embedded within the schema of global finance it is impossible to avoid given their permanent reach.

State autonomy and the structural powers

In the FATF's 40 Recs. we have a quintessential example of the sheer power of external quasi-regulatory influences on the polities of nation states. AML laws and related regulatory guidelines implemented by countries in the post-1990s are founded on these dictates and convey not only the present-day structure of international finance but, in particular, its long arm of *influence*. The expression "a picture is worth a thousand words" is well depicted in the FATF's ability to supra-territorially extend its influence into the affairs of independent nations to gain their conformity to unilaterally contrived mandates. These mandates, once adopted by countries possessing greater industrial power and political muscle, are sculpted into a standard or regulatory norm for un-decided nations. Resistance is not an option due to the looming threat of marginalisation and other sanctions engineered and controlled by the same powers. Hence, the small island state is constrained into acting in a manner consistent with the expectations of the global crowd and not necessarily after exercising its own carefully considered, federal opinion. It is this intrinsic positional power enjoyed by onshore nations that seems to challenge state sovereignty and, further, emphasises how regulatory capacity has been subtly transitioned from the hands of elected local authorities to external governance entities.

Legitimacy and legality

To be fair, one must concede that this power did not suddenly appear; neither was there a specific moment when it was formally handed over. Rather, it would have developed incrementally, at least in part, over a period of time through a process of social interaction, transaction and exchange (Blau, 1964). This in turn opened up a political door that created the legitimacy to exercise a degree of influence over the accepting party.

Johnson (2003) also presents plausible input in seeking to explain the legitimacy factor in global relations. The point of her argument is that legality is not necessary for power to be asserted. Rather, what is required within a community is the agreement of key influential parties that the actions undertaken or proposed to be undertaken by an organisation, coincide with their own expectations. This concord effect is sufficient to endorse the entity's intent and simultaneously create assent by other parties, even though the latter may have dissenting views (Johnson, 2003, pp. 38–40).

Whereas the legitimacy tool is the subtle first step leveraged by the OECD/FATF to exert intended change, the American methodology is more overt and begins with legitimising intentions in the national judicial framework. Once the relevant congressional Act is passed, change is effected by exercising prevailing hegemony over capitalist mechanisms. Perhaps the first diffusion of a US law in this manner and within the AML space occurred following the 9/11 tragedy in New York in 2001, with the swift passing of the USA Patriot Act. This law immediately placed significant accountability on the shoulders of foreign financial institutions using networking systems such as correspondent banking and SWIFT.[1] By expanding the legal net to include foreign financial actors operating within its commercial space, the US government's ability to curb money laundering and terrorist financing within its banking system was now strengthened. This was further emphasised with the legal power to enforce due process against foreign financial institutions through these entities' US affiliate company/office.

Notions of legitimacy when combined with the extension and influence of foreign laws are major highlights in the onshore/offshore debate. In their own way, each poses a real threat of disruption to island business, particularly where there is delay in implementing the necessary controls as dictated by external forces. However, despite the associated harshness on reputation for non-compliance, there is a strong argument for retaining this approach: an integrated financial system and the speed of capital flows when triaged with the real and present danger of illicit funds being co-mingled with licit monies militate against any one state's ability to adequately manage its own regulatory space. Throw in global terrorism, organised crime and transnational disease and we have a category five hurricane against national security.

But does this necessarily signal a death knell for the state? Or does it, in fact, provoke a reconfiguration of an old trusted model? Certainly, as it relates to financial intermediation there remains an opportunity for countries in the forefront to set expectations of behaviour for entities doing business on their soil, through their territories or in their electronic space (Scholte, 2002, p. 31; Sica, 2000, pp. 47–48). This means that more co-operation might actually be needed than less, despite sovereignty postures. Again, can the model of sovereignty as we know it continue to hold true?

Acts of the transnationals

The apparent consignment of the state to the background on matters of global regulation is a phenomenon worth sifting through. Overall, this seems to feature strongly in contemporary finance. It is a dynamic not to be taken lightly as it could be seen to represent a form of imperialism which, unlike its earlier, more visible configurations – and which could be rebuffed by civil rebellion – must be dealt with differently, due to its more subtle and complex nature.

Let us for the moment expand our notion of society to include the wider community of nations. At this high level one could better appreciate the need for regulations, controls and other governance mechanisms if only to mitigate the risk of negative occurrences and the resulting potential impact upon millions. Surely in this context, rules of engagement must be formalized and, indeed, respected by all. In this regard, there is an important role for organisations such as the OECD/FATF (Keohane, 2001). But what about the expectations of citizenry of the OFC who have democratically empowered their government to conduct the nation's affairs? Should decisions such as whether or not to tax and the rates to apply thereof, not continue to lie within the domain of the sovereign nation and this, regardless of geographic size or location? Should bullish behaviour by other nations or groups of nations or organised factions purporting to represent such be condoned?

In addressing these behaviours and the legality thereof, Hartman (2000) argues that where there is absence of a duty to comply with a standard, the threat of sanction for non-compliance is spurious. Not helpful either is the self-referential perspective of onshore nations which, at the outset, drove global discourse around both money laundering prevention and harmful tax competition. In seeing past the shenanigan and inputting into the tax debate, Antoine suggests there is neither legal nor moral obligation to assist onshore states in increasing fiscal revenue through tax collection (Antoine, 2001, pp. 9–10). Rahn joins the fray, asserting a nation's right of fiscal self-direction underscoring the notion that external impositions to act otherwise would be "nothing short of financial imperialism" (Rahn, 2002, p. 344).

The matter of sovereignty is also of particular concern to Morris (2001), but more so from the failure of nations to recognise their own power and thus act from a self-determinant position. This, however, is easier said than done since it is evident the interaction of the state and financial system is not as simple as it was before the era of technological revolution. In fact, it is espoused by some, including Strange (1996) and Shelley (1995, 1998, 1999), that the structural power of the international financial system may have permanently overcome the state's regulatory capacity. Sica notes this manifestation in the financial system's vast, extra-territorial reach and states' inability to keep pace with the effects of technology (Sica, 2000, p. 47). This perspective is identifiable in part through the execution and arrogation of non-legal, transnational clout by non-state actors over sovereign states, discussed earlier. Imperialist overtones notwithstanding, the resulting island fear and scramble to transform regulatory regimes reinforces this reality.

The notion of structural power is also applicable to the inordinate, highly organised criminal networks whose inherent capacity and extensive reach (political, financial and economic) can potentially lead to state capture. This is a malevolent section of the cast of transnational actors who execute their corruptive part on the stage of global finance (Shelley, 1995, 1998, 1999; Strange, 1996).

Despite the state's apparent lack of control over the mobility of capital – licit or illicit – in an ever-evolving electronic age, there is a response mechanism which may be exploited, but it first has to be "perceived" (Sica, 2000). In short, the same technology that facilitated the globalisation of financial markets in the first place may be leveraged by states to increase their monitoring and control of financial capital (Sica, 2000, p. 71). At the level of political sophistry, Russia certainly picked up the utility of technology in its quest to influence the outcome of the 2016 US elections, overtly promoting the incumbent president as its preferred leader over Hillary Clinton.

In terms of the level of global collaboration deemed necessary for the re-regulation of international financial markets and, as such, international financial flows, some examples are clear (Heillener, 1998). These include the Basel Capital Accord of 1998.[2]

The second example of note according to Heillener is what is referred to as the "cooperative initiative" by member states of the FATF to regulate money laundering (Heillener, 1998, p. 4). This latter example unsurprisingly brings us back to square one. For it is the very apparent disregard for the input of small nation states that the issue of blacklisting was challenged by these nations in the first place, duh! This only strengthens the point of the need for greater collaboration and co-operation with and amongst all nations, when it comes to tackling global concerns. While larger countries may possess the physical resources with which to engage these issues, small island nations can contribute at the level of ideas and technical expertise. No longer should they be overlooked simply because of geographical size or the depth of their national coffers. Thankfully, this strategy appears to be a thing of the past with the advent of initiatives such as the OECD's BEPS undertaking. Although its initial structure appears to have been constructed in-house albeit with G20 input, the OECD's invitation to all interested nations in developing a global consensus-based (tax) framework is a step in the right direction.

Hampton and Levi (1999) weigh in on the matter of state sovereignty, suggesting that the framework for contemporary money laundering is based on the growth of three "spaces" of offshore finance namely – secrecy, regulation, and politics. The authors contend that:

> In geopolitical terms, the war on drugs and other assaults on financial crime offer an apparently neutral rationale for intervention in the affairs of (states) … regardless of the extent of evidence that money laundering has occurred to facilitate the supply of drugs, or whether the areas are perceived to be producers, distribution zones or conduits.
>
> (Hampton and Levi, 1999, p. 646)

Interventionist measures are likely to be engaged, argues the authors if countries are "politically weak" that is, in need of aid; lacking in military might; have no significant corporate connections and not needed "for strategic purposes" (Hampton and Levi, 1999). This, needless to say, is the position of most if not all Caribbean IFCs. On the other hand, it is felt that countries able to provide push-back have "greater freedom to commit financial crime and traffic in drugs, at least while Western needs are current" (Hampton and Levi, 1999). By way of example, the strategic need for Pakistan's allied support immediately following 9/11 superseded the fact that the Musharraf government was – up to the time of his impeachment in August 2008 – a military one which assumed power by coup, that democratic elections had not been forthcoming and also that the country had a nuclear capability which it had threatened to use against India.

Such international polities can only undermine the sanguine efforts of IFCs' regulatory compliance initiatives and their ability to comply with external dictates as well as their involvement in the noble ethic of fighting against money laundering. Given such political dynamics, one is left to wonder if the real "war against money laundering" is not really a war for political power. If so, can such a war be won?

As discussed before, extrinsic motivators can only go so far and this pertains to countries in the same way as it does to individuals. The fact is that the issue of money laundering is bigger than any one nation and certainly falls well beyond the capacity of any one country to unilaterally handle. Therefore, rather than hold fast to early models of statehood and sovereignty at all costs, the time may now be ripe to revisit them to see to what extent a revival may be required and a new gospel of statehood preached.

Statehood model

What is understood of sovereignty and statehood is derived mostly from the tenets outlined in the Westphalian tradition. The first guiding principle identifies the notion of territoriality (Menzel, n.d.). Inherent in this concept is geographical location and, thus, a boundary. The boundary implies separation and distinction from other locations and also sets up a monopoly of power over the defined geographic space. It is not clear how boundaries are defined in extensive non-island land masses, comprising multiple territories, although this may be derived from a colonial imprint over time. The second principle is that of sovereignty. This takes the idea that there is no authority superior to the state and hence the state's internal affairs are the state's business. Also there is no recognition accorded other entities outside the state itself (Menzel, n.d., p. 3). In short, states are the only actors when it comes to matters of the state. Additionally, the idea of sovereignty leaves the choice of political system enjoyed by the state left up to the state itself (Menzel, n.d.). This position is consistent with de Vattel's idea that "a dwarf is as much a man as a giant is; a small republic is no less a sovereign state than the most powerful Kingdom" (de Vattel, 1758, p. 75).

The other two principles highlight notions of legality and the balance of power. The former promotes states as having innate, equal rights. And these rights are neither transferable nor can they be distilled based on size, location or any other factor. The balance of power element is an offsetting mechanism which keeps states in check and evens out behaviours that are demonstrably out of sync with the tenor of the state system in general (Menzel, n.d., p. 4).

There is today a wholesale challenge to this classic model of statehood. For now, the challengers are vying for the sovereignty title; only, not to wrest it from the rightful owners, but to refine the meaning for future generations. In the red corner we have new patterns of governance (Djelic & Sahlin-Andersson, 2006) attended by a party of networking, interdependencies and diffusions of power. In the blue corner is the venomous IT revolution known for its capacity to overpower opponents to change, rendering actors easier access to markets in a new virtual territory known as cyberspace. The bout being fought is like no other thriller. What is different though is the outcome. The "greatest" will not be a person, but the conjoining of contenders in a re-ordering of the world, whose seamless engagement blurs national boundaries and promotes governance as a "shared experience" (Djelic & Sahlin-Andersson, 2006).

Notes

1 Acronym for the "Society for Worldwide Interbank Financial Telecommunications". SWIFT is a global network that supports the electronic transfer of funds among member banks and other financial institutions.
2 This accord seeks to promote common standards for capital in the international banks of industrial countries. It is a model incorporated as part of the larger, more encompassing Basel Standards of Banking Supervision, the benchmark protocols for nationally registered financial institutions. The standards are also the chief reference point of regulatory compliance during inspections and/or reviews of the operations of financial institutions. Further details may be found at: https://www.bis.org/publ/bcbs04a.pdf

References

Antoine, R., 2001. The offshore financial services sector: Legal policy issues on the path to development: A legal defense. *Journal of Eastern Caribbean Studies*, 26(4), pp. 1–27.

Atiyah, P. & Summers, R. S., 1987. *Form and substance in Anglo-American law: A comparative study of legal reasoning, legal theory and legal institutions*. Oxford: Clarendon Press.

Barrow, V., 2004. A genealogy of Barbadian tourism: The welcoming society and contemporary narratives of resistance. *Journal of Eastern Caribbean Affairs*, 29(2), pp. 50–75.

Blau, P., 1964. *Theory and exchange in social life*. New York: John Wiley and Sons Inc.

Blum, J. A., Levi, M., Naylor, R. T. & Williams, P., 1998. Financial havens, banking secrecy and money laundering. *Criminal Justice Newsletter, United Nations*, 8(34 and 35), pp. 1–72.

de Vattel, E., 1758. *The law of nations*, eds., Kapossy, B. & Whatmore, R. Translated by Nugent, T. 2008. London: Liberty Fund.

Djelic, M.-L. & Sahlin-Andersson, K., 2006. Introduction; A world of governance: The rise of transnational regulation. In: Djelic, M.-L. & Sahlin-Andersson, K., eds. *Transnational governance: Institutional dynamics of regulation*. Cambridge: Cambridge University Press, pp. 1–28.

Financial Stability Forum, 2000. Report of the Working Group of Offshore Centres. Basel: Financial Stability Forum.

Hampton, M. P. & Levi, M., 1999. Fast spinning into oblivion? Recent developments in money laundering policies and offshore finance centers. *Third World Quarterly*, 20(3), pp. 645–656.

Hartman, B., 2000. Cooercing cooperation from offshore financial centers: Identity and coincidence of international obligations against money laundering and harmful tax competition. *International and Comparative Law Review*, 25(2), pp. 253–290.

Heillener, E., 1998. Electronic money: A challenge to the sovereign state? *Journal of International Affairs*, 51(2), pp. 387–409.

Johnson, J., 2003. Repairing legitimacy after blacklisting by the Financial Action Task Force. *Journal of Money Laundering Control*, 7(1), pp. 38–49.

Keohane, R., 2001. Governance in a partially globalized world. *American Political Science Review*, 95(1), pp. 1–13.

Marshall, D., 2007. The new international financial architecture and Caribbean OFCs: Confronting financial stability discourse. *Third World Quarterly*, 28(5), pp. 917–938.

Marshall, D., 2008. Gaining fluency in finance: Globalization/financialization and offshore financial centers. *Contemporary Politics*, 14(3), pp. 357–373.

Maurer, B., 2001. Islands in the net: Rewiring technological and financial circuits in the "offshore" Caribbean. *Comparative Studies in History and Society*, 43(3), pp. 467–501.

Menzel, U., n.d. Westphalian state system or hegemonic world order? A theoretical introduction [Online]. Available at: http://www.ulrich-menzel.de/vortraege/Vortrag_Westph_Statesystem_or_Hegemonic_World_Order.pdf [accessed 1 September 2017].

Mitchell, D. J., 2003. US government agencies confirm low-tax jurisdictions are not money laundering havens. *Journal of Financial Crime*, 11(2), pp. 127–133.

Morris, G., 2001. The future of offshore private banking: Understanding the effects of the OECD/FATF and IRS initiatives on international finance. Speech.

Palan, R., 2003. *The offshore world: Sovereign markets, virtual places and nomad milllionaires*. New York: Cornell University Press.

Pratt, M., 2007. *Imperial eyes: Travel writing and transculturation*. 2nd ed. London: Routledge.

Rahn, R., 2002. Taxation, money laundering and liberty. *Journal of Financial Crime*, 9(4), pp. 341–346.

Rogers, S., 2002. The case for international tax competition: A Caribbean perspective. *Prosperitas*, 2(2), pp. 1–6.

Roper, P., Roberts, G., Odendaal, H.& Pelser, C., 2003. *The practical guide to offshore financial centres*. Bryanston:The International Publication Trust.

Sanders, R., 2002. The fight against fiscal colonialism: The OECD and small jurisdictions. *The Round Table*, (365), pp. 325–348.

Scholte, J., 2002. Civil society and the governance of global finance. In: J. Scholte & A. Schnabel, eds. *Civil society and global finance.* New York: Routledge, pp. 11–32.

Shelley, L., 1995. Transnational organized crime: An imminent threat to the nation-state. *Journal of International Affairs*, 48(2), pp. 463–489.

Shelley, L., 1998. Crime and corruption in a digital age. *Journal of International Affairs*, 51(2), pp. 605–620.

Shelley, L., 1999. Transnational organized crime: The new authoritarianism. In: H. Friman & P. Andreas, eds. *The illicit global economy and statepower.* Maryland: Rowan & Littlefield Publishers Inc, pp. 25–51.

Sica, V., 2000. Cleaning the laundry: States and the monitoring of the financial system. *Millennium Journal of International Studies*, 29(1), pp. 47–72.

Strange, S., 1996. *The retreat of the state: The diffusion of power in the world economy.* Cambridge: Cambridge University Press.

3   Unmasking the darkness

Prologue

Let us try to understand money laundering a bit more. Of course, to do so effectively, we also have to factor in the notion of terrorist financing. As criminal acts, these variables, together, form the basis of the work of the FATF and have found a prominent place in national legal and financial regulatory frameworks. To therefore discuss one and not the other will hardly paint the holistic picture required to assess the extent to which they negatively impact international financial services markets. However, while the outright consequences of the latter might be more easily understood, we are still not quite clear about what makes the laundering of money such a threat. Moreover, why is systematic attention to its prevention and control considered necessary by countries the world over?

So what the heck is it?

Factors common to the various definitions of money laundering as provided by international bodies such as the FATF, the IMF and the United Nations Office on Drugs and Crime (UNODC), include:

a   the transfer or movement of funds;
b   the disguise or concealment of the illegal origin of funds; and
c   their subsequent utilisation by perpetrators, with full knowledge of the illegal derivation.

The backdrop for this characterisation of money laundering was the formal setting of the United Nations Convention against Illicit Traffic in Narcotics Drugs and Psychotropic Substances held in Vienna in 1988[1] and a subsequent gathering of nations at a Convention against Transnational Organized Crime in Palermo in 2000.[2]

The notion of money laundering itself is metaphorical. The expression connotes the idea of something which is dirty – in this case money – being taken a through a washing cycle for the purpose of cleansing. The French equivalent terminology – "blanchiment d'argent" – literally the bleaching of money implies a purification process aimed at removing stains or what is described by Lilley as the washing of black money such that it "appears whiter than white" (Lilley, 2006, p. 6).

By application, the proceeds of crime (dirty money) are said to be taken through various transactional rotations (washing) in order to sanitise the funds such that they appear legitimately derived (clean). The transactional rotations or stages mirror a washing machine's cycles through which the dirty money is run. In turn, these cycles are known as placement, layering and integration.[3]

Placement refers to the initial effort to introduce illegally derived money into the banking system mostly through cash. This medium is regarded as almost fool proof because there is no apparent trail back to the original source as there is with a cheque, wire transfer or other paper-based instrument. Small cheque deposits and other instruments can also be used and placed into accounts at multiple locations of the same bank or different banks. The banking system itself is utopia for illegally derived money. It is a place of conjoining and concealment and does not necessarily allow for distinction between licit and illicit funds. Notwithstanding, of the three stages, placement is the best point of identifying illegality since the transfer and conversion elements of banking are not yet fully engaged at this juncture thereby providing a window, albeit a brief one, for discovering or detecting nefarious activity (Woods, 1998).

The activities employed at the layering stage occur after the funds have entered the financial system and can vary considerably. The idea of layering is understood through the lens of an individual living in a cold country: protection from the cold is supported by appropriate dress. This protective covering essentially hides one's core from discovery by, in this case, the wind! Over-exposure might result in sickness or something worse. Likewise, to protect illicit funds from discovery by enforcement authorities and by extension the criminal from sanction, layering involves cloaking (covering) your tracks (underlying crime) with the various types of facilities and offerings made available by financial institutions. These include electronic remittances; the purchase of bank drafts, foreign cheques, credit cards and other financial instruments. This stage will also include the use of multiple financial institutions; the creation and use of corporate vehicles or other complex legal arrangements such as trusts; the use of bearer instruments such as third-party cheques and bearer shares, and the buying and selling of property.

In terms of the facilitators of money laundering, that is to say, persons whose services may be co-opted to veil the criminal origin of funds, professional intermediaries such as lawyers, accountants, bankers and the like are among a smart criminal's foremost targets. The procedures which must take place to effect lawful transfer and/or the conversion of property requires involvement of counsel. High finance activities such as mergers and acquisitions, initial public offerings, securitisations and syndications also involve legal processes at various levels. Furthermore, with legal privilege at the centre of the attorney-client relationship, an additional veil may well be cast over underlying transactions, naturally serving the criminal client's preference for further cover up. In the layering stage, the objective is to employ the strategy of conversion and movement to further deepen or conceal the true (illicit) source of funds. Finding and, indeed, fitting together the pieces of the laundering puzzle is made all the more difficult when there is distance between the evil money and its original source.

This successful iterative progression leads to integration where the original tainted funds have been so mutated as to appear to be legitimate. This is also the illusory stage of laundering where funds are normalised and any inkling of illegality is inhumed in regular commerce (Ali, 2003). Clean funds can therefore be invested in tangible assets such as real property (e.g. land, arts and antiques); luxury assets or business ventures. This stage is said to be perhaps the most difficult point to detect that money laundering has, in fact, occurred.[4]

In terms of its utility, the benefit of clean money is in its ability to be used out in the open and without fear of law enforcement repercussions (Alldridge, 2001). Not so with evil money. This is where the "operational principles" inherent to the money laundering process come in, notes Blum et al. (1998). Each carefully choreographed stage not only minimises the uncertainty of being able to access the funds, but also aids in ongoing concealment of the underlying crime.

Practical money laundering

Stages notwithstanding, we should not entertain the thought that money laundering is a neat and tidy process which flows easily from stage to stage. In fact it is more dynamic than we could possibly think (Lilley, 2006). The dynamism of the process refers not only to the speed with which it can unfold, but also its seamless often non-linear nature. In reality, the process can be engaged at any of the stages, based on a number of factors including:

a   the intention of the launderer;
b   format in which the illicit monies are held at any point;
c   what exchanges or conversions have gone on before funds are brought to the vaults of a financial institution.

For example, if illicit funds are already exchanged and reformatted outside the banking system, thereby already constituting some form of laundering or concealment, the point at which the funds are actually received for deposit into an account may, in fact, begin the placement and layering stages simultaneously. It could also be the end stage of integration! Another example would be useful here. Let us look at a classic.

Box 3.1 Day at the races

Forty-five minutes before the end of the day, MJ Gabrosky finally got lucky. His bet on the 5–1 favoured horse, fortuitously dubbed Winning Streak, netted him earnings of $10,000. "At last!", he bellowed, in earshot of jealous, cheering punters, his right hand raised in clenched victory and the other clutching, for dear life, the only evidence of his rights to the ten grand – the cashier's receipt of the original punt.

Unknown to MJ, Fraulein Luceefra – a nickname spieled by squeaky high school co-eds because of her natural competence in the German language and her equally alluring looks – had been stalking him the whole day, oohing at his losses, ahhing at his near wins, hoping he would secure the spoils. MJ was, after all, her 13th mark for today. With her handler shadowing her every move, it took Fraulein Lu only moments to profile MJ: a recovering gambler who lost his young family to the same addiction in which he now gloried. She surmised the volatile Bahamian software developer had forever blamed himself, quite rightly, for a near tragedy. He was at the track to win back the money he had borrowed from the friend of a friend to settle the debt.

The Fraulein was spot on.

After the kidnapping of his two-year-old son – later found strapped in and crying in the back seat of a stolen SUV some seven miles from the rest stop he had pulled into for a cup of Colombian coffee, to assure himself he'd be awake for the next 100 miles back to Fort Lauderdale – MJ was a changed man. Or so he thought. He should have known not to mess with the Kahoots gang and to pay the money back as promised only the week before. But the risk-taker in him – and not the gambler – wooed his spirit to reinvest the winnings in multiple losing horses only to be back at square one. But not anymore, this win was it for him. After this he was out, he convinced himself.

He was tempted to throw his hat in again just for a last hoorah even as he hastily, half-hurried to the cute male cashier, only to be softly side-lined by a voice and a face out of Weinstein's Hollywood.

Lu could tell he was a lot less confident than he thought and went in for the kill. "Well done", she affirmed, with a smile of intangible contempt, deliberately crossing MJ's path and immediately extending an elegant palm to his, forcing a greeting – and a touch – all the while looking directly into his exploitable eyes, dilated and distracted with delight at his windfall.

"Do I know you?", queried MJ, now blocked from engaging the cashier's inviting eyes. His innocence was disgusting, Lu thought to herself. "No, but I'd love to", she sprouted back. "How much did you win if I may ask?" It was easy for MJ to boast of his lucky largesse, while throwing in his disappointment that it was not a bit more; just what Lu was waiting to hear. "I could help with that darling", she propositioned, knowing how to deploy her practice-perfect English accent at the most opportune moment, enough to add an aura of sophistication and trust to the game she played 12 times earlier in the day.

"Would you mind terribly if I buy that ticket from you, darling?" edging a little closer with lips ever so slightly, pursed, "I've got the cash and can give you a $1,000 more for your trouble". In the very moment MJ pondered the encounter and the offer, Lu's handler accidentally bumped into his co-criminal and wife, causing her to lose her balance and fall forward into a pair of reflexive arms MJ realised were his own.

It was all over. Her near accident brought the now suddenly reformed heterosexual MJ into proximity of a female body, something he had not felt for years. Parting with his ticket was all he could do to help the Fraulein in distress and with a $1,000 premium for his "trouble", all cash. Hell yeah!

Lu then took the ticket-for-cash to Arty, the cute but confederate cashier, slipping him another hundred bucks for falsifying the documentation and issuing a cheque in her name drawn on the company's account. Nobody saw the wink. "Just what the doctor ordered", Arty thought to himself. Having made an additional $1,300 extra for the day, he could now stock up on an additional month's supply of marijuana to treat his chronic back pain.

With evidence of her "winnings" in hand from the race track, Lu could deposit several of the 13 cheques into her own bank account over the course of the next six months; allowing a few to become stale-dated, so she could request a re-issue from the racing company. She would also be happy to invest in her brother-in-law's start-up bakery and have the remaining funds wired to her nephew, a final year resident at Johns Hopkins. So what if the underlying source was the last portion of the $250,000 she and her husband got from their lucrative drug trade? And the $2,400 between MJ and Arty? A mere cost of doing business.

As for MJ, without a receipt or some other indication of the source of his $11,000, he could find himself in a spot of bother trying to explain the origin of his alleged winnings to the credit union teller. He may find it necessary to break down his deposits into smaller amounts to beat the regulatory threshold, unaware that this kind of smurfing would likely be flagged by the institution's monitoring systems and potentially instigate the filing of a suspicious activity report. MJ then, in failing to pick up on the con, may find himself at the centre of surveillance or worse, an investigation.

He would talk through these concerns with his new friend Lu, when he would call her later that night.

In the back of the car, Fraulein Lu threw off her wig, peeled away her contacts and leaned forward to massage the neck of her chauffeuring husband on the way to the airport. "Always a pleasure doing business with you darling", cooed the Fraulein. "And with you my sweet", replied the handler.

Multi-coloured laundry

The money laundering cycle could also be deemed completed when dirty funds are comingled with the daily earnings of a regular store (in reality a "front" business), with total earnings reported as emanating from the cover business. Virtual accounting procedures may be engaged to reflect the combined income which is integrated into the financial system when deposited. As noted by Blum et al., all stages of the laundering process are satisfied; in this case in that: (a) the money is distanced (physically or meta-physically) from the crime; (b) hidden in the accounts of a legitimate business; and (c) resurface as the earnings of the firm with plausible reasons for generating that much cash (Blum et al., 1998, p. 11). Hence with the money laundering cycle completed well before funds hit the financial system, it is clear that either of the formal stages of the laundering process can be re-engaged separately, jointly or severally thus highlighting its dynamism and non-linearity. Moreover, it is the business environment itself which also can create opportunities for concealment of illegal monies. This will be further highlighted as we take a moment to visit the origin of money laundering and discuss why there is such attention being paid to it by the global community.

Once upon a time

Outside its metaphorical association, the notion of money laundering is also colloquial. Anecdotal evidence suggests the term appears to have originated alongside the activities of organised crime in the depression years of the 1920–1930s in the United States (Lilley, 2006). Prominent organised crime figures of that era were said to have used cash-intensive businesses such as laundromats and car washes as vehicles through which the financial proceeds of crime such as bootlegging and other types of racketeering were deposited into the financial system. Money laundering in that era was also used to avoid the aggression of corrupt police officers who, aware of the illegal activities engaged in by merchants, would demand to be paid "protection money". In return, the officers would look the other way. It was also used as a means of hiding criminal proceeds from one's competitors in illegal activity and evading the attention of tax authorities (Blum et al., 1998, p. 11).

Origins aside, it would be safe to suggest that attempts by perpetrators of criminal acts to conceal criminal proceeds are not contemporary phenomena. A criminal, regardless of the particular dispensation, would want to be able to derive benefit from illegal activities in much the same way as the ordinary individual would from licit endeavours (Taitt, 2006). Said benefit would be the ability to re-access ill-gotten gain at the expense of the institution or individual who (presumably) acquired it legally. Another key advantage would be the ability to employ the filthy lucre as working capital to fund more crime (Blum et al., 1998, p. 9).

One could also surmise that money laundering activities have existed as long as there was a need, be it commercial, legal, political or otherwise, to hide the nature and existence of financial transfers (Blum et al., 1998, p. 8; Masciandaro, 2004, p. 63). This seems to suggest there could come a time when there is a *legitimate* need to mask money movements and conceal the true nature of funds. An example that comes to mind is the situation involving the illegal garnishing of assets by state bodies under repressive governments or, worse yet, invading powers. In the case of the latter, the German occupation of surrounding nations in the Second World War and the subsequent rendition of Jewish wealth offshore to countries such as Switzerland, while meeting the criteria of concealment, does not necessarily fit the bill of a crime in the circumstances. Also the lack of restraint by national governing powers can place legitimately derived assets at risk of confiscation or forfeiture. Should right standing business stand by and allow this to happen without pushback, that is to say, by doing all that is possible to protect shareholder interests especially where there has been a breakdown in law and order or a blatant abuse of power? What about cases where the identification of witnesses must be protected in perpetuity having exposed the activities of organised crime networks? In the absence of an underlying crime per se it must be that concealment has an otherwise utilitarian benefit.

That said, attempts to legitimise money laundering money fall into questionable territory in circumstances where governments overstep their boundaries. A case in point might be where laundered funds are used to influence the course of conflicts between and among nations, factions and sects. Or where liabilities owed to countries are embedded within a forest of transactions to throw off would-be plaintiffs (Blum et al., 1998).

Although the term money laundering only seemed to have emerged in the twentieth century, it is accepted that the process may have been going on long before. In fact, it can be said that the idea of proceeds of crime is not restricted to epochs. Neither is the criminal's intention or expectation to benefit from its use. However, by developing a language and defining the various processes involved, modern societies are better able to articulate a perpetual reality made more poignant by certain contemporary environmental factors.

Financing acts of terror

This is not necessarily the same for terrorist financing. First of all there is nothing colloquial about using money to fund the killing of people in the name of something bigger or "someone" higher. By hitching the combating of terrorist financing to the money laundering coach simultaneous attention is accorded key global scourges in a focused manner. As to what constitutes terrorist financing itself, we get substantive insight from Article 2 of the United Nations (1999) International Convention for the Suppression of the Financing of Terrorism:[5]

> Any person commits an offence within the meaning of this Convention if that person by any means, directly or indirectly, unlawfully and wilfully, provides or collects funds with the intention that they should be used or in the knowledge that they are to be used, in full or in part, in order to carry out:
> (a) An act which constitutes an offence within the scope of and as defined in one of the treaties listed in the annex; or

(b) Any other act intended to cause death or serious bodily injury to a civilian, or to any other person not taking an active part in the hostilities in a situation of armed conflict, when the purpose of such act, by its nature or context, is to intimidate a population, or to compel a government or an international organization to do or to abstain from doing any act.

Based on this definition, the distinction between money laundering and terrorist financing is skewed to the *purpose/use* of funds not their *origin*. Of note also is that, whereas the source of illicit monies may constitute a predicate offence for money laundering, the same cannot be said of the source of funds deployed to support terrorism. As for the latter, funds can be either lawfully or unlawfully derived. In fact, terrorist monies can originate from the simplest and smallest non-public donation to the very large conspicuous gift by a prominent international corporation. Such legitimate monies may be passed to charities, community groups or other civil organisations. There is no telling how the money will be used. Also, unless there is legal requirement for customers to disclose the use of funds, the matter of determining whether funds are terrorist-related may be difficult to prove. In any case, the disclosure of how funds are intended to be used does not mean they would be used in the manner disclosed.

This matter of the source and use of funds are important distinctions. For, although it is known that legitimately earned funds may be used to finance terrorism, what seems weakly represented in the literature is the use of legitimately earned funds that are applied towards future crime, that is, crimes outside terrorism. There appears to be little articulation of this reality as a societal transgression in contrast to the redundant clarionisation of the illegal source/proceeds of crime discourse, which has been an important plank of money laundering legislation in both developed and developing countries.

The proceeds of crime may be concealed in myriad ways notes Casella (2003). But the construction of money laundering on the basis of an underlying past crime alone means that a potentially important area of criminal coverage – that of the intended unlawful use of funds – is missed (Casella, 2003, p. 92). A more complete determination of money laundering should therefore capture the movement of funds through the financial system with the prospective criminal application of these monies (Casella, 2003, p. 93). That said, how exactly is one to prove that funds are intended for criminal use in the absence of the occurrence of a crime? Worst yet, from the point of view of the financial institution, what are the circumstances that could trigger the filing of a suspicious transaction report apart from failure to disclose the intended use of funds? And to what extent are clients allowed to change their minds when determining the amount required for use and in what format? Lastly, should the tracking of the intended use of funds be placed in the domain of financial institutions?

While there is added value in preventing the financing of criminal acts, the untold numbers of persons using the services of financial companies means substantial thought should be given to *how* such value is to be effected before venturing into this area.

Evil money and the economy

Unsurprisingly, the perspective of international institutions regarding the effects of money laundering is economic in nature. Prevailing rhetoric pegs money laundering as negatively impacting business; potentially undermining financial markets; also that money laundering endangers banks and/or national banking systems. It is also said to invite the corruption of professional service providers. In light of the systemic nature of global finance, the case is made for it to be controlled (Masciandaro, 1998; Johnson and Lim, 2002). Complementing these views is the FATF's targeting of financial institutions as a primary buttress point. Commercial banks are, in particular, the major broker of financial assets, linking deficit units to surplus units (Whitehead, 1969). Also, as noted in an earlier chapter, these entities are the first port of call in effecting monetary policy. Given their public interface, the stability of the financial system requires their conscription in stemming the flow of evil money.

Whether these economic "harms", notes Alldridge (2001), are sufficiently valid and real to merit wholesale criminalisation of money laundering is a question worth pursuing. If we look at the impact on business, for example, it is plausible that additional financial capital which has been illegally obtained and actively employed within a business can provide leverage over the competition, assuming prudent application. Competitors who are unable to nimbly respond within the change window due to the absence of matching financial input will eventually lose out. Closed businesses often result in unemployed people who, in turn, are hard pressed to pay their bills, service their loans, educate their children, buy insurance and acquire the necessary health care. There is also potential dampening of the economy where those who are eligible for jobs cannot find them. But would there not be a similar outcome if additional licit funds were deployed by the receiving business with competitors unable to respond? Furthermore, what if in the *illicit* scenario those funds were genuinely applied to enhancing the enterprise, delivering more innovative products at a reasonable price, creating employment and the requisite taxes paid to government? In other words, that no further illegal activity is engaged, funded or supported. Any notion of a threat in this context asserts Alldridge might, in fact, be an issue of "cross subsidy" which is better resolved within a competition law framework (Alldridge, 2001, p. 307). That may be so. However, the merging of, let us say, apples (licit funds) with oranges (illicit monies) for argument's sake, while expanding the basket of fruit in general will temporarily misrepresent the true flavour (intended impact) when pressed together. In an economic sense, illicit funds, because of their short shelf life – that is, the fact they are subject to removal from the economy on demand – can potentially distort both the quantitative and qualitative levels of output, investment, growth and other indicators of economic health believed to have been derived from a prescription of monetary policies (United Nations Office on Drugs and Crime, 2011).

As regards the notion of money laundering undermining financial markets, the concern here no doubt are the inefficiencies created as a result of the *underlying* reason for moving laundered funds, which is, to avoid disclosure rather than to maximise returns (Tanzi, 1996). The idea of making the most of one's money fares better in a preferential interest rate regime for high volume funds and over the long term. Given this time horizon, funds may be utilised more efficiently within an economy and bring about higher yield for households. However, non-disclosure is no fan of high premiums and for practical purposes relishes the short term. As we have learned, it is concealment achieved through movement (layering) and ready accessibility (hence the short term) which maintain the darkness required for criminal control. Thus with vast sums of laundered money jumping across borders and entering and exiting markets in this manner, instability at both national and international levels cannot be ruled out (Tanzi, 1996, p. 7). Of specific concern at the jurisdictional level would be the movement in value of one's currency against others. As such movement is not trade-based but premised on capital flight, liquidity is put under pressure resulting in an increased cost of borrowing (Tanzi, 1996, p. 8). Such a threat is worth noting, particularly for import-dependent IFCs, whose bills must be settled in foreign currency.

But what of the so-called harm or potential compromise to which professionals might fall prey through their unwitting or even deliberate engagement of criminals in the course of their job? Do cultural mores and personal values not have some kind of role in those moments of choice? Are corrupt professionals ubiquitous in certain jurisdictions and less present in others? Most assuredly, the degree of supervisory effectiveness and the robustness of a legal framework in general exert equal influence in restraining atypical behaviour (Alldridge, 2001).

As to how exactly money laundering may be harmful to a bank or a particular banking system, is a compelling question indeed. A bank's insolvency relates to the inability to meet its obligations and is easily one of its primary risks. However, with laundering (hiding evil money using the bank's conversion and transfer mechanisms) there is no *direct* threat as such to ongoing viability. This is also true of other informal financial transfer networks such as bureaux de change. Nonetheless, there is still a potential hazard and a significant one at that. The hazard is rooted in the frailty of a commercial system of exchange grounded, historically, on trust. Trust itself relies on and lives in, perception. And perception we know to be the lens through which we, as customers ourselves, interpret reality. Therefore, when our trust is eroded, our behaviour as depositors can be powerfully influenced. Bank runs can be triggered when we as individuals or corporate depositors perceive our funds and the access thereof, to be at risk. This might be less so for sovereign depositors who wish to retain their deposits in an otherwise risky institution, for political purposes. Sovereign withdrawals would be, after all, the primary indicator that something is, in fact, wrong. Such perception may be shaped or instigated by a single or multiple variables. For example, although largely responsible for the poor state of its economy, Greece's government had to intervene to restrict clients' access to their own funds to avoid such a bank run following failed austerity measures emerging out of the Great Recession of 2008.[6]

Overzealous media reporting can also tap into public emotion by conveying the impression that all may not be well within an economy, thereby setting and/or reinforcing a tone of disquiet among the citizenry. Our perception is also influenced by the behaviour of an institution's top management where it is believed they are conducting the bank's affairs in a manner inconsistent with the institution's mandate; that the institution's management is dishonest, is in bed with criminal elements and believed to be engaged in assisting criminals in laundering funds, let us say from arms trafficking. These are merely a few examples, yet present in each of them is an ounce of perception in influencing reality and hence, actions. The fact that financial institutions bank with, lend or otherwise do business with each other and that government is also involved in the mix, so to speak, means the potential for contagion is a serious one and the overall harm can be significant. We see this idea of contagion fleshed out once more in the 2008 crisis where inferior debts were repackaged and traded across several financial institutions, resulting in some cases in these institutions' destabilisation, ultimate demise or bail-out by government. I return to this in the upcoming chapter.

In terms of the corruption of professionals, I believe it is a viable concern in the AML debate. While right thinking people might assume probity, the truth is we do not really know for sure what goes on behind the confidentiality veil underpinning these professions. Such legal cloaks can protect both felon and upright, much like the financial system may be used, simultaneously, for criminal and legitimate purposes. Even as I contemplate this idea, what comes to mind are the nuanced, unsolicited assertions by the former Attorney of President Trump, Michael Cohen, as being the leader of the free world's "fixer". While Special Counsel Robert Mueller's probe into Russia's meddling in the 2016 US elections remains fluid at the time of writing, it is the mere job description inherent in Cohen's self-processed role which borders on subtlety and comes to rest on suspicion.

Having to some extent addressed the money laundering rhetoric and the case for its criminalisation, what of the actual precipitators or underlying influences that result in its proliferation?

The criminal and work

Effective criminals make use of essentially the same framework of systems and procedures available to the honest business person. Thus, the idea of planning, organising, controlling and leading are not actions foreign to malefactors. Indeed, these are the very elements which are necessary for the execution of illicit activity and the attainment of "business objectives".

Certainly, when we think of the activities of the professionally networked criminals, we think of an organised system operating out of a structure set up with defined roles and responsibilities, internal controls and feedback mechanisms including audits and assessments of various kinds. The only difference is the *product*. This differs widely from the standard goods and services of the licit economy (Friman and Andreas, 1999). They include, but are not limited to, trafficking in psychoactive substances such as heroin, cocaine and marijuana; human trafficking (including child slavery and prostitution); arms smuggling; blackmail; trading in endangered species; toxic waste dumping; kidnappings; black-market currency operations and most other illegal and inhumane commercial activity. As if this were not enough:

> there is even a growing illicit transnational trade in human body parts, thanks to the modern technologies that make it possible to store and ship high-demand organs such as kidneys, livers and bone cartilage.
>
> (Friman and Andreas, 1999, p. 2)

Given their sinister and unlawful nature, these deviant activities would hardly ever be represented in the regular domain of business far less as stand-alone corporatised ventures. Rather, they might well be hidden from public view under the cloak of a "front" organisation or cover business, portraying to an unsuspecting public, an image of corporate citizenship and ethical altruism. Lilley (2006, p. 3) asserts that "the proceeds of crime are so massive that they and the people who control them can yield great influence in relationships with legitimate businesses hungry for profit". I take this to mean that a "front" organisation may not necessarily be owned outright by criminal elements. Rather, it may be the lure of prospective capital gains that an otherwise honest proprietor would allow his or her business premises to be knowingly used in the commission of crime; the prospective gains being a share in the profits. Another useful option for the acquisition of business capital in this way would be simply agreeing to facilitate the comingling of illegal wealth from organised crime sources with legitimate revenues. In either case, such enterprises become particularly vulnerable to extortion.

Fanning the flames

It is important to underscore the pervasive reality of this influence since this epoch, like no other, is dominated by certain enabling forces which aid, albeit unintentionally, the expansion of the activities of organised crime. These forces include the technological revolution, which as we know allows for seamless financial transfers and electronic trading; the ascendance of capital markets, a trading hub for global money (of all stripes); higher living standards and with that great expectations of more educated populations, which in turn demand a constant flow of financing income, irrespective of the source. The increase in knowledge is not exploited by the good guys alone. Organised crime, like any business, requires investors. And these investors expect a return on their stakes. Actually, if you think about it, there is little stopping cash-rich organised syndicates from plying their trade on a global scale. Nor can we forget the erstwhile increase in competition which provides consumers with a greater range of options at competitive prices. Low prices we know can result from various actions including effective cost management, but also criminal subvention. The cultural exchange which takes place through the transmigration of labour could also mean a commutation of personal moral codes and therefore potential susceptibility to criminal wrong doing.

The increased knowledge base of investors in organised crime would also suggest an increase in demand for the types of products/services that will yield increased criminal proceeds. The elimination of barriers to trade will allow cash-rich organised syndicates to invest abroad thereby expanding reach. The movement of labour enables crime bosses to employ the best and brightest to further entrench themselves and their influence in government, business and society.

When taken together, these attributes make the financial system all the more appealing to organised crime in that it provides cartels, mafias and their associations with just the framework and, indeed, the camouflage needed to transport huge quantities of illegal funds on a global scale. The ability to detect, trace or furthermore recover illicit monies in such circumstances is thus extremely difficult.

Although the notion of globalisation is often viewed from the standpoint of OECD countries (Mittlelman, 2000), these push factors are the offspring of a capitalist engagement which stimulate professionally networked criminals to expand their activity. Conditions favourable to their work are, after all, handed to them on a platter. Thus, electronic commercial gateways are exploited to reinforce the disguise and concealment of illicit wealth. Through its conversion to "megabyte" money, its potential movement is made so exponential as to traverse more jurisdictions than most persons would visit in their lifetime.

Crime cartels and institutional corruption

A common modus operandi of transnational crime groups is to deliberately infiltrate corridors of power, particularly government, business and law enforcement with the ultimate aim of wielding influence, commanding resources, and tilting decision-making in their favour (Shelley, 1999). Often, their aim is to gain access to parliaments or their equivalents by paying off officials in order to secure lucrative contracts and licenses and also to ensure their illegal enterprises are able to operate securely. This is why the movement of labour across the world is of significance to crime bosses. It enables the deployment of skilled and trusted lieutenants to further entrench themselves and their influence across societies.

Under public regulatory programs for example, notes Shelley (1998, p. 18), firms may pay to get a favourable interpretation of the rules or to lighten the regulatory load, pointing to the reality that rules can be leveraged by officials possessing discretionary power, to their financial advantage. Often, the motivation to accept bribes has to do with the lack of motivation of bureaucrats which in turn is also linked to their low remuneration. With such conditions present, the work of the criminal is made easy as the tenets of corruption are simply waiting to be exploited. To Rose-Ackerman (1999), bribes therefore can be seen as incentive payments for bureaucrats, even though taking bribes is arguably a crime in most countries. This inevitably makes bribery a predicate offence for money laundering and as such derived proceeds will need to be hidden in order to obscure the source.

Organised crime can infiltrate financial institutions through its employees as well. Walker (2000), Levi (2001) and Wright (2002) all agree that money laundering is often effected by inside assistance. Walker for example proposes that money laundering is made easy by the complicit behaviour of key bank officials with criminals (Walker, 2000, p. 6). Basing his assertions on the results of a review of the BCCI scandal, Walker concludes that through deliberate errors of omission by senior officials aware of the criminal source of funds, a culture of deception was allowed to perpetuate within the bank. Mention is also made of pay-offs to political figures in the 73 countries where BCCI operated, implying corruption at government level.

According to Levi (2001, p. 206), some reliance is placed on public and corporate agents to exercise the appropriate discretion the would-be money launderer requires in handling funds, particularly where co-operation is required by law enforcement authorities. Consistent with this notion, Wright draws upon observations made by the UK's Serious Fraud Office that:

> Money laundering can only take place where there are sophisticated professionals, e.g. lawyers, accountants and bankers, who are willing to be actively engaged in criminal acts or simply shut their eyes to the truth.
>
> (Wright, 2002, p. 240)

These conclusions, particularly those drawn by the law enforcement practitioners Walker and Wright from actual cases are consistent with the posture of the US Federal Reserve Board. In his testimony before the Committee on Banking and Financial Services Financial Services in 1998, Deputy Associate Director of Banking Supervision and Regulation, Herbert A. Biern, affirmed that banks and their employees are the "first and strongest line of defense against financial crimes and in particular, money laundering".

More importantly these views are in alignment with the agent-principal theory espoused by (Bowles, 1999). The phenomenon of corruption is viewed as a problem of asymmetric information involving collusion between agents and outsiders, against principals, or between supervisors and agents against principals. In crafting this theory, Bowles distinguishes corruption from the actions of extortion and fraud, proposing that the latter two involve a unilateral action by a person or group aimed at advancing their own interest at the expense of others (Bowles, 1999, p. 460).

Corruption has its place where efficiency is enhanced, notably so in emerging economies (Rashid, 1981). Addressing the issue of shortage should be paramount within these countries and once there is willingness and an ability to pay a premium – that is, a bribe (within reason of course) – access to the supply should be facilitated. Within such constraints greasy palms are just the oil needed to activate rusty bureaucratic wheels.

However, outcomes could change where unchecked dependency on bribe-paying patrons ends up doing more harm than good (Rashid, 1981, p. 449).

Rashid's philosophy while steeped in economic theory and development is disputable. For example, Seyf (2001) asserts that while powerful individuals may, in fact, benefit from corruption, the upshot is actually a waste of already scarce resources at the macro-economic level. Rather, the origin of shortage in a developing context is a weak productive base (Seyf, 2001, p. 602). If Seyf's perspective is applied to the economic framework of contemporary Caribbean economies, clear evidence suggests a deficiency in the natural resource base.

Disputing Rashid's argument further, is it really that corruption is pervasive in the developing Caribbean due to lack of resources? A brief perusal of the Transparency International Corruption Perceptions Index[7] over the three-year period 2007–2009 demonstrates that this is not necessarily the case, as several Caribbean island developing nations were ranked among the least corrupt in the world. In some cases, the rankings of these nations actually improved over time. Barbados, for example, moved up the rankings from 23 in 2007 to 20 to 2009. In 2007 St. Lucia was ranked 24th, 21st in 2008 and 22nd in 2009. From a ranking of 30 in 2007, Saint Vincent and the Grenadines moved up to 28th in 2008, falling to 31st in 2009. The small island nation of Dominica also featured relatively high in the overall rankings in the review period moving from 37th in 2007 to 33rd in 2008 and falling one place to 34th in 2009. It should be noted that these rankings are out of a total world sample of over 170 countries. A snapshot of 2017 rankings showed some fall-off in the noted jurisdictions, with Barbados in 25th place, St. Lucia in 48th, St. Vincent and the Grenadines in 40th and Dominica in 42nd.

In fairness to Rashid, though, it may be the public sector reforms engaged by these countries in the decades following his 1981 observation which support the, generally, favourable rankings noted. Be that as it may, neither he nor Bowles (1999) addresses the impact on the individual engaging in the corruptive act. This brings to the table the moralist perspective of Wright (2002). According to her, "assisting criminals has a corruption and corrosive effect on the professionals who associate with them". This seems to imply that once an individual engages in the initial corruptive act a rub-off effect is precipitated, resulting in actions which may be difficult to shake over time. The fleshing out of such a perspective may be immediately and easily applied to virtually any situation anywhere in the world involving the exchange of goods and services.

It must be pointed out that corruption, while often associated with low- to mid-level bureaucrats unhappy with the system, is certainly not confined to them. Rose-Ackerman (1999, p. 113) suggests that politicians at the highest level in both democratic and non-democratic states fall prey to corruption. This is evident in the plethora of examples in modern-day governments whose leaders appear bent on personal enrichment. What this implies is that where there is an absence of appropriate checks and balances via internal governance systems, power can be centrally controlled such as to facilitate corruption. In fact, the notion of discretionary power is deemed by Doig and McIvor (1999) and Jain (2001), respectively, as precursors to corruption. The former particularly, note that:

> Corruption has frequently taken place in societies where there is considerable discretion for public officials, limited accountability, and little transparency in governmental operations. In such societies civil institutions are often weak or undeveloped and the public voice silenced.
>
> (Doig and McIvor, 1999, p. 657)

Notably, discretionary power is attractive to rent-seekers and may be exploited by interest groups or others in a position to do so (Jain, 2001, p. 77). Weak judicial and accountability systems further compound this issue by allowing wrongdoers on both sides to go unpunished thus reinforcing the cycle of corruption.

Walking the talk

It is fair to say that how actors in an organisation conduct themselves depends on the tone set and modelled by top leadership. If this tone is one of compromise tending towards corruptive behaviour, such would be the prevailing spirit or attitude within the bounded territory of the organisation. Under such conditions, a ripe environment is created for corruption and self-dealing. On the other hand, where an ethical tenor is struck at the highest level and backed by appropriate control and governance mechanisms, deviations from established norms and principles will stand out as aberrations. Offenders can then be adequately disciplined. Similarly, tone and standards are especially critical at the political level, as they send a message through bureaucratic ranks as to the kind of conduct desired and expected down the line. They also send a message to the electorate and broader society as to the manner in which government conducts its business and therefore the type of culture it has chosen to embrace. This notion of tone may also be extended beyond national boundaries to a transnational space. Here, influential bodies depending on their purpose, convey expectations in regard to the type of conduct preferred within their sphere of authority and towards specific outcomes. Therefore, understanding these powers, their derivation and underlying motivations is fundamental to our question of the effectiveness of regulatory controls in solving the money laundering problem. It is these concerns to which we now turn our attention.

Notes

1 See Resolution adopted by the UN Nations via Articles 3 (b) and 3 (c). Available at: http://www.unodc.org/pdf/convention_1988_en.pdf
2 See Resolution adopted by the UN General Assembly via Articles 6 and 7. Available at: http://www.unodc.org/pdf/crime/a_res_55/res5525e.pdf
3 FATF website at: http://www.fatf-gafi.org
4 See Money Laundering FAQs at: http://www.fatf-gafi.org
5 Available at: www.un.org/law/cod/finterr.htm
6 See https://www.thedailystar.net/business/greece-banking-shutdown-sparks-global-markets-slump-104914
7 Corruption Perceptions Index © 2007–2009 by Transparency International. Licensed under CC BY-ND 4.0.

References

Ali, S., 2003. *Money laundering control in the Caribbean*. London: Kluwer Law International.
Alldridge, P., 2001. The moral limits of the crime of money laundering. *Buffalo Criminal Review Law*, 5(1), pp. 279–319.
Blum, J. A., Levi, M., Naylor, R. T. & Williams, P., 1998. Financial havens, banking secrecy and money laundering. *Criminal Justice Newsletter, United Nations*, 8(34 and 35), pp. 1–72.
Bowles, R., 1999. Corruption. Refereed entry 8500. In: B. Boukaert & G. De Geest, eds. *International encyclopedia of law and economics*. Vol. V. *Criminal law, economics of crime and law enforcement*. Cheltenham: Edward Elgar, pp. 460–491.

Casella, D., 2003. Reverse money laundering. *Journal of Money Laundering Control*, 7(1), pp. 92–94.

Doig, A. & McIvor, S., 1999. Corruption and its control in the developmental context: An analysis and selective review of the literature. *Third World Quarterly*, 20(3), pp. 656–665.

Friman, H. & Andreas, P., 1999. Introduction. In: H. Friman & P. Andreas, eds. *The illicit global economy and state power*. Maryland: Rowman & Littlefield Publishers Inc., pp. 1–17.

Jain, A., 2001. Corruption: A review. *Journal of Economic Surveys*, 15(1), pp. 71–121.

Johnson, J. & Lim, D., 2002. Money laundering: Has the Financial Action Task Force made a difference? *Journal of Financial Crime*, 10(1), pp. 7–22.

Levi, M., 2001. Money laundering: Private banking becomes less private. In: R. Hodess, J. Banfield & T. Wolfe, eds. *Global corruption report*. Berlin: Transparency International.

Lilley, P., 2006. *The untold truth about global money laundering, international crime and terrorism*. London: Kogan Page Ltd.

Masciandaro, D., 1998. Money laundering, banks and regulators: An economic analysis. *Issue Working Paper* 73.

Masciandaro, D. ed., 2004. *Global financial crime: Terrorism and organized crime, money laundering and offshore centers*. Farnham: Ashgate Publishing.

Mittlelman, J., 2000. Globalization: Captors and captive. *Third World Quarterly*, 21(6), pp. 917–929.

Rashid, S., 1981. Public utilities in egalitarian LDC's: The role of bribery in achieving Pareto efficiency. *Kyklos*, 34(3), pp. 448–460.

Rose-Ackerman, S., 1999. *Corruption and government: Causes, consequences and reform*. Cambridge: Cambridge University Press.

Seyf, A., 2001. Corruption and development: A study of conflict. *Development in Practice*, 11(5), pp. 597–605.

Shelley, L., 1998. Crime and corruption in a digital age. *Journal of International Affairs*, 51(2), pp. 605–620.

Shelley, L., 1999. Transnational organized crime: The new authoritarianism. In: H. Friman & P. Andreas, eds. *The illicit global economy and state power*. Maryland: Rowman & Littlefield Publishers Inc., pp. 25–51.

Taitt, K., 2006. Regulation and the burden on banks and client services. *Offshore Investment*, February, pp. 21–22.

Tanzi, V., 1996. Money laundering and the international financial system. *IMF Working Paper 96/55*.

United Nations Office on Drugs and Crime, 2011. *Estimating illicit financial flows resulting from drug trafficking and other transnational organized crimes*. Vienna: UNODC Studies and Threat Analysis Section.

Walker, L., 2000. *Corruption in international banking and financial systems*. Canberra: Australian Institute of Criminology in association with Australian Federal Police and Australian Customs Service.

Whitehead, G., 1969. *Commerce made simple*. Oxford: Butterworth-Heinemann Ltd.

Woods, B., 1998. *The art and science of money laundering: Inside the commerce of the international narcotics traffickers*. Colorado: Paladin Press.

Wright, R., 2002. The hiding of wealth: The implications for the prevention and control of crime and the protection of economic stability. *Journal of Financial Crime*, 9(3), pp. 239–243.

4   Ruling the darkness

Prologue

From personal reflection we appreciate that our tendency as individuals, to act in a specific manner may be influenced by various factors. These factors may originate from within ourselves, in terms of our own value composition and personal motivations or, alternatively, from an external source which compels our actions in an intended direction. Either way, there is an outcome. With stemming the flow of evil money top of mind, this aspect of our discussion addresses the institutional stimuli shaping compliance and the complementary role of values and other intrinsic motivators in producing the desired results.

Control framework

The FATF is the principal standard-setting body responsible for the global framework around the prevention and control of money laundering. And in the aftermath of the 9/11 attack on the World Trade Center, the control of the financing of terrorism. The actions of non-state actors in proliferating weapons of mass destruction have received the attention of the UN Security Council and efforts to counter the financing of proliferation have been included in the FATF's work. Underpinning this work are the FATF's 40 Recs.,[1] essentially guidance as to what a country's legislative and regulatory frameworks should look like if they are to effectively mitigate these risks. In order for these recommendations to take hold, they must be reflected within a nation's legislative and regulatory reality. This, in turn, creates substance at a national level against which compliance becomes necessary and regulatory monitoring and supervision responsibilities perpetuated. Not to be forgotten is the gap analysis necessary within the financial institution and the consequent adjustments required to internal policy and procedures. Supplementing these expectations is an independent, mutual evaluation of national frameworks by the FATF agents with a view to determining their degree of robustness and adherence to the 40 Recs. Consistent with the work of auditors, a report of findings is then prepared and drafts sent to competent authorities for input and comment. The final report is made available to the government of the day and also posted on the internet for public viewing. An important control mechanism deployed by the FATF, mutual evaluations reveal this entity's mind-set regarding stemming the flow of evil money and the extent to which it will hold nations accountable for failure to engage reasonable efforts to do so.

The work of the FATF and its ongoing influence create a platform of sorts for a deeper dive into the nuances of regulation and the kinesis of its next of kin, compliance.

Let us see where this dive takes us in our understanding of the importance of rules and the extent of their role in maintaining a sense of order within a social system, in this case the banking system.

Understanding what we do not know

Up to the end of the 20th century, the idea of regulation had received the attention of scholars mostly from the fields of law, politics and economics (Morgan & Engwall, 1999). Quite naturally, the legal slant was initially concerned with the utility of compliance in the administration of justice. However, in the work of Ogus (1995) we see an integration of economic theory into regulatory analysis in part to gain a better understanding of the extent to which efficiencies (cost savings) were realised through public legal interventions. As to be expected, the policy side was of key concern to political science scholars, mainly from the angle of causation: how and why different forms of regulatory processes emerged in industry and society. Also featuring in these analyses were assessments relating to the extent to which regulatory systems were captured by regulated constituents (Morgan and Soin, 1999, p. 166).

Common amongst the highlighted streams, though brief, is an economics dialectic – a prevailing intercourse between markets and regulation. And this is understandable when the context is laid bare: deregulation of financial markets unfolded in the 1980s and into the 1990s and scholarly interest had piqued in terms of seeking to understand its economic effects. Fast forward to Haines (2011) and we find affirmation of the economics of business as a good starting point for building understanding of what constitutes the idea of compliance in the first place. Here is where competitive pressures and organisational culture entwine to influence regulatory compliance outcomes (Haines, 2011, p. 288). Of course, while compliance has been traditionally hinged to a legal framework of some kind what makes its achievement challenging in part, is understanding the underlying purpose of the governing law or rule and the context of its origination (Haines, 2011, pp. 287–288). The resulting dissonance occurring from time to time can give rise to antonymous interpretations of what, in fact, is required to be compliant and is perhaps why regulatory inspectors at times apply various working definitions of compliance when operating in the field (Hutter, 1997).

Reverting briefly to the initial rationale of a governing law, it is generally understood that laws for the most part are enacted to shape the behaviours necessary for an ordered society. However, there is also the reflexive enactment of laws based on harm perpetrated on and experienced by a community. In this regard, an influencing factor intrinsic to law making often considered by incumbent governments is the idea of legitimacy. For the political directorate, this is important if only to give their base the impression their interests are being taken care of, when in fact they are acting out of self-interest in order to mitigate political risk. Inevitably, this posture of legislative enhancement is not adopted to truly reduce threats; rather it is engaged to quell public anxieties in the short term sufficient to enable policy-makers the opportunity to live to fight another term (Haines, 2011, pp. 292–293).

Prison break

Earlier, failure to expand studies in such a way as to embrace the insight and thoughts of other stakeholders would eventually limit the effectiveness of analyses conducted from within the noted streams at the time. Often, these parties would independently cultivate and interpret their own reality leading to self-referential conclusions as to how markets and structures should operate. Unfortunately, what bearing these perceptions had on the regulatory process were not necessarily considered (Morgan and Engwall, 1999). The missing link from the political science analysis was the incorrect alignment of market dynamics with the ways in which organisations and managers understand and construct forms of regulation (Morgan and Engwall, 1999, p. 2). A not dissimilar conclusion was also made in assessing the approach of the economist movement. Notably, that little attention was paid to the "historical construction of systems and styles of regulation (and) the social interaction of consumers, governments and firms in the regulatory process" (Morgan and Engwall, 1999, p. 2).

In general, what this says to us is that the historical bases on which regulation was analysed would only have provided us with a fractional view of what was to become an important distinctive in the globalised world of the 21st century. Shortcomings not-withstanding, a path was created for new insight and approaches to emerge such as the organisational approach to regulation as seen in the work of Morgan and Soin (1999), Parker (1999, 2000) and Caroll and McGregor-Lowndes (2002), to name a few. In addition, approaches examining the socio-economic influences on regulatory compliance through the insight of Sutinen and Kuperan (1998) and psycho-social motivations for compliance through studies conducted by May (2004) and Tyler (2006), respectively, would add further to the historical discourse. Other contributions seeking to explain compliance from an inside out perspective, that is to say, through the lens of the business enterprise, expand on earlier work in some cases. In particular, compliance motivations, capacity and enforcement as well as the influencing nature of the broader social and economic environment on compliance, are mustered by Parker and Nielsen (2011). In the meantime, environmental regulation had been consistently carving out its own space throughout, providing the initial language and rendition to the contemporary problem of climate change, see Gunningham et al. (1998), Gunningham and Sinclair (1999), Gunningham et al. (2003) and McClanahan and Cinner (2012).

The bare bones of compliance

For persons[2] involved in dealing either directly or indirectly with public funds, compliance with the laws and regulations governing their operations is critical. Particularly for financial institutions involved in retail and wholesale banking activities, specific disclosures relating to the product on offer and associated conflicts are legally required. At the foundation of these rules is consideration of the consumer, who lacks the specialist, institutionalized knowledge (Persaud, 2015). Laws and regulations are also critical if systemic risk is to be properly mitigated across a financial system (Persaud, 2015, p. 13). Failure to abide by these rules could invoke sanctions of various degrees including monetary fines; license revocation and jail terms for individuals acting on behalf of the entity at the time of regulatory breach. Sanctions are necessarily aimed in part at affirming public trust by ensuring accountability for actions inconsistent with agreed standards and also as a deterrent to potential wrongdoers. This contemporary reality helps in our processing of earlier rationales and strategies relating to regulatory compliance.

You see, compliance is established on the basis of regulation or the making of rules. In short, the need to comply can only be predicated on the fact that a set of directives have been created by an authority empowered to do so (Hutter, 1997). Thus in order to assure respect by those persons constituting the regulated group, appropriate adherent mechanisms, must be implemented (Hutter, 1997). Chief among such mechanisms would be control methods or checks and balances which further promote and reinforce compliance at an operational level (Baldwin et al., 1998). This view is consistent with that of Dodd and Hutter who deem regulation as a means of controlling economic behaviour; essentially the state's application of the law to "constrain and organize the activities of business and industry" (Dodd and Hutter, 2000, p. 2).

The gap that, unavoidably, obtains between the proclamation of a rule and its implementation by constituents would imply that compliance is fluid in nature (Hutter, 1997). As such, the journey to full compliance status will include *ongoing* efforts to achieve and maintain regulatory requirements, to phased-in progress *towards* future compliance. In this regard, there will likely always be a state of justifiable, albeit temporary, non-compliance (Hutter, 1997, p. 80). It is in this regulatory setting that compliance becomes "complex, flexible and dynamic" (Hutter, 1997, p. 237). Viewed in this way, if one considers the detailed inputs necessary to bring about the desired end-state – as in gap analyses, testing and reporting, communicating expectations across the enterprise and tweaking the policy and control framework – then from the regulatee's perspective, compliance is best located within a change-management framework. This in turn points to the need for a suitable implementation strategy, which, if executed correctly, has the effect of improving business processes and enhancing organisational effectiveness (Sadiq and Indulska, 2008).

Compliance models

Going deeper still, early strategies of regulatory compliance and enforcement unfurl in the work of Hawkins (1984) and Reiss (1984). These were the compliance (voluntary) model and the deterrence (command and control) model, respectively. The former was a deliberate, relationship-based effort that saw ongoing engagement with the regulator and the regulated. The approach featured these two actors as together being responsible for resolving emergent problems with the ultimate goal of avoiding penalties for non-conformance. In this context, sanctions were seen as the failure of the regulatory system.

In contrast, the deterrence model involved neither co-operation nor collaboration. In fact, the regulator deliberately distanced itself from constituents. The implication was as powerful as the intended effect and immediately shaped expectation of how engagement was to occur. This military style approach to regulation saw punishment and the use of threats and/or incentives being employed as the primary instruments to deter rule-breaking. Sutinen and Kuperan note these factors as extrinsic motivators and challenge their credibility as being the only policy mechanisms for improving compliance with regulations (Sutinen and Kuperan, 1998, p. 175). Similarly, May (2004) views the use of legal instrumentalities as negative motivations driven by fears of the consequences of being found in violation of regulatory norms. His outlook seeks to promote a broader appreciation of regulation as exceeding the mere enforcement of edicts to more of the fulfilment of a social contract (May, 2004, p. 42).

In viewing compliance as "more than an outward conformity with a regulation", Feest argues that external conformity and internal intention may not always jibe given the absence of information, in this case – the unawareness of what is considered the norm or regulation (Feest, 1968, p. 448). There may also be other influencing variables that have nothing to do with norm awareness such as the fear of sanctions (Feest, 1968, p. 448). But what about other possible compliance compulsions?

Behavioural considerations aside, the basic human tenet of personal choice would suggest it would be somewhat short-sighted to assume the primary reasons for rule adherence by actors could, in fact, be sanctions or for that matter incentives. What about one's internal compulsion to do the right thing? Also, what about the influence of peers in the decision-making process?

Sutinen and Kuperan (1998) observe that extrinsic factors fall short in providing a full explanation for compliance motivations. There are, in fact, other intrinsic factors that have to do with one's internal moorings and the impact of social influence. This perspective is again consistent with the standpoint of May, who points out "affirmative" motivations as "emanating from good intentions and a sense of obligation to comply" (May, 2004, p. 42).

Despite these views, it is noteworthy that the dominant approach to maintaining social order into the 21st century continues to be deterrence-based (Nagin 1998). It insinuates a greater level of confidence and certainty of adherence in a regulatory model in which public sanctions hold sway. What it also does is reinforce the significance of branding and reputation, essentially having a good name, in an interconnected world and the ease with which deliberate or unwitting acts of stigmatisation, regardless of source, can raise doubts. A common response in the form of hesitancy, in such circumstances, just goes to show how perception often has greater effect than reality, among global actors.

The other consideration is that a sanctions-based model sends a clear signal of intolerance for dealing in and benefitting from the proceeds of crime, reinforcing the good guys' mantra that "crime must never pay". The question of whether a sanctions approach *by itself* is, in fact, a successful deterrence tool in money laundering control and the extent to which it is effective in enforcing regulatory compliance – in the long term – are explored later.

Regulatory change

Modern-day business is fraught with incessant transformation. However, the advent of new laws and/or updated guidance from regulatory agents, particularly for financial commerce, should not be regarded as necessarily *originating* with them, although they may be *initiated* by them, at least to some degree.[3] Instead, legal insertions take their cue from the creativity and ongoing innovation of business actors vying for clients and the attendant potential profits. Thus in order to protect the consumer and/or investor in this competitive process from being disadvantaged, regulation becomes important to achieve the broader societal goal of order. Given the change intrinsic to the business of banking, it may be better therefore for regulatory compliance not to be regarded as a terminal point, but rather as an incremental movement towards objectives, which on near-achievement could suddenly change again, thereby precipitating a new compliance cycle alongside its earlier rotations. In addition, while singular deterrence may impact regulatory compliance positively in the short term, a more strategic view may be required for banks operating in small sized vulnerable economies such as in the Caribbean region. The responsiveness to change may be a factor in achieving positive regulatory outcomes. Here the simultaneous development of regulatory relationships alongside deterrence strategies may constitute a better option.

Also, responsiveness to regulatory change should not be mixed up with responsive regulation. The former relates to constituents' ability to manage the presumptive gap between new requirements and the incumbent institutional reality. Responsive regulation, on the other hand, is a means of ordering the environment over which the regulator has oversight. Context, history and regulatory culture play a defining role in this paradigm (Ayers and Brathwaite, 1992). And since it is allows for creative problem solving, the idea of responsive regulation is more of an attitude than a prescription-based form of engagement (Ayers and Brathwaite, 1992, p. 5). The notion allows for diversity amongst regulated entities even in terms of their conduct, whether positive or negative. Negative behaviour, for example, will trigger a greater degree of intervention than would positive behaviour (Ayers and Brathwaite, 1992, p. 4). This is perhaps why under the responsive model there is difficulty in identifying a clear-cut way forward. This is not an insurmountable problem, but is considered par for the course. In the end it is the outcome of the interplay between supporting and opposing forces, coupled with an understanding of what is required at that specific moment of consideration that will win out (Ayers and Brathwaite, 1992, p. 5).

Compared to the earlier deterrence model of compliance, responsive regulation enjoys greater latitude and as such is not impositionary (Ayres and Brathwaite, 1992). That said, is this specific model suited to money laundering prevention? More particularly, are the tenets of this regulatory strategy sufficiently sound to reduce the threat of a global concern given the apparent immediacy of the risk to national and institutional reputations and, indeed, a financial system? Although proactive laws are not possible for the simple reason that there are no suitable sanctions for a crime which is *not yet* committed, different approaches to regulation should be explored in order to ensure maximum exploitation of possibilities before honing in on an optimal approach. For example, the flexibility of the responsive model while configured to account for various types of movement within business would be considered inadequate when the problem of regulation is viewed through the lens of the environment. To regulate in such a context demands understanding that decisions can potentially impact future generations (Ayers and Brathwaite, 1992). This does not appear to have been taken into consideration by President Trump in his effective annulment of the Obama administration's efforts at forestalling climate change, through the latter's clean energy policy.[4] And this despite the broad based engagement with and sign off by 195 of the world's nations at a Paris summit in December 2015. That said, it should be understood that while stakeholder assent is a critical step in addressing a matter that touches all of us, consequential laws and rules on their own will be limited in their ability to *solve* this unique problem given its planetary scale (Gunningham et al., 1998).

Regulatory compliance and legitimacy

Another motivation for compliance has to do with the idea of legitimacy (Tyler, 2006). The thought is that an individual was likely to give deference to an authority in the form of self-regulatory behaviour where, in the eyes of the individual, the authority is assessed as authentic and acts in ways that are consistent with the individual's value system. Whether or not there was the risk of detection of breaches was immaterial. Such authenticity or genuineness finds its moorings on a public discernment that laws are being executed on an even-handed basis by legal archetypes, notably the police and law courts. Procedural justice is therefore instrumental to rule adherence in a context of juridical expectations (Tyler, 2006, pp. 161–169).

The Tyler application of legitimacy as a basis for conformity to legal rules may be contrasted to the organisational theory of legitimacy as a basis of conformity to social norms. In the latter case, legal officialdom is not required to forge compliance. According to Johnson, organisational legitimacy is conferred when influential parties constituting a group perceive that the desired outcomes of an entity are consistent with their own and endorse the actions and activities of the entity (Johnson, 2003, p. 38). As a result, the parties of lesser influence who may not necessarily agree with the activities of the entity find themselves having to conform to expectations. Inherent in this organisational approach is the issue of power where compliance is based neither on procedural justice nor intrinsic motivations, rather extrinsic motivations arising out of the instrumental fear of marginalisation from the main grouping and/or negative sanctions agreed upon within the main group (Tyler, 2006).

This specific notion of power relations in shaping compliance is reminiscent of the theory of social exchange as espoused by Blau (1964). According to him, voluntary actions by an individual are not always triggered by an internal proclivity, but sometimes by a social pressure to conform. Using the gift exchange process as an illustration, Blau observes that the real benefit accruing to the giver is their access to the broader society to which the recipient is party. Within this wider group the act of giving is itself highly regarded and viewed as consistent with group norms. Against this background, it is the broader social influence which forges conformity (Blau, 1964, pp. 88–111).

At the level of global relations, this is how the FATF appeared to have been able to exercise blacklisting measures against countries whose national AML regimes were not up to the standards it mandated and which were endorsed by the larger and more influential nations. We see a repeat of this scenario in 2009 when, in its ongoing attempt to level the playing field, the OECD issued a variegated list highlighting the extent to which countries had implemented tax information exchange agreements effectively allowing home countries the ability to elicit financial information as regards the external assets of its citizenry.

Regulatory compliance and anomie

An examination of the concept of anomie provides an additional social theoretical impetus into the literature dealing with regulatory compliance. Anomie was first addressed in European sociology by Durkheim (1897, 1951)[5] and developed later in American sociology by Merton (1938). Its derivative term "anomia" which deals more with one's psychological state, was later propounded according to Caruna et al. (2001), by theorists such as MacIver (1950) and Srole (1956).

Durkheim's theory of anomie is based upon a social condition whose main tenets comprise the absence of structure in the form of standards and/or rules and diminution in values. In such a state, the rudder of regulation is compromised eventually leading to a situation of normlessness. Durkheim viewed the *collective order* as the external regulating force which defined and ordered the goals to which men should orient their behaviour (Durkheim, 1951, pp. 248–249). This posture was borne out from the idea that man did not have the capacity to control his passions and therefore such control had to be exercised by a "force exterior to him". Thus with the disruption of this force or collective order there was nothing to keep man's aspirations or desires in check. The incessant demand for more would soon come to exceed the reality of being able to fulfil these proclivities resulting in "de-regulation" or "anomie". It is these conditions which ultimately, set the tone for deviant behaviour or non-compliance.

In analysing the relationship between anomie and deviant behaviour in the marketing domain, Caruna et al. (2001, p. 323) discuss anomia as a value internal to the individual and as such, a possible "antecedent variable to dishonest behaviour". Such insight is particularly useful in this book and helps us understand, at least in part, the link between personal and institutional values and regulatory compliance outcomes.

One of the precipitants of this de-regulatory state – anomie – considered of particular import to this study is the external environment of trade and industry; a context described by Durkheim as being in a chronic state of anomie (Durkheim, 1951, p. 256). This condition is perpetuated by the lure of vast and virgin international markets whose striking assets are made proximate by advanced technologies. The prospect of eternal riches stimulate further man's appetite for what he is yet to have but imagines he does. As a corollary to this perception, Durkheim felt that the constant pressure to strive for what he called "infinite" or "receding goals" was a material contributor to a breakdown in regulatory norms (Durkheim, 1951, pp. 249–257). Based on this Durkheimian concept, there appears to be some correlation with the 2007–2008 global meltdown as, for the most part, corporate greed and the vagaries of the capitalist system have been touted as key reasons for the depression.

Merton (1938) is able to build on this concept of social order by suggesting that anomie arises out of the disjunction occurring between societal goals and the means by which these goals are achieved. Different *modes of adaptation* are assumed by individuals according to their perception of social reality. Thus an individual may consider the goal of wealth accumulation to be attainable due to what is perceived to be the equally available access to acceptable means of goal achievement such as education and employment opportunities. In this case, one should expect the individual's actions to be integrated, resulting in behaviour compliant with social norms. However, deviant behaviour arises when it is perceived that one's access to societal goals is blocked. Notwithstanding these challenges, one's aspirations are not dampened and, as a result, *innovation* is deployed by the individual as an alternative vehicle to the closed institutionalised means. In other cases, where culturally accepted means of goal achievement are not respected, individuals may begin to manifest a behaviour that is ritualistic in nature as the means themselves become a focal point of ultimate value. The other adaptive means of *retreatism* and *rebellion* occur as a result of the perception that one's aspirations may never be reached and, as such, both the goals and the institutionalised means of attainment are rejected by the individual.

Whether positive or negative, the outcome of Merton's (1938) analysis highlights his concern about how social structures operate to pressure certain persons in society to engage in non-conformist rather than conformist conduct. Although his advancement of anomie theory addresses the individual's modes of adaptation to social pressure, the extant literature does not appear to suggest an application of anomie theory to the corporate "individual", that is, the institution. Modern legal jurisprudence denotes a company as being able to engage in business under its own recognisance such that it may sue or be sued. This legal persona allows the company to engage the world of trade and commerce on a competitive basis and in its own name. If one is to extend Mertonian theory into this business context, an argument may be made that suggests societal pressures (fuelled by the capitalist system of economics) are, in fact, exerted upon business entities or even nations to act in ways that are either consistent or inconsistent with social norms, such that adaptive modes are employed to deal with any apparent gaps between prescribed goals and the accepted means of achieving these goals.

If we raise the discussion to the level of nations, we find ourselves seeking to identify the mode of adaptation deployed by nations involved in the competition for international business in the pursuit of state goals. More specifically, how do larger nations respond when they perceive access to macro-capital as being hampered by the upstart micro-state known as the OFC? Lacuna aside, I see here an opportunity to augment present literature to potentially explain deviant or non-compliant behaviour such as institutional money laundering; complicit behaviour by institutional agents in facilitating it; and complicit behaviour by like-minded nations to reclaim power over global capital. By exploring these applications, we will be in a better position to assess whether the money laundering problem is really a problem. And if indeed so, to identify whether regulatory insertions alone can save the day.

Conclusion

Early discourse pertaining to regulatory compliance was rooted within the legal, political and economics streams, somewhat to the detriment of the sociological, psychological/ behavioural and, indeed, other perspectives. The strong emphasis on extrinsic motivations for compliance, that is to say, the incentives/sanctions that reward/penalise (deviant) behaviour, is evidence of this historical reality. Applied in the context of this book, the public disciplining of nation states by the OECD/FATF is, arguably, based on a sanctions or deterrence model of compliance. It would be unwise to view this model as a silver bullet, given the dynamic nature of finance and the verity that its institutions are manned by human beings possessing the ability to choose their response to occurrences within their environment. Scope is therefore opened up to build out the intrinsic motivations discourse, particularly the role of values in compliance formations, thereby adding to knowledge.

In the course of time, other regulatory compliance slants would emerge placing the spotlight on contemporary issues including the universal concern of climate change. Also, dialogue relating to the regulation of evil money flows within the Caribbean island financial centre, particularly concerning such matters as the impact of AML compliance rules on the business of this sector, appears less than substantive.

One must also not forget the social role played by regulation in maintaining an ordered society and the resulting disruption when societal codes are undermined by self-seeking miscreants at both the individual and corporate levels. The underlying motivations for such behaviour, such as the intensity of commercial capitalism, is a path that has opened up and one which merits further exploration to determine utility to the policy-making architecture of small island developing states. Simultaneously, there is the opportunity to augment prevailing insight, considering the global attention accorded money laundering risk and the enhanced regulatory governance measures required at strategic and operational tiers.

Notes

1 Available at: http://fatf-gafi.org
2 In addition to the individual, this term also refers to the corporate entity which, for legal purposes is regarded as a "person" in its own right.
3 Lobbyists, non-governmental organisations and other non-state actors are also involved in the regulatory process.
4 See Editorial, President Trump risks the planet. *New York Times*, 28 March 2017.
5 Durkheim's 1897 work is mentioned here as an antecedent to Merton's subsequent and further development of the idea of anomie. Thereafter, I refer to the reprinted (1951) version.

References

Ayers, I. & Brathwaite, J., 1992. *Responsive regulation: Transcending the deregulation debate.* New York: Oxford University Press.

Baldwin, R., Scott, C. & Hood, C., 1998. *A Socio-legal reader on regulation.* Oxford: Oxford University Press.

Blau, P., 1964. *Theory and exchange in social life.* New York: John Wiley and Sons Inc.

Caroll, P. & McGregor-Lowndes, M., 2002. *Managing regulatory compliance.* Melbourne: Australian Institute of Criminology.

Caruna, A., Ramaseshan, B. & Ewing, T., 2001. Anomia and deviant behaviour in marketing: Some preliminary evidence. *Journal of Managerial Psychology,* 16(5), pp. 322–338.

Dodd, N. & Hutter, B., 2000. Geopolitics and regulation of economic life. *Law and Policy,* 22(1), pp. 1–24.

Durkheim, E., 1897. Reprinted 1951. *Suicide: A study of sociology.* 2nd ed. New York: The Free Press of Glencoe.

Feest, J., 1968. Compliance with legal regulations: Observation of stop sign behaviour. *Law and Society Review,* 2(3), pp. 447–462.

Gunningham, N., Grabosky, P. & Sinclair, D., 1998. *Smart regulation: Designing environmental policy.* Oxford: Clarendon Press.

Gunningham, N., Kagan, R. & Thornton, D., 2003. *Shades of green: Business, regulation and environment.* Palo Alto: Stanford University Press.

Gunningham, N. & Sinclair, D., 1999. Regulatory pluralism: Designing policy mixes for environmental protection. *Law & Policy,* 21(1), p. 49–74.

Haines, F., 2011. Facing the challenge: Hercules, Houdini or the charge of the Light Brigade. In: C. Parker & V.L. Nielsen, eds. *Explaining compliance: Business responses to regulation.* Cheltenham: Edward Elgar Publishing Inc., pp. 287–304.

Hawkins, K., 1984. *Environment and enforcement: Regulation and the social definition of pollution.* Oxford: Oxford University Press.

Hutter, B., 1997. *Regulation and environment.* Oxford: Clarendon Press.

Johnson, J., 2003. Repairing legitimacy after blacklisting by the Financial Action Task Force. *Journal of Money Laundering Control,* 7(1), pp. 38–49.

MacIver, R., 1950. *The ramparts we guard.* Macmillan: New York.

May, P., 2004. Compliance motivations: Affirmative and negative bases. *Law and Society Review,* 38(1), pp. 41–67.

McClanahan, T. & Cinner, J., 2012. *Adapting to a changing environment: Confronting the consequences of climate change.* New York: Oxford University Press.

Merton, R. K., 1938. Social structure and anomie. *American Sociological Review,* 3, pp. 672–680.

Morgan, G. & Engwall, L., 1999. *Regulations and organizations: International perspectives.* London: Routledge.

Morgan, G. & Soin, K., 1999. Regulatory compliance. In: G. Morgan & L. Engwall, eds. *Regulations and organizations: International perspectives.* London: Routledge.

Nagin, D., 1998. Criminal deterrence research at the outset of the 21st century. In: M. Tonry, ed. *Crime and Justice: A review of research.* Chicago: University of Chicago Press.

Ogus, A., 1995. *Regulation: Legal forum and economic theory.* Oxford: Clarendon Press.

Parker, C., 1999. How to win hearts and minds: Corporate compliance policies and sexual harassment. *Law & Policy,* 21(1), pp. 21–42.

Parker, C., 2000. Reinventing regulation within the corporation: Compliance-oriented regulatory innovation. *Administration and Society,* 32(5), pp. 529–565.

Parker, C. & Nielsen, V. L., 2011. *Explaining compliance: Business responses to regulation.* Cheltenham: Edward Elgar.

Persaud, A., 2015. *Reinventing financial regulation. A blueprint for overcoming systemic risk.* California: Apress.

Reiss, J. A., 1984. Selecting strategies of social control over organizational life. In: K. Hawkins, ed. *Enforcing regulation*. The Hague: Kluwer-Nijhoff Publishing.

Sadiq, S. & Indulska, M., 2008. The compliance enabled enterprise – process is the product. *Compliance and Regulatory Journal*, 5, pp. 27–31.

Srole, L., 1956. Social integration and certain corollaries: An exploratory study. *American Sociological Review*, 21, pp. 709–716.

Sutinen, J. & Kuperan, K., 1998. Blue water crime: Deterrence, legitimacy and compliance in fisheries. *Law and Society Review*, 32(2), pp. 309–338.

Tyler, T., 2006. *Why people obey the law*. Princeton: Princeton University Press.

5 Working a hunch

Prologue

When it comes to following up questionable transactions or securing the necessary level of satisfaction with a client's bona-fides before on-boarding, compliance officers tend to encourage front-line staff to follow their gut; that headless brain which functions outside logic, hard evidence and pituitary analysis. Lenders also know of this emotion. It is not every borrower, after all, who will meet every requirement under regular rules. In fact, even though some borrowers meet all the requirements, the lender herself may remain uneasy with the overall lending proposal. It is nothing lenders can put their hands on per se, but to all intents and purposes the discomfort remains. In a nutshell, the lender has a hunch the client can be trusted to keep his or her side of the bargain, or not.

In this chapter, I lay bare my analytical framework and follow a hunch. The hunch being that my reflections on the effectiveness of regulation in curbing the evil money problem are best decoded within an institutional framework. I also set out the way in which I went about gathering the data I felt would be useful to my analysis.

Life without rules

I start by agreeing with Burrell and Morgan (1979) that without some form of regulation the governance of social life would prove difficult. To therefore root this work in functionalist theory is axiomatic. Moreover, to further explain my position and the questions at the heart of this work, the approach I took was from an integrative theoretical slant that drew on the work of Durkheim (1951), Merton (1938) and Blau (1964), respectively. These studies were in relation to social structure, regulation and anomie.

Durkheim's work, for example, sets the stage for our understanding of the role of the collective order as a regulative force aimed at curbing the passions of man and preserving the collective from disruption. His thinking enables an analysis of the capitalist agenda and structural power to energise intense competition. Additionally, the notion that the lack of governing standards or rules within an economy engenders anomic conditions supports the need for regulation in maintaining social control (Durkheim, 1951, pp. 248–249). However, the collective order he sees as the regulative force necessary to mitigate individual passions does not appear to promote personal responsibility in maintaining social norms. Rather, it seems to delegate primary responsibility to the external regulative force. By application to our key question of whether a purely regulatory fix – that is to say, a response from the collective – answers the threat of evil money, one notes from mere observation that it does not. Why?

The answer lies beyond amendments to and redeployment of the FATF's 40 Recs., systematic national legislative reforms and implementation of regulatory compliance systems in financial institutions. In fact, Durkheim admits that the business environment is generally in a *chronic* state of anomie (Durkheim, 1951, p. 254). To wit, as there is no end to man's appetite for wealth, goals recede – or put differently – the goal post keeps moving, resulting in an ultimate breakdown in the regulatory system (Durkheim, 1951, pp. 249–257). Thus, economic depressions, upturns, busts and booms notwithstanding, there is no defined end to wealth accumulation under capitalism. No zenith to profit maximisation. No end to organisational expansion. As a matter of fact, the achievement of one goal in the form of financial wealth brings with it a propensity to undertake a risk or risks to achieve another and still another, ad infinitum. In the same manner, within financial globalisation there is no defined barrier to either of capital access, capital retention, or the movement thereof. Therefore, with the ready availability of wealth (licit and illicit) to both institutional and private purchasers, how realistic is it to even attempt to assuage constantly renewed appetites? There is absolutely no shortage of contemporary examples of corporate and personal indiscretions. In fact, there is a glut! The most all-consuming instance post the year 2000 marker was the conspicuous 2008 financial crisis, the tail-wind effects of which would be experienced by island nations well after instigating economies had settled back down.

With a virtual inability to curb the appetite for wealth maximisation, a breakdown (anomie) is inevitable if the gap between the new goal set by business innovation and the implementation of countervailing regulatory guidance is too wide. I am of the opinion that, embedded within this interstitial space is a temporary lack of accountability – the absence of controls both at the personal and corporate levels – which means the tendency to take risks is higher than usual and remains so until the gap is closed by external (regulatory) insertion. It is also during this hiatus where new norms have not yet been established and, akin to Durkheim's rationale for anomic suicide, that personal and/or corporate mis-behaviours can, in fact, bring an end to burgeoning careers as well as the ruination of financial organisations. Criminal exploitation is also possible during this regulatory downtime. Such a situation appears to have been the case with the advent of virtual currencies, in particular, bitcoin, as early as 2011. In the absence of guiding rules of engagement for this disruptive innovation at the time, early adopters exploited the lack of regulatory oversight and, indeed, understanding of the crypto-currency market. Criminals used the apparent anonymity of the block chain to hawk drugs and engage in all forms of illegal activity. Despite its transformational tenets, intermediation was still required to bring together criminal buyers and criminal sellers. This demand gave rise to companies such as Silk Road, more than charmed to fulfil the call. However, in February 2015 its proprietor, Ross Ulbricht, was put away for life on seven counts ranging from aiding and abetting the distribution of narcotics, money laundering and various conspiracy charges.[1]

More of Merton (1938)

In terms of another precipitant for contrary behaviour, invoking Merton stimulates our understanding further. Taking Durkheim's anomie discussion to a different level, Merton speaks of anomie as occurring when there is a disjunction between societal goals and the means to achieve them (Merton, 1938, pp. 674–676). When persons come under pressure to achieve these goals, there are certain *modes of adaptation* which they engage. The method of adaptation adopted will correlate to their perception of whether or not they consider the means to achieve these expectations as being available to them or alternatively whether or not they wish to avail themselves of the means. Their choice will be to conform, deviate or adopt a neutralising mode of behaviour (Merton, 1938, p. 676). The potential value of Merton's insight is to demonstrate how the interpretation of social reality – for business entities this would be the competitive environment – influences corporate direction and actions. Take, for example, the decision-making paradigms of a company's senior executives. Among the primary judgements required from time to time are choices relating to enhancement of the bottom line, for example, how to (re)position the company to take advantage of future opportunities and how to respond to an innovative product launched by a competitor or pending restrictive regulatory ruling. It may be that deliberately pursuing clients functioning in illicit markets is considered acceptable in the circumstances and for the sake of institutional prosperity.

A parallel may also be made to the individual. For example, if an employee of a financial institution, upon surveying his or her own corporate everyday life notes for example that the path to promotion is being blocked by nepotistic behaviour. Or that access to educational opportunities – an important tool for advancement – is lacking; the employee may respond to this perceived reality purely out of self-interest. A tool of choice is that of conjoining with criminal elements (within or outside the firm) to achieve the goals in mind. In this respect, the case studies to follow later examine the collusive behaviour of employees and the possible underlying reasons inciting such misconduct.

Integrating Blau (1964)

Another brand of integrative theory being leveraged for this work is conjecture behind *exchange and power* espoused by Blau (1964). As with Merton (1938), we acquire a comprehensive understanding of social reality by linking micro and macro level assertions. The notion of how simple social interactions give rise to more complex ones, ultimately legitimising the operation of future relations, is potent. It shows just how subtly power can be accrued to an entity or person through the postures adopted in earlier and ongoing engagement. Blau's perspective will help analyse at a macro level, the relational interface of small emerging economies and their larger industrial neighbours who carry significant weight in standard setting bodies such as the FATF.

The theory of exchange and power may also be applied at a micro level to analyse individuals' interaction with the organisation, specifically their place of work. In the employer-employee relationship, either party (*ceteris paribus*) can, as it were, fire the other. Yet in practical terms there is, arguably, an imbalance of power, with the scales tipped in favour of the paying party. For the employee, constraints of conscience may emerge where the organisation's way of doing things clashes with personal mores. For all this, the employee may opt to go along with the company's wishes, in deference to institutional power. In short, since rocking the boat could impact the ongoing ability to support one's family, compliance might be deemed preferential amongst limited options.

Valuing offshore

Notwithstanding the centrality of offshore nations in the swirl of financial globalisation, their value remains, generally, unacknowledged. And, if acknowledged, then grudgingly so. Although questions of the legitimacy of standard setters arise whenever some new criticism is levelled at IFCs or a new compliance demand arises from left field, the cry of foul appears to have waned over time. There is now a posture of acclimatisation which has been adopted by targeted island states even as they continue to forge their way ahead. My sense is that these conflicts have their root in a power dynamic from which it may be difficult to self-extricate given the dependency variable. This makes Blau's work all the more relevant to this question of unresolved tensions. Hence, while Durkheim's and Merton's perspectives help to explain the potential forces which exert performance pressures on state and non-state actors alike, Blau's exchange theory is complementary in so far as it speaks to the relational component of social structure and the conduct of actors.

The ties that bind

Entwining my research was what I deemed a *trinary code*. On one strand, we have the encryption of international finance, characterised by hostility between the symbol economy and the real economy (Marshall, 2008). On another strand, we have the encryption of international crime, an equally dominant reality featuring commercial trading on the dark side and from which enormous illicit sums are transacted (Leacock, 2001). This architecture, though new, is not unlike the old one in that it can neither control how funds are sourced nor how they are utilised. In fact, despite its profound power to shape modern day commerce, the new international financial system, when stripped of its padding, is purely vehicular in nature when it comes to capital. Nonetheless, this feature is exactly what makes it dangerous: according to Friman and Andreas (1999), IMF accounts put the figure of annually laundered funds at upwards to $500 billion. Exactly how this figure was derived is not clear. That said, the Ponzi-schemes of Madoff and Stanford took early shape in this environment, gaining full flight in the universal escalation to financialisation and, until uncovered, played out at the poker table of "casino capitalism" (Strange, 1997).

The linkage of these two scoundrels to IFCs adds fuel to an already well-stoked fire and provides further ammunition to the onshore establishment in making an erstwhile point, created in part through recurring variables such as discourse, jest and criminal folklore. For example, perceptive movie-goers would note the sometimes subtle and not so subtle pokes at island financial centres by Western media. The unflattering depiction of certain of these states in Hollywood-made movies in high throttle scenes where a gunman takes hostages and predicates their safe release on the transfer of millions of dollars to a "numbered offshore account" always, it would seem, in the Bahamas or the Cayman Islands, insinuates that:

a   IFCs are a suitable repository for criminal monies, the source of which will never be known; or
b   IFCs are a safe haven for villains to enjoy ill-gotten booty without fear of recrimination.

As conceivably the most powerful medium through which ideas are communicated, the Arts are a bridge to the soul. They stir our emotions and help distil meaning. The Arts also shed light on what is hidden and unspoken. Artistic licence is what empowers the writer, the film producer and director among others, to address, portray and, indeed, challenge accepted norms as a means of supporting societal transition to new norms.

Artistic licence fashions narratives, shapes discourse and feeds ideologies. Depending on the creator's artistic agenda, so too their political suasion, Hollywood can be co-opted to declare what offshore is and what it is not, despite it being something totally opposite. The power to transmit just the right mix of nuance, tinged with a soupçon of doubt around comparative quality, transparency, integrity and legality, all in a real-time mental moment, is second to none. It is striking that the Manhattans and New Jerseys, Chicagos and Wyomings have, for some time, had a system of offshore financial services in place in which non-resident holders of local deposits/capital are not charged withholding taxes on their capital/interest gains when compared to residents of those countries. Why then does Hollywood not point to the offshore enclaves in its own country?

The remaining strand to the *trinary code* is the longest. It pertains to the now decrypted financial tempest experienced by most world economies in some form in the ensuing years of its genesis, circa 2007. Wrapped in the swaddling clothes of capitalism, it was only a matter of time before its unveiling. Still, a reprise is useful here.

In the spirit of one-upmanship otherwise known as competition, US banks turned their attention to a market niche which they believed could enhance their bottom line, at least in the short term. For low income householders, the prospect of owning your own home when coupled with apparently modest interest rates at inception was a more than effective lure. However, in practical terms these advances were really sub-prime mortgages and therefore carried an inherent risk of default, particularly where interest rates began to trend upward, which they eventually did. The subsequent repackaging, conversion and intra-trading of these debts across multiple financial entities in and beyond US shores, presumably to spread the risk (but really the infection), resulted in the sub-prime mortgage crisis. Falling property values, increasing interest rates and fiscally out-manoeuvred borrowers created a perfect storm which saw previously delighted home-owners literally walking away from their homes. Interest yields on securitisations could not be paid since before you knew it, intended funding from mortgage payments had dried up. And because of the systemic relationships germane to banking business, the high level of non-performing loans placed gambling financial institutions under severe pressure, impacting their operational viability. Liquidity was sucked out of global financial markets where sub-primes were traded in significant volumes alongside other exotic innovations and, one by one, infected US financial institutions were either taken down through acquisition, nationalised or simply allowed to go under.

That said, for entities whose systemic reach was too deeply embedded in the global economy, failure was not an option. Hence, those financial institutions considered "too big to fail" were bailed out by the then Bush administration in an arrangement known as the Troubled Asset Relief Program or TARP.[2]

Déjà vu, I hear you say? It is certainly not the only financial crisis experienced in modern times. It is, however, the most far reaching. With common themes of unfettered financial innovation, risk-taking and the absence of governing rules and accountability mechanisms at the time, the Durkheim (1951) and Merton (1938) conventions are easily called to mind to help explain this phenomenon, in particular the self-seeking, questionable actions of certain bankers and their role in a near cataclysmic global financial crisis.

Asserting myself

I made additional assertions in cultivating my analytical framework. One was to adopt a realist approach. The problem of money laundering and the sufficiency of regulation, after all, are not part of my own consciousness but externally observable. At the episte-mological level, I chose a positivist stance to maintain the requisite level of rigour throughout. In terms of my view of human nature, a middle ground outlook was assumed. I believe both situational and voluntary factors influence the relationship between humans and their respective societies or contexts. In other words, although we are shaped in part by our environment, there remains the agency of free-will we all have. We are each cap-able of exercising that free will (sense of choice) within the milieu of human relationships.

Lastly, the nomothetic basis of this work is epitomised by a scientific protocol which enables analysis of the problem using a mixture of quantitative and qualitative techniques. Useful, therefore, in this exercise was the deployment of questionnaires, the analysis of secondary data from government, non-government and other sources. I also seized the opportunity to speak directly with experts in the field. What I also thought useful was to analyse the content of a number of significant cases (scandals in some instances) specifi-cally occurring in the financial services industry.

Line of attack

I focused my attention on the domestic and international financial services experience of a limited number of Caribbean Commonwealth nations. This helped with the important aspect of manageability and also allowed for a more focused analysis. As it relates to my engagement with Caribbean financial regulators, my sampling approach was a purposive one. The major criterion had to do with the regulator being located in a country involved in both traditional banking services as well as international financial services. While several countries met this criterion, I thought I should dispatch my survey instrument to both mature and emerging jurisdictions. My rationale for this was altruistic. It was to understand these jurisdictions' regulatory mandate; how they each viewed their role in the jurisdiction; how they went about achieving their goals and what they con-sidered to be the issues surrounding effective AML/combating the financing of terrorism (CFT) from the regulator's perspective and that of their constituents.

Responses were forthcoming from three regulatory entities. Since this response rate was 60% of the total, the final sample was deemed appropriate for research purposes. A content analysis method was subsequently employed to extract data. Supplemental data was pursued by reviewing the website of each regulatory institution. This proved useful in obtaining a better understanding of what was recorded. The findings are presented under confidentiality and discussed in Chapter 6.

Talking with the experts

There is always important insight to be gained through dialogue. Talking with high level experts and practitioners was therefore a priority. In this regard, what I did was to secure consultation with an official of a foreign consulate with the expectation of understanding the perspective of a G20 nation. From the practitioner side, I held discussions with individuals possessing significant experience in the international business sector.

Given the senior level of the persons noted, it was felt that an open-ended question approach would prove most fruitful in stimulating discussion and the expansion of comments. As with the regulatory surveys, content analysis was employed to mine data for further scrutiny. Transcripts are presented and discussed further, under confidentiality, in Chapter 6.

What do the documents say?

As the major proponents of global AML policy diffusion since the 1990s, the OECD and FATF are closely associated with the subject of this research. In particular, the implementation of the FATF's 40 Recs. serves as the global indicator of the strength of a country's AML/CFT frameworks. It is against these protocols that the FATF or FATF-style regulatory bodies (FRSBs) test member countries' compliance. Within the Caribbean region such testing, known as a mutual evaluation, is carried out by the Caribbean Financial Action Task Force (CFATF).

My review took in evaluations conducted on a sample of six IFCs. In terms of the selection criteria, I focused my attention on those three jurisdictions which also completed the regulatory survey. The other three countries were included on the basis of their relative maturity in the offshore space. Coincidentally and quite fortunately for this research, the AML/CFT framework of those countries in question were independently assessed within reasonable proximity of each other, thereby enabling close comparison of findings. Outcomes are presented again, under confidentiality, in Chapter 6.[3]

To supplement my document analysis strategy, I brought into the picture a series of other reports, this time emanating from the office of the US State Department. These were the International Narcotics Control Strategy Reports (INSCRs) issued over the five-year period 2006–2010.

... and the cases what do they tell us?

Consistent with the design of this work, there was one thing left to do. That was to energise discussion by including live examples of money laundering and other financial crimes, specifically fraud and organised theft. My reason for this is the delineation of these areas, (although there are others) as being predicate or underlying offences for the laundering of money. In short, these underlying offences often generate criminal proceeds. The subsequent actions aimed at concealing their original derivation are deemed money laundering.

As regards the extraction of data, common threads and consistencies were identified and a final juxtaposition made against the grandfather case involving BCCI. More than twenty-five years after its historic collapse in 1991, the circumstances precipitating the bank's fall have become a reference point for academic enquirers, regulatory review and (financial) law enforcement training. The entity's demise, which was brought about mostly through corporate misbehaviour, precipitated a string of changes to the supervision of banking entities and regulatory enforcement globally. One notable change was the strengthening of the paradigm of consolidated supervision. Underpinning this idea is ensuring there is adequate knowledge of the operations of branches and/or subsidiaries irrespective of their location. The Basel Core Principles of Banking Supervision suggests this function as most suitable to the host Regulator/Supervisor. Having this kind of centripetal oversight allows for an enterprise wide view of the financial institution's general condition at a more granular level, assisting with the determination of capital adequacy levels and operational risk management. While the other financial institutions analysed in this research did not necessarily collapse as BCCI did, there were certain influencing factors present in each of them. To my mind, it is these factors which triggered subsequent events of such magnanimity as to merit their inclusion here. This brings us to the rationale for case selection.

Manageability aside, the choice of specific cases at the exclusion of others was based on a purposive sampling approach, with a predilection for *significance*. The idea here was to identify occurrences in the international financial services industry which stood out in their own right. In this regard the prominence of the entity in the broader industry or global context was noted as a key factor. The event should also have either affected the institution's fiscal operations as it relates to footing the monetary cost of non-compliance or threatened its continued existence as a business enterprise. In short, the sanctions may have been of a *financial* significance, for example, a hefty fine; *operational* significance, such as the loss of a licence to operate or the dissolution of operations through purchase/absorption of assets by another entity or some similar action. The resulting *reputational* impact would also be considered operationally significant since a smear to an entity's brand can have negative connotations in the market place, potentially resulting in a loss of client base. Lastly, the sheer size in money terms of the financial crime was another major consideration.

Legendary US investor and Chairman of Berkshire Hathaway, Warren Buffet, knows of these consequences very well. Reiterating what he had previously conveyed to employees in the wake of the Saloman Brothers' Inc. scandal of 1991, in an opening statement before the Sub-committee on Telecommunications and Finance of the Energy and Commerce Committee of the US House of Representatives, Buffet was quoted as saying, "… lose money for the firm and I will be understanding; lose a shred of reputation for the firm and I will be ruthless".[4]

To round off the selection criteria, I considered the extent of regulatory/law enforcement intervention in terms of the depth of investigation. Alternatively, the degree of collusion on the part of state agents and the extent to which evidence of complicit behaviour was deemed to have compromised the agents' ability to act responsibly were also considered. The complicit behaviour criterion was also applied to the financial institution and their agents in the same manner. Briefly introduced below and with at least *one* of the noted criterion present, the following cases – along with BCCI – were identified for further analysis. Figures are quoted in US dollars unless otherwise stated.

Bank of New York Mellon Corporation 1998 (BONY)

Easily one of the oldest banks in the United States, BONY was established in 1794. Unfortunately, though, the bank became embroiled in a $7 billion money laundering scandal through Russia at a time when that country's economy was going through structural adjustment. In the end, the bank received a $38 million fine by its US regulators, one of the largest in US history at the time. Two years after being fined, BONY would merge operations with the Mellon Corporation to become Bank of New York Mellon Corporation.

Citibank 1998

Like the BONY case before, this matter unfolded at the cusp of the 21st century, although federal investigations covered transactions occurring in the two-year period 1992–1994. Positioned among the top 50 banks worldwide in 1998, Citibank found itself under regulatory scrutiny for its alleged involvement in the laundering of up to $100 million for a client, Raul Salinas. Raul was the brother of former Mexican President Carlos Salinas. The case is one which helped to shape the FATF's concept known as *politically exposed person* as explained in the FATF's 40 Recs.

First International Bank of Grenada 2001 (FIBG)

As part of its effort to attract alternate investment, the Grenada government decided to build an offshore sector following in the footsteps of its eastern Caribbean neighbours such as Barbados, St. Kitts and Nevis and Antigua, to name a few. However, as a result of massive institutional fraud amongst other things, FIBG suffered a revocation of licence with most of its clients losing their deposits. In the end, the Grenada authorities would close down the sector for several years following this embarrassing scandal. Although predicated on fraud, this case had far reaching consequences not only on the reputation of Grenada as an offshore financial centre, but also on the Caribbean offshore sector as a whole.

Riggs National Corporation and Riggs Bank 2004

Back in its heyday, Riggs' client base was adorned with the glitz of diplomats and the glamour of presidents, not to mention the elegance of statesmen and women. Its location in Washington DC brought relationship managers within proximity of commuting VIPs, whose chauffeur-driven vehicles and agency-protected parties aspirated a righteous air in a forever busy metropolis, much to the envy of rivals. With more than a century and half experience under its prestigious belt, Riggs had a strong, trusted brand and its principals knew it. However, the bank became a casualty of its well-earned pride when the Financial Crimes Enforcement Network slapped the apparently venerable institution with a concurrent fine of $25 million. Among the main reasons for the levied sanctions was the alleged concealment of assets of the former Chilean dictator, Augusto Pinochet. The bank's failure to report suspicious transactions, consistent with its own compliance program, was called into question. The transactions involved the withdrawal of tens of millions of dollars in cash and international drafts from accounts controlled by the Saudi Arabian embassy and Saudi Arabian officials. Similar occurrences were also identified with accounts relating to the African nation of Equatorial Guinea. Like BONY, Riggs' operations were absorbed by another financial institution; in this case, the Pittsburgh-based PNC Financial Services Group – in a merger worth over $700 million.

Bernard L. Madoff/Bernard L. Madoff Investment Securities (BMIS) LLC 2008

Global eyes were affixed on this case formally brought before the US law courts in December 2008 as white collar crime reached its dizzying heights. Although there was no bloodshed involved, the human carcasses left in Madoff's wake told a different story.[5] How, after all, could a $65 billion fraud go unnoticed for so long? And what punishment could possibly befit a crime which killed off the hopes, dreams and futures of present and yet to be conceived generations? The three life sentences totalling 150 years, no doubt, was to eternalise Madoff's punishment, debiting his accountability across both tangible and spiritual planes. With interest on investments permanently extinguished, retirees and pre-retirees were now both penniless and powerless, some resorting to food stamps and others scavenging around in garbage cans. Court documents also record grandparents acknowledging the decreased standard of living as impairing their ability to visit and, indeed, be visited by family. Regulatory authorities came in for a tongue lashing, with blame laid squarely on the shoulders of the SEC for failure to act swiftly on intelligence brought to its attention over a prolonged period.

LIBOR scandal (2012)

Fundamental to the core lending function that is the business of banking and the work-ings of global financial markets, is the London Interbank Offered Rate. LIBOR's deri-vation is predicated on the world's biggest banks submitting an indication of the cost at which they are likely to borrow amongst themselves on an overnight (short term) and unsecured basis. Previously managed by the British Banking Association, the submitted rates were centrally aggregated by a third party and the resulting set of indices published to guide the industry's base lending.

Over time, heavy reliance came to be placed on LIBOR which, in turn, was used as a gauge for on-lending to market actors (consumers, companies, sovereigns). A high LIBOR would be passed on to the market as would be a low one, with a resulting impact either way. In terms of its utility to monetary authorities, LIBOR interacts with economic models to support determination of potential future shifts in market performance and changes in interest rates (McBride, et al., 2016).

As early as 2003, the activities underpinning LIBOR's daily calculation attracted the cross-border scrutiny of regulators, culminating several years later in a major investigation into its apparent rigging by its chief proponents, the big banks, among them Barclays, UBS and Deutsche Bank. Ongoing investigation apart, LIBOR is juicy ripe for our review, given the theoretical framework outlined earlier.

With my approach clarified, I now turn to address the findings culled from each of the noted methods.

Notes

1 See https://www.docketalarm.com/cases/New_York_Southern_District_Court/1–14-cr-00068/ USA_v._Ulbricht/183/
2 The TARP was signed into law by the Bush administration just when he (President Bush) was about to demit office. However, it was President Obama who presided over the allo-cation of the remaining funds (several hundred billion) to those banks considered "too big to fail".
3 Formal permission to reuse country statistics in relation to the outcome of mutual evaluations conducted was not obtained. Therefore, specific country names, related statistical tables and other information which might potentially indicate the jurisdictions involved have been redac-ted and a brief overview of overall findings presented instead.
4 See *Wall Street Journal* at http://blogs.wsj.com/marketbeat/2010/05/01/ buffetts-1991-saloman-testimony/tab/print/
5 See Vancouverite News Services at https://vancouverite.com/2009/06/29

References

Blau, P., 1964. *Theory and exchange in social life*. New York: John Wiley and Sons Inc.

Burrell, G. & Morgan, G., 1979. *Sociological paradigms and organizational analysis*. Aldershot: Gower.

Durkheim, E., 1897. Reprinted 1951. *Suicide: A study of sociology*. 2nd ed. New York: The Free Press of Glencoe.

Friman, H. & Andreas, P., 1999. Introduction. In: H. Friman & P. Andreas, eds. *The illicit global economy and state power*. Maryland: Rowman & Littlefield Publishers Inc., pp. 1–17.

Leacock, C., 2001. Internationalization of crime. *Journal of International Law and Politics*, 34(1), pp. 263–280.

Marshall, D., 2008. Gaining fluency in finance: Globalization/financialization and offshore finan-cial centers. *Contemporary Politics*, 14(3), pp. 357–373.

McBride, J., Alessi, C., Sergei, M. A. & Sergei, M. A., 2016. Understanding the LIBOR scandal [Online]. Available at: https://www.cfr.org/backgrounder/understanding-libor-scandal [accessed 8 April 2018].

Merton, R. K., 1938. Social structure and anomie. *American Sociological Review*, 3, pp. 672–680.

Strange, S., 1997. *Casino Capitalism*. Manchester: Manchester University Press.

6   The eyes have it

Prologue

I deal, first, with the results arising from *four* of the five sources used to gather information for this research. Due to their wide-ranging nature, my analysis of the case studies – which constitutes the fifth and final element of my mixed methodology approach – is reserved for the upcoming chapters.

Where am I headed?

I begin by assessing the outcomes relating to my engagement with regional regulatory authorities obtained via questionnaires. Thereafter, I undertake an analysis of the content of mutual evaluation/detailed assessment reports compiled by the CFATF/IMF on a cross-section (sub-set really) of both mature and emerging IFCs. The intent is to acquire a more comprehensive view of the state of compliance in Caribbean nations doing business in the international financial services sector, from the standpoint of the CFATF/IMF.[1] To triangulate my efforts, I then seek to make sense of the US State Department's International Narcotics Control Strategy Reports (INSCRs) over the five-year period 2006–2010. Lastly, the insight acquired from key practitioners by way of face-to-face interviews is presented and discussed. We then form our conclusion at the end of the chapter.

Eye of the eagle

Mindful of confidentiality, the names of the overseeing regulatory institutions responding to the survey are not explicitly identified. Instead, they are referred to as Bravo, Delta and Zulu regulators, respectively. The questions posed to them and the resulting coding structure employed to extract data are itemised in Table 6.1. Concerning the motivation behind the line of questioning, this was to ultimately establish the regulatory philosophy underpinning rule-making in these offshore states. To this end, questions raised sought to establish regulators' key objectives; determine the extent to which there was commonality to these objectives and approach; and identify the challenges experienced in the financial services sector with regard to money laundering compliance. The intention was to also find common ground in regulators' understanding of the catalysts of change in their respective jurisdictions; the bases for regulatory design and the contestations experienced in effecting such.

In addition, an attempt was made to assess the level of co-operation from regulated entities and to gain a better understanding of the perceived reasons for these entities'

Table 6.1 Regulatory responses analysis

Questions	Bravo regulators	Delta regulators	Zulu regulators	Recurring themes and frequency
In general, what is (are) the objective(s) of regulation as it pertains to the financial services sector?	(1) A framework that supports laws; (2) Preserves safety and soundness of financial system; (3) To clarify meaning of statutes.	(1) Maintain financial stability and market confidence; (2) Protect jurisdiction's reputation; (3) Deter criminal elements.	(1) Provide quality environment for business; (2) Promote country's economic interest; (3) Sound financial system; (4) Deter criminal elements; (5) Market confidence, consumer protection, reputation of jurisdiction; (6) Maintain balance between ability of jurisdiction to compete on international scale without compromising high quality regulatory standards; (7) Transparency and fairness.	Soundness of financial system (3); Market confidence (2) Delta/Zulu; Reputation (2) Delta/Zulu; To deter criminal use of financial system (2) Delta/Zulu; Breakdown legal requirements in practical form to enable implementation (1) Bravo; Consumer Protection (2) Delta/Zulu; Promote competitive business environment based on efficiency, transparency and fairness (1) Zulu.
Describe the Authority's approach to the regulation of the financial services sector.	(1) Industry Consultation; (2) Intra-regulatory consultation.	Independent approach.	Risk-based approach.	Consultative (3) (Delta from website; Zulu from website).
Has this approach changed materially in the last two decades? If yes, what were some of the main factors driving that change?	Yes, with regard to level of interaction with sector. Changes in international standards driven by external events.	Yes implied – approach changed on establishment of independent regulator in 2002 (no response to latter part of question).	Yes implied – risk-based approach is in place. Approach adopted due to external influences; viewed as more efficient and effective.	Yes (3); External influences (2) Bravo/Zulu.
In general, what are some of the elements taken into consideration in the design of AML/CFT guidelines/regulations?	(1) International standards and best practice; (2) Nature and size of sector; (3) Industry views/feedback; (4) Harmonisation of base line rules across regulatory agencies overseeing financial groups.	International standards, i.e. FATF.	(1) Type of business being undertaken; (2) Type of client; (3) Turnover of funds; (4) Source of funds.	International standards (3); Nature/size of sector (1) Bravo; Industry feedback (1) Bravo; Regulatory harmonisation (1) Bravo; Type of client/business (1) Zulu.

(Continued)

Questions	Bravo regulators	Delta regulators	Zulu regulators	Recurring themes and frequency
What is the Authority's function in relation to combating money laundering/terrorist financing in the jurisdiction?	(1)To assess licensees' AML/CFT program adequacy against statutes/regulations/guidelines; (2) To advise on adequacy and effectiveness of national framework.	To monitor licensees' compliance with laws/codes/regulations.	(1) To monitor compliance with money laundering regulations; (2) The prevention and detection of money laundering thereby protecting the industry, stakeholder interest and ability to compete globally.	Compliance monitoring (3); Detection of financial crime (1) Delta; Advise on national status (1) Bravo.
What (if any) are some of the major challenges faced by the Authority in executing this mandate?	Effective use of resources in ensuring balance between safety and soundness and AML/CFT compliance.	Adequate training of staff of financial institutions to ensure compliance.	(1) Inability to capture every money laundering event owing to criminal innovations; (2) Training of staff to keep up to date with new trends; (3) Training of staff in industry.	Training of financial institution/regulatory staff (2) Delta/Zulu; Resource allocation (1) Bravo; Criminal innovation (1) Zulu.
As regards the adherence of licensed financial institutions to AML/CFT protocols, how would you describe the level of co-operation from these entities?	High level of co-operation.	Full co-operation.	Very good.	Overall, very good (3).
What do you consider to be the main factors influencing these institutions' compliance with regulatory requirements?	(1) Risk to operations; (2) Risk to jurisdiction (reputation implied).	Reputational damage to institution.	Reputation.	Reputation (3); Risk to operations (1) Bravo.

Questions	Bravo regulators	Delta regulators	Zulu regulators	Recurring themes and frequency
Beyond compliance programmes, are there any additional actions financial institutions can take to protect themselves from money laundering/terrorist financing? Explain.	(1) Keeping abreast of international trends; (2) IT enhancements.	Staff training.	Staff training.	Ongoing training/education (3); IT investment (1) Bravo.
In light of the consolidated approach to banking supervision presently employed by regulatory authorities in the examination of authorised financial entities, how possible would you say is institutional money laundering/crime in your jurisdiction? Explain.	(1) (Risk is mitigated) through integrated risk management; (2) Adoption of highest standards across group.	(1) There is some level of risk: mainly as a result of the Caribbean's proximity to North and South America and its use as a trans-shipment point for drugs.	Minimal risk: (1) Most of the regulated entities in Zulu jurisdiction are banks of international standing; (2) Only banks from countries with equivalent AML/CFT standards are admitted into jurisdiction.	Possible (3); Geographical location (1); Integrated risk management/high group standards (1) Bravo; International standing of financial institutions/equivalent jurisdictional standards (1) Zulu.

adherence to protocols in the first place. Also, with compliance programs and systems forming the primary defence mechanism against money laundering, the survey attempted to evince from regulatory authorities whether financial institutions could do anything more beyond these systems to protect themselves against money laundering. It was here that the broader term "financial crime" was introduced into the mix to capture other variables such as fraud, embezzlement and so forth.

Lastly, with regard to the global standard of consolidated supervision I inquired about the extent to which institutional crime – corporate wrongdoing – that is either allowed and/or engaged in by top management/owners, could still be possible.

What I found

An analysis of the comments would suggest, in the first instance, that safety and soundness of the financial system is the *foremost* regulatory concern of Caribbean regulators. It is viewed as a critical feature to market confidence particularly to Delta and Zulu regulators whose seamless engagement with mainland nations has proved of historic value to their economies.

The protection of the jurisdiction's reputation was highlighted as a key objective among regulators. Financial institutions' compliance with protocols was, ostensibly, motivated by an analogous desire and intent to protect their own brand from the scars of association with evil money. Consumer protection was also regarded highly by Delta and Zulu regulators. When it came to deterring the criminal use of the financial system, there was no doubt where the sampled regulators stood.

Delta regulators considered their jurisdiction's overall business efficacy as a key objective and appeared to link money laundering deterrence with promoting an environment conducive to good business. Bravo regulators saw granularity as necessary in bringing about clarity. In short, breaking down legal requirements into practical prescriptive terms was seen as providing important utility, directly enhancing the ability of regulated entities to effectively implement compliance protocols. This is perhaps why compliance monitoring was also valued highly across the board, with Bravo, in particular, viewing its ability to provide advice on the adequacy and effectiveness of its national framework as a central function.

Staff competence both in terms of the regulator and their constituents was identified as a key challenge to executing regulatory mandates. For example, Delta considered criminal innovation as being so iterative as to require staff training on an ongoing basis simply to be able to keep up with new trends. Bravo was confronted with the effective deployment of resources considering its broader safety and soundness mandate. From the perspective of the regulated entity, ongoing training and education would have an impact on operational expenditure and hence the ability to maximise profits. To be fair, this reality must also be viewed from the other side, that is, although infusing a cost to the business, the benefit of training may be measured in the avoidance of financial and other sanctions, and hence the retention of institutional reputation through the enhanced ability to follow regulatory protocols. It is interesting that the matter of training was also viewed by the collective sample as the main action banks should engage to protect themselves, even outside the standard compliance programs.

Although Bravo regulators identified the need to stay abreast of trends (as did Delta) and also improving the institution's information technology capability, there was not an explicit reference to the role of values or ethics in ensuring positive regulatory outcomes. I was left to assume that the term "training" was meant to be all-encompassing and, as such, should include a values component for completeness purposes.

Generally, the deliberate act of money laundering or financial crime by a financial institution was acknowledged as still possible despite the global standard of consolidated supervision deployed by regulating bodies. In the eyes of the Bravo regulator, financial crime at the level of the institution was felt to be linked, in part, to the failure to adopt the highest standards on a group-wide basis and also to manage risk in an integrated manner. However, the argument may be made that standards are implemented by people and their adoption across the board depend on the *willingness* of agents to act in *accordance* with those standards.

Bravo viewed the geographic location of the Caribbean as a major influencing factor. The region's use as a transshipment route for drugs, was noted a possible avenue of illicit funds entering the financial system. However, this limits criminal proceeds to illegal drugs and necessarily excludes other predicate offences involving the proceeds of crime, including fraud, corruption, embezzlement and the like. From Delta's perspective, although considered possible, the risk of *institutional* crime was felt to be mitigated by allowing in only institutions of the highest international repute. As we see, however, in the case studies to follow, the standing of banks, international or otherwise, is irrelevant when the institution or its agents acting on their own or on behalf of the institution purposely act in a deviant manner. From a reputation perspective, there is an overall sense among island regulators that jurisdictional character is, indeed, the cornerstone to maintaining an international product which attracts the right type of business.

My findings also confirmed that, generally, regulators engaged the industry through consultation. Consultancy also traversed sibling agencies for the purposes of harmonisation of rules across the sector and ensuring a common appreciation of the types of risk to which the sector may be exposed, while at the same time providing a lucid environment for business. Such a collaborative approach no doubt leads to "buy in" from the broader commercial borough, thus consolidating the control needed to meet the overarching obligation of safety and soundness. What also happens is that the tendency to compel compliance is nullified and is more likely to promote voluntarism since entities would have had an opportunity to input into the regulatory process. A possible outcome of this type of industry engagement is the level of co-operation displayed in following regulatory protocols. Indeed, the sampled authorities were satisfied in this area. That said, as pointed out before, banks have a vested interest in complying given the symbiosis between institutional adherence and reputational protection.

Mapping Durkheim (1951)

The way I see it, the overall tone secreting this regulatory analysis is an intention of empowered entities to maintain a kind of social order, in this case the financial system. Of course, intrinsic to this understanding is the minimisation of the tendency towards deviant or non-compliant conduct. Under this regime, threats to the system must be dealt with firmly, quickly and preferably publicly, in order to retain jurisdictional system stability while indirectly keeping the broader external system safe and sound. In this way, the potential harm to the social order is circumvented. It should be noted here that the maintenance of the social order is promoted as a collective accountability occurring at the external quasi-regulatory level, which is then transmitted to the internal substantive regulatory (country) level. Then comes the trickledown effect to the institution being regulated.

The value of Durkheim's (1951) functionalist outlook in regard to avoiding the potential breakdown in social order by the imposition of regulatory governance is especially critical to our analysis. Crucial also is Merton's (1938) articulation of anomie when it comes to understanding the actions of individuals which, in running counter to societal norms, also undermine the proper functioning of its multivariate systems. The outlook of both these functional theorists provides us with a composite mirror through which we are able to enhance our perception of the social reality of financial regulation using the findings arising from engaging regional regulators.

Beginning with Durkheim (1951), we note the assertion that the fulfilment of biological needs in individuals, rather than satiating the desire only serves to stimulate the desire for more. The argument is made that since man's unlimited desires ultimately produce a breakdown in regulatory norms, behaviour could only be constrained by a "force exterior to him" (Durkheim, 1951, pp. 248–249). Durkheim further suggests that this regulative force must not only play the same role for moral needs which the organism plays for physical needs, but since physical restraint is ineffective in containing the emotions of the heart, the regulative force must be moral and recognised by the individual as just and worthy of respect. The outcome would be to stimulate a spontaneous and submissive response from man (Durkheim, 1951, pp. 248–249).

Although originally contrived with the individual in mind, there is a possible application of this model to a pseudo-individual, that is to say, a country (jurisdiction) or an institution. That each of these entities constitutes individuals, albeit on a collective basis, I consider it appropriate to attempt the application.

We recall the research question which examined the objectives of regulation, and we have already noted that the jurisdiction, personified, can be regarded as the regulator's consort, whose beauty (economic environment) is to be protected and well-being (financial system) kept safe and sound. If the desires of the consort are not kept in check, there is the strong possibility that untamed cravings could intensify, leading to the establishment of relationships and associations that do not conduce to the collective order and its maintenance. Put another way: by virtue of their comparatively weak natural resource base, and thus natural "hunger" for investment, Caribbean IFCs are compelled to seek out other viable sources of capital. If one is to follow Durkheim's thinking, to leave such aspirations unchecked by regulatory standards is to set the stage for anomie, for in the absence of regulations aimed at protecting the financial system, a tendency could arise among banking institutions or their host countries – competing for investment – to develop alliances with corruptive capital sources, for example, organised crime groups (which are traditionally not deficient in this area), corrupt officials (who are always on the hunt for suitable avenues to park stolen monies), and so forth. The end result could be a state whose national commerce is imprisoned by criminally derived capital whose sudden appearance and precipitous flight destabilises the social order or financial system. The unreliability of the long-term presence of capital may hinder national advancement, through uncertain job accessibility, education possibilities and health care resources, and indeed compromise all the other factors which make for an ordered and developed society.

Such a situation is felt to be the case in Russia in the aftermath of its devolution from the Union of Soviet Socialist Republics (Soviet Union) according to Shelley (1999). The rapidity of privatisation of state assets without the appropriate legal framework, governance standards and transparency opened up the state to manipulation by crooked, yet influential bureaucrats and politicians connected to organised crime groups. Consequently, this led to the cementing of control over a vulnerable economy. The implication here is that deviant behaviour is stimulated at least in part in conditions of social disorder, a position consistent with Finckenauer and Voronin (2001) in their study of the organised crime threat in Russia.

Enter Merton (1938)

In order to explicate the notion of anomie in relation to the disruption of an ordered financial system, a departure from the Durkheim (1951) hypothesis to the Merton (1938) postulation is essential. In his quest to understand the influence of societal structures in shaping non-conforming behaviour among citizenry, Merton sought to identify the "non-biological conditions" that tended to induce normative digressions. To suggest that man's biological drives were the precursor to the social regulatory breakdown was to confine the notion of social order into being "solely a device for impulse management and the processing of social tensions" (Merton, 1938, p. 672). While acknowledging the nature of man in this regard, Merton isolated two elements of social and cultural structure in an effort to provide an alternative explanation for the possible breakdown in the collective order.

The first element related to what he termed "culturally defined goals, purposes and interests" (Merton, 1938, p. 672). Together, these constituted an aspirational frame of reference for the collective and were themselves integrated as they appealed to composite societal emotions. Although acknowledging that these aspirations were related to man's original biological drives – with deference to Durkheim (1951) – Merton proffered the observation that they were not *governed* by them (Merton, 1938, p. 672).

To further set up his explanation of societal deviance, Merton pinpointed a second element of social structure. This element "defined, regulated and controlled the acceptable means of achieving these goals" (Merton, 1938, p. 673). The argument is made that within a collective order there exists moral or institutional strictures that shape what is considered the permissible and required procedures for goal attainment (Merton, 1938, p. 673). Furthermore these "moral imperatives" as Merton puts it, "did not necessarily coincide with technical or efficiency norms" (Merton, 1938, p. 673). In short, one's personal skill or professional ability had little to do with regulatory protocols at the societal level. Indeed, the behaviour adopted to achieve goals is thought to be confined to what aligns to institutionally accepted norms. Therefore, although illicit activity may be viewed by certain persons in the collective as an efficient means to societal aspirations, this vehicle would be naturally abhorred by the group if legal expedients constituted the general norm.

This thrusts our discussion into an iterative realm as Merton singles out different modes of behaviour that could potentially ensue when a strain or disjunction occurs between societal goals and institutionally acceptable means of achieving them. To begin with, conforming behaviour occurs when there is a match between goals and means. In short, where there is no perception of blocked or restricted access to means, goals are viewed as attainable and the methods used to attain them are embraced. Thus where individual success is promoted as an objective in the collective, matching means of attainment such as employment opportunities, education and health care facilities will emerge as key instrumentalities, thus stimulating conforming tendencies in the population. At the level of our pseudo-individual – let us use the emerging nation state in this example – a key success goal may very well be the attainment of developed country status as alluded to before. In which case, alongside political liberties and other social freedoms, access to development capital at suitable terms would be expected. The withholding of such facilities for whatever reason or the perception that they are not accessible by the qualifying state can effectively hinder national aspirations, precipitating a different course of capital acquisition which may fall outside institutionally accepted means. This could, in part, account for the lax approach by some OFCs in securing inward investment prior to the global clamp down by the FATF. This dynamic is explored in Chapter 7 in the case study dealing with First International Bank of Grenada.

Applying the same Mertonian theory to the financial institution, success goals may be linked to relative performance in the industry that highlight measures of profitability and a fair return on shareholder investment as commercial triumph (success) in the marketplace. Access to capital again, in this case through a qualitative increase in the bank's depository base would provide the institution with the necessary resources it needs to at least have a chance at satisfying its corporate aspirations of financial prosperity set by the economic collective. Organisational conformity will occur where congruence between goals and means exist thus maintaining an ordered financial system.

Merton's second mode of adaptation relates to behaviour which ensues when cultural goals are embraced, but the means of attainment are perceived by aspirants to be unavailable or inaccessible. Means may also be flat out rejected by success incumbents. In the first case, unfair competition, inadequate regulation, institutional nepotism or even corruption can shape perceptions resulting in a new behaviour that adapts to prevailing conditions. In the latter scenario, a total rejection of means while holding cultural goals constant will also evoke new behaviour, as alternative means located outside the scope of what is deemed acceptable to achieve success, are actively sought. In either case, a deviant type of behaviour which Merton dubs "innovation" is engaged.

Now if we were to transition to the individual within the organisation, commonly acceptable goals would include promotion, increase in pay and recognition for good work. The means in this case would be linked to the range of opportunities available to prove one's ability – leading projects, developing an idea, building a model, presenting a new theory, the list is not exhaustive. An enabling environment would also help – human resource systems that provide transparent and effective conflict resolution measures; management who are fair and just in exercising their responsibilities, and an enterprise culture which stimulates intrapreneurship, the exercise of initiative, and so forth. Where tension exists between these two bands, the employee may still embrace the broad goals of expectation, but consider non-conforming behaviour such as fraud and other activities which undermine the corporate collective code to be legitimate alternatives in their own eyes, given the perceived blockages in the path to success within the organisation. This interpretation of their surrounding social reality could lead employees to act in ways that are wholly detrimental to the reputation of the institution.

The other adaptive mode espoused by Merton (1938) to explain non-compliance and which is considered of relevance to this study, occurs when means are prized over goals. The resulting impact on the institution is one of ritualism where bureaucratic rules previously developed to facilitate organisational objectives are now so embraced as to become a hindrance to the entity's advancement. Employees are therefore unable to think creatively and are constipated when it comes to the application of rules in the solving of problems, particularly those occurring "out of the box". This adaptive mode will help us reconcile the challenges encountered with client service delivery when regulatory rules become deified. We discuss this further in the section dealing with practitioner insight.

Hawk-eye

Mutual evaluation exercises are carried out by the FATF or FATF Style Regulatory Bodies (FRSBs) as part of a broader Mutual Exercise Program (MEP).[2] The objective of the MEP is to scrutinise progress made by member governments in implementing the FATF Recommendations and also to assess the effectiveness of the AML and counter-terrorist financing systems in member jurisdictions. These exercises are carried out periodically across member states and take the form of a multilateral peer review where resources (experts) *external* to the country under review and led by an FATF/FRSB designate are utilised at each stage of the exercise. The team of experts is drawn from the financial, legal and law enforcement areas. The exercise consists of an on-site visit to the jurisdiction under review and comprehensive meetings with government officials and the private sector over a two-week period. The findings of the assessment team are compiled in a mutual evaluation report in which ratings are applied to defined areas of the standards, specifically: legal systems, preventative measures for financial institutions, institutional and other measures and international co-operation. Generally, the degree of compliance applied is enshrined in the terms – *fully compliant, largely compliant, partially compliant* and *non-compliant.*

The reports analysed in this research were based on a round of mutual evaluations occurring before the present fourth round, which is presently in execution mode at the time of finalising this book (spring 2018). These evaluations would have been carried out against the FATF's 40 Recs. of 2003, IX Special Recs. of 2001 and related AML/CFT methodologies.

What I found

In Oscar jurisdiction

As at the reporting period, Oscar had achieved either full compliance or a measure of compliance in all but a few of the FATF's 40 Recs. The areas noted as deficient or non-compliant had to do with the AML/CFT measures to be taken by financial institutions and non-financial businesses and professions. In terms of the FATF's IX Special Recs. against terrorist financing, Oscar did not meet the criteria in one area, namely the rules governing wire transfers.

In Bravo jurisdiction

At the time of review, 13% or five of the FATF's 40 Recs. had not been addressed by Bravo, thus yielding a non-compliant rating in these areas. Like Oscar, these deficiencies fell under the category of AML/CFT preventative measures. Similarly, only one area of the FATF's IX Special Recs. was deemed non-compliant.

In Tango jurisdiction

This jurisdiction's assessment revealed a relatively high non-compliance rate (30%), representing 12 items at the time of review. However, there was a mere one item outstanding as it related to the FATF's IX Special Recs.

In Zulu jurisdiction

Zulu's level of compliance with the FATF's 40 Recs. at the time of review was a direct reflection of ongoing efforts to set in place the global standards. The jurisdiction was identified as largely compliant in just under half of the required areas and either fully compliant or partially so in the ones remaining. The FATF's IX Special Recs. pertaining to terrorism were also receiving adequate attention with all areas either fully addressed or having achieved some measure of compliance.

In Delta jurisdiction

At the time of review of its legal and regulatory framework, Delta was either fully compliant or had achieved a measure of compliance in all of the FATF's 40 Recs. The jurisdiction was also well on the way to resolving issues pertaining to the implementation of CFT measures.

In Romeo jurisdiction

Of the FATF's 40 Recs., Romeo was fully, largely or partially compliant in 90% of the areas. The jurisdiction had also taken clear measures in the majority of the FATF's IX Special Recs.

Discussion

The bulk of the FATF's 40 Recs. (Recs. 4–25) revolved around the preventative measures category, accounting for 22 or 53% of the 40 Recs. in total. The heavy focus in this area essentially related to the work/duties of financial companies and/or designated non-financial businesses and professions, effectively placing these entities at the locus of AML/CFT risk mitigation efforts. The other 18 of the 40 Recs. pertained to the enabling legal framework for money laundering prevention.

Under confidentiality, my observations in reviewing the various evaluation reports are as follows:

a   The high average of 89% compliance across the sample was due directly to the solid efforts of the Oscar, Delta and Zulu jurisdictions in aligning their legal and regulatory framework to international standards.

b   On average, there were 15 areas (representing 38% of the FATF's 40 Recs.) in which the composite jurisdictions were only partially compliant. This inferred that, although on track for full compliance, the regional AML/CFT framework might not have been as robust as it could, in the intervening period, and could therefore have been exposed to money laundering and terrorist financing risk.

c   Delta jurisdiction had carved out a compliance path in the sampled jurisdictions being fully, largely or partially compliant with *all* of the FATF's 40 Recs. This was also true of Zulu, whose implementation efforts yielded compliance outcomes of some form in 39 of the 40 Recs.

d   In general, the difference in compliance levels may have been due, in part, to the timing of the evaluations undertaken. It may also be as a result of the varying speeds with which legal and regulatory wheels turn in the sampled jurisdictions. Another reason might be due to the physical proximity of some IFCs to a larger mainland and hence the subtle pressure to live up to international standards. Having said that, Oscar should have been more advanced in its compliance efforts at the time of review. However, the risk mitigating efforts were clear: Oscar had quickly reinvented its legal framework, strengthened institutional and other measures as well as opened up the doors for legal co-operation across borders.

e   With Tango removed from the equation, the remaining jurisdictions were observed as being only *non-compliant*, on average, in just two areas. When included, Tango's non-compliant assessment in 30% of the FATF's 40 Recs. was disbursed across and absorbed within the low frequency of non-compliance across the other five jurisdictions. This resulted in a doubling of this average to four areas of non-compliance.

f   While Tango's non-compliance levels could be deemed rather high for its mature offshore economy, this was offset by that country's efforts to meet FATF standards in other critical areas. In fact, in terms of these critical areas (not mentioned deliberately to maintain confidentiality) there were, notably, no areas of non-compliance.

Falcon Crest

International Narcotics Control Strategy Reports (INCSRs) are prepared by the US Department of State to its Congress and span the wide-ranging efforts of key countries in addressing all aspects of the international drug trade in the particular year under review.[3] The section of the reports denoted *Volume II* specifically covers money laundering and financial crimes. In this brief review, I make reference to reports for the five-year period 2006–2010.

As it relates to categories, three primary delineations are used in the reports. These are: (a) countries/jurisdictions of primary concern (CPC); (b) countries/jurisdictions of concern (CC); and (c) countries/jurisdictions monitored (CM).[4]

Jurisdictions of primary concern are also regarded as major money laundering countries under INCSR reporting criteria. These are locations "whose financial institutions engage in currency transactions involving significant amounts of proceeds from international narcotics trafficking". Amongst the criteria for being allocated to the two remaining categories are the jurisdiction's money laundering culture (whether it involves drugs or other contraband); the legislative environment in relation to: money laundering prevention; and regulatory effectiveness in terms of licensing and oversight of business and offshore finance.

A determination as to whether the country is vulnerable to terrorist finance and the extent thereof is also considered. The State Department also makes it clear that any government – including the United States and the United Kingdom:

> Can have comprehensive anti-money laundering laws on its books and conduct aggressive anti-money laundering enforcement efforts but still be classified a "Primary Concern" jurisdiction. In some cases, this classification may simply or largely be a function of the size of the jurisdiction's economy.[5]

The INSCRs under review are consolidated at Table 6.2. However, to get a better picture of US concerns with the region as it pertains to money laundering, the scope in this circumstance is extended to include multiple Caribbean IFCs and non-IFCs. In addition, larger industrial nations are included for completeness.

Table 6.2 Consolidated international narcotics strategy reports 2006–2010

Country	2010			2009			2008			2007			2006		
	CPC	CC	CM	CPC	CC	CM	CPC	CC	CM	CPC	CC	CM	CPC	CC	CM
Australia	Y			Y			Y			Y			Y		
Bahamas	Y			Y			Y			Y			Y		
Barbados		Y			Y			Y			Y			Y	
Bermuda			Y			Y			Y			Y			Y
BVI		Y			Y			Y			Y			Y	
Canada	Y			Y			Y			Y			Y		
Cayman Islands	Y			Y			Y			Y			Y		
Dominica			Y			Y		Y			Y			Y	
Dominican Republic	Y			Y			Y			Y			Y		
France	Y			Y			Y			Y			Y		
Germany	Y			Y			Y			Y			Y		
Grenada		Y			Y			Y			Y			Y	
Haiti	Y			Y			Y			Y			Y		
Hong Kong	Y			Y			Y			Y			Y		
Jamaica		Y			Y			Y			Y			Y	
Luxembourg	Y			Y			Y			Y			Y		
Netherland Antilles		Y			Y			Y			Y			Y	
Singapore	Y			Y			Y			Y			Y		

Country	CPC	CC	CM	CPC	CC	CM	CPC	CC	CM	CPC	CC	CM	CPC	CC	CM
St. Kitts and Nevis		Y			Y		Y			Y			Y		
St. Lucia		Y			Y			Y			Y			Y	
St. Vincent and the Grenadines		Y			Y			Y			Y			Y	
Switzerland	Y			Y			Y			Y			Y		
Trinidad and Tobago			Y			Y			Y			Y			Y
Turks and Caicos		Y			Y			Y			Y			Y	
United Kingdom	Y			Y			Y			Y			Y		
United States	Y			Y			Y			Y			Y		

Source: US State Department.

Notes: CPC – countries of primary concern; CC – countries of concern; CM – countries monitored.

What I found

From Table 6.2 we note that, from among Caribbean IFCs, Bahamas, Antigua and Barbuda and the Cayman Islands have remained of high concern to US authorities over the entire five-year period. In fact, these jurisdictions are identified alongside OECD nations, as "major money laundering countries" and as pointed out in the allocation criteria earlier described, the extensive economies of large nations are a key factor in these countries' allocation to this high-risk category. However, in terms of the Caribbean IFCs, it is noted that their mere *exposure* to "intense offshore financial services activity" is a major factor. In addition, Antigua and Barbuda along with the Bahamas and Cayman Islands were identified as drug transshipment points. Illicit drug proceeds are said to then make their way into the financial system. The prevalence of financial fraud in Bahamas and Cayman is also said to yield criminal proceeds. Bahamas was also identified as having criminal proceeds concealed (laundered) via the purchase of real estate, large vehicles, jewellery, through legitimate businesses operations and also the extensive network of international business companies it hosts. Additionally, the internet gaming industry, though legislated, in Antigua and Barbuda is still cause for concern to the US State Department.

Although not as acute as their sister Caribbean states in terms of money laundering concerns, several IFCs still remain of "concern". Among IFC states, Barbados and BVI over the review period maintained their lesser rating as "countries of concern", with other jurisdictions such as Grenada, Netherland Antilles, St. Kitts and Nevis, St. Lucia, St. Vincent and the Grenadines, Turks and Caicos as well as Jamaica, also maintaining a similar holding pattern. Anguilla, Bermuda and Dominica and, to some extent, Trinidad and Tobago generally required monitoring and hence were not of material concern to US authorities.

Discussion

Allocation to the various categories of lesser or higher risk does not appear to be based on empirical considerations, rather disparate iterations of the notion of "concern". What drives this concern appears to be;

a   the assessed IFC's exposure to and engagement in offshore business itself;

b   the apparent tendency of certain IFCs to attract predicate offences for money laundering; and

c   the immutability of islands' physical location relative to bigger countries and the latter's commercial trading activities in the business of vice.

In my view, the built-in flexibility of this approach is just what hegemony requires to exercise control over what is outside its power but which, nonetheless, has aggressively crossed into its cyber (financial) space to take up a kind of self-imposed "permanent residence". For what is clear is that the mitigation and prevention measures as delineated by OECD nations in the FATF's 40 Recs. and the evidence of reasonable compliance actions obtained through independent, formal evaluation, have been overlooked and separate self-referential criteria made up and established around an introspective idea of "concern". That said, INSCRs derive from the US State Department. Its authors can therefore establish and craft whatever criteria they feel is required – including (drug supply) chain management – to enhance their own objectives in relation to restricting illegal narcotics from penetrating their nation's shores.

Pelican brief

Operating at or near the water's surface, these birds' skills are best exercised in a front-line environment. Their activities have a type of metaphorical link to the work of practitioners whose field of vision provide us with an unmatched level of insight into the waters offshore, so to speak. Questions were therefore posed to two sources of high value as they relate to the offshore finance discourse. While some questions were posed to both agents, others were not. This was not only in order to capitalise on the knowledge base of the individuals, but also to account for the variation in their respective professional roles as attorney at law/businessman (ALB) and financial investigator/diplomat (FID). The distinction in the questions posed and to whom they were put is made clear by the use of this nomenclature. The actual questions are recounted below, followed by the responses.

How would you define offshore financial services/centres?

ALB:

Unfortunately the definition of offshore financial services/centres has been left up to on-shore domains. It derives from a US posture that business on an international scale which is not conducted on their shores is offshore. What the so-called offshore domains are doing is nothing different from what US states such as Vermont, South Carolina, Guam and Hawaii. It is just that it is being done in small island nations.

It is preferable that the notion of offshore financial services be regarded as *international financial services*, particularly as it relates to a country like Barbados, which has a long tradition of (financial services) trading with a notable strength in the insurance sector. Barbados has also had a vast array of double taxation treaties for some time. In this regard Barbados should not be viewed in the same mould as new IFCs such a Vanuatu. Additionally there are huge differences in the offerings of each jurisdiction and to the degree of attention paid by a nation's government to the sector; outcomes would be expected to be of a higher level.

Barbados needs to see itself as an international financial centre; as a mature banking domain based mostly on its legislation, regulation and its cadre of professionals. However to improve its competitiveness against countries such as Guernsey and Jersey it must improve on its administration of its international business offering.

What would you say accounted for the movement towards an offshore financial strategy by the Barbados government?

ALB:

The movement to offshore financial business was triggered by the perception that there was a need to divest from the traditional sugar industry – which had its financial constraints – to explore other foreign exchange earning opportunities.

What are your views in regard to the notion that offshore financial services are an alternative economic solution for small-island nations?

FID:

The make-up of offshore financial services is such that only service-type jobs are provided. Workers are not paid a premium salary rather they are paid at a service rate. These types of jobs are not helpful to the community in the long run. The breath of skills at the disposal of the offshore entity, are not fully utilised.

Financial resources are an important requirement for government projects. Funds are merely parked in IFCs suggesting they are not invested to assist the communities in which the offshore entity is domiciled. Reinvestment is not taken seriously by offshore entities. It is a matter of leadership since government must decide the minimum quality of life it wants for its citizens.

An alternative approach to offshore business could be to have a wider industry strategy that say focuses on software development. Such a strategy would naturally draw on the UWI community. National efforts should be aimed at finding the best match between what the country currently has and what its future needs may, that is, identify the industries which are lacking in the community which could enhance our standard of living.

What do you believe is the source of tensions which appear to exist between offshore financial centres and traditional banking domains?

ALB:

It is mostly political and stems in part from the contemporary reality that offshore nations cut into the onshore banking business market in a big way such that potential tax revenues of onshore nations are materially reduced.

FID:

IFCs were previously perceived as a harbour for the proceeds of crime. In the past they allowed the criminally minded to move the proceeds of crime with impunity and under the cloak of anonymity. The funds from the proceeds of crime ultimately belong to someone and/or people who have been put at a disadvantage. Where is the social conscience?

What are your views on the necessity of increased regulation in an era of globalisation?

ALB:

It should be easier to regulate in a context of regulation *(and by implication to do business)* as a result of technology and greater co-operation that comes through clear and closer relationships among regulatory bodies and across countries.

Regulation should not hinder business but facilitate it. As it stands (locally) regulation is being used as a show of power in the hands of bureaucratic functionaries. Regulation must be viewed as developmental, that is, a strategy that is aimed at ensuring integrity; compliance with standards; the promotion of transparency and general efforts to move the jurisdiction *forward*. A developmental approach creates the notion that the jurisdiction is not hindered although in fact it is well regulated.

What are some of the factors influencing proliferation of money laundering?

ALB:

This mostly has to do with the drug trade and the actions of corrupt governments in interfering with international transactions.

FID:

The whole laundering experience is driven by greed. The more you have the more you want. The drug trade and government corruption are also important to this process. The integrity of public officials should always be a guiding light for them. The difficulty comes when these officials recognise the power they have over procurement/allocation of funds to which they have access (via loans, grants business, etc.) and fail to separate their own personal interest from the interest of the people. Corruption is a hindrance to advancement. It is based on the selfishness of leaders. The corruption of public officials hinders the cascading of benefits to the population.

Some governments still view funds from *any* source as useful in building the economy. One cannot justify the acceptance of "dirty" money to advance a society. To do so would make the country beholding to organised crime.

There may also be the perception that the laws of the land are not applicable to all. Such a perception must change to curb the tendency to engage in money laundering. There must be a willingness to apply laws fairly and evenly across the board.

Do you consider money laundering to be a problem in the jurisdiction?

ALB:

There is no more money laundering happening offshore than in onshore nations. Due to the high standards applied to IFCs one can assert it may in fact be cleaner than onshore jurisdictions. At the same time the cleverness of criminals is such that the illicit provenance of money may be disguised well before funds hit the banking sector thus making them appear clean. So it is possible money laundering could be happening in the region. However this would be the case in *any* region.

FID:

The money laundering threat is not specific to the Caribbean. Money laundering is committed by the non-poor. The poor is used as "mules" and would likely not allow themselves to be used had they jobs and/or access to the means of achieving goals.

Do you consider the war against money laundering to be winnable?

ALB:

The fight is a noble one but it has its limitations. Given the sophistication of international commerce and the larger number of corrupt systems globally it may be difficult to develop a uniform standard for money laundering prevention.

How engaged is the wider society in the prevention process?

ALB:

They are not well informed. Greater education of society is desirable. This should extend to law firms; businesses in general and also to those engaged in international services. Specific attention should be paid to the importance of being alert to suspicious transactions. There must also be an attempt to counteract the tendency of some to be attracted to scams.

What are your views on client privacy and the requirements to disclose under money laundering reporting requirements?

ALB:

Essentially, we may have to live with this requirement as classic English law, which is our reference point, does not necessarily respect the right to privacy and this notwithstanding the "Tournier" Case. The notion of privacy has also been gradually redefined in US law as well.

FID:

The purpose of AML is to keep people honest; act as a strong deterrence mechanism; establish a link to criminal activity resulting in apprehension of the criminal; confiscation of the proceeds of crime and repatriation of said funds back to the affected community. Take for example the matter relating to the former New York Attorney General Elliott Spitzer: The suspicious activity report submitted by a financial institution highlighted Spitzer's attempts at structuring transactions, which is a crime in the US. Additional tracking also exposed his links to prostitution, which further cemented the case against him. The SAR filed not only exposed a financial crime but also pointed to underlying criminal activity. New laws are being developed to protect the non-criminal individual from malicious reporting by a financial institution or other entities. Malicious reporting may soon be a prosecutable offence in US courts.

How can small island nations influence the international rule making process with regard to money laundering prevention?

FID:

International bodies would want to know they are dealing with one national/ common voice. An effective national/Caribbean voice would be based on the consistency and stability of government. Haiti is an example of the erratic nature of a country which lacks a common voice. International bodies should not be expected to take them seriously. The establishment of regional entities such as the CFATF and other similar styled bodies would also assist small island nations in maintaining their federal voice in a global environment. It is preferable to see a unified Caribbean emerge with a collective thinking on areas such as commerce, advancement, autonomy, "good fellow" funds. Such a move would take the Caribbean further than it is.

Beyond compliance systems how can financial institutions protect themselves against money laundering/terrorist financing?

FID:

Outside of national (laws/regulations) and institutional control, staff should be encouraged operate out of a value system which promotes their integrity and family as not for sale.

How do we correct the international perception of IFCs as havens for money laundering/tax evasion?

ALB:

Government must embrace the industry more and take a definitive leadership role. It must have a good story to tell. There was a time when the Central Bank would promote the sector internationally e.g. at the RIMS conference, but at that time they had no control over the sector. That input worked to assist in the promotion and development of the industry. In the absence of such input today we must find alternative credible voices to assist in the international "selling" process. This would prove useful in counteracting the negative portrayal of the Caribbean offshore jurisdictions in the international media.

FID:

By boldly approaching the international media and engaging such media houses as *Time Magazine* and others. In addition, there is a need to begin to send positive messages with respect to the strong regulatory framework currently in place in the region. A strong message must also be sent to would-be investors that you do not want their "dirty" money. Rather, they will need to show you how they intend to better the lives of your people by giving back/reinvesting some of their profits in the region.

Birds of a feather

The definition of offshore financial services emanates from and has been fashioned by those core nations which previously enjoyed capital supremacy. A realignment has taken place in the global economic order and smaller nations have emerged to command a space in the business of global capital. Now is as good a time as ever for island financial self-confidence to follow suit. To this end it would be useful to leverage specific strengths and further develop capabilities. Promotion of the region as historically strong in delivering high quality international business solutions within well-regulated jurisdictions may be used as a countervailing activity against the incessant discourse of weak regulation, ultra-secrecy, money laundering, etc.

Although the divestment objective (into offshore financial services) may have been achieved, its full benefit is yet to be maximised by divesting countries and, by extension, island regions. This is particularly so from the point of view of the low levels of reinvestment into the community by regulated entities. When compared to the financial breaks these companies enjoy, the degree of financial reciprocation is incongruent. Therefore, offshore businesses should be considered *not* to be as socially responsible as they ought to be. Anecdotal evidence might suggest the level of societal reinvestment is generally inconsistent with the fiscal benefits of offshore finance to the receiving entity. However, there is always the matter of Allen Stanford, who, before his exposure as a fraudster, had invested millions into the then branded Twenty-20 cricket as a means of stimulating renewed interest in the regional game. Although not the best example given the emphasis in this book on governing "evil" money and Stanford's umbrous money-making means, it does speak to an inherent uncertainty of the true source of funds whether or not compliance protocols are in place and are being followed. The truth is, illegally obtained funds that have been reinvested into society, in other words, put to good social use, have in fact activated the end stage of money laundering, that of integration. What better way to cover an illicit money trail! Having said that, there must be a willingness on the part of national leadership to ensure there is a clear, tangible and mutual benefit for host communities and international business guests operating within its shores.

In an earlier chapter, I proposed that the conflict existing between IFCs and traditional banking domains could be due to the former's success in attracting capital away from those nations. Naturally, from the outside in, the view might be somewhat different, that is to say, the tendency of these centres to lure the criminal element and their seemingly deliberate involvement in promoting secrecy/concealment without due regard for the social harm it could cause. A taciturn response may be that outsiders should be more concerned about money laundering in their own jurisdiction than in somebody else's. With that, legal systems need overhauling to effectively execute the enforcement and sanctions component of enacted laws. Opportunities for greater interaction have arisen for criminals due to the ever-evolving technological nature of financial globalisation. The good guys also need to maximise the opportunities technology brings as well. Hence as there is international "co-operation" and dialogue amongst criminal networks, there must be the same on the part of local/regional regulators and similarly supervisory bodies. Such regulatory interface would be critical since the large number of small and geographically separated island nations already make criminal migration somewhat easy, in addition to the establishment of related potentially criminal enterprises in other jurisdictions.

The notion of regulation, particularly in relation to its aims, is in need of clarification. Else, its innate power may be misused. The bureaucracy, which may arise out of the misapplication of rules or the misuse of the power in the execution of rules, can negatively impact client service delivery. This observation by ALB is interesting as it seems to directly correlate to the adaptive behaviour which Merton (1938) dubbed ritualism. According to Merton, this mode of behaviour is engaged when institutional means of achieving cultural goals become so prized above the goals themselves as to result in a state of over-conformity, ultimately leading to the "displacement" of goals. Thus, the rule itself, rather than maintaining its instrumental value as originally intended, becomes the focus in and of itself, thereby engendering a state of bureaucracy (Merton, 1957, pp. 195–206). The apparent ritualism by mostly front-line bureaucrats would suggest that training should be accentuated at the operational level and at the strategic level, the objective of regulation should be revisited. A balanced approach to compliance and the fluidity of business is critical if island IFCs are to improve their ability to efficiently process institutional approvals and effectively compete with jurisdictions which do not have similar problems.

There is common understanding that money laundering is a universal experience. With the level of regulation currently in existence in Caribbean IFCs, the chances of it occurring are neither higher nor lower when compared to advanced countries engaged in similar international financial services. This may have to do, in part, with the innovatory capability of criminals and their skill at activating the concealment process well before primary entry into the banking system, and not necessarily weaknesses in the legal and regulatory systems of IFCs. Equally, the failure of political authorities to provide adequate opportunities for its citizens could entice certain classes into deviant behaviour. Such behaviour is instigated when higher (non-poor) classes exercise their social power to entice lower classes into acting against societal norms and is equally abnormal when the latter actually carry out the deviant acts.

There also appears to be unanimity when it comes to the potential causal factors of money laundering. One notes the familiar theme of greed, which again speaks clearly to Durkheim's (1951) notion of receding goals in the relentless pursuit of wealth. However, one wonders if the receding goal dynamic, which features strongly in the capitalist domain, may not also be applicable to the unending war against money laundering. That could turn out to be a receding goal itself.

The corruption motif is consistent with what has been discussed before as regards the agent-principal interface and the conflicts of interest which come about when trust on either side is breached. Personal choice, therefore, to act in concert with or against the collective becomes a key flashpoint beyond internal control systems and legal frameworks. This aside, the intensity of leadership and their engagement in setting national standards for maintaining a pristine jurisdiction and their willingness to ensure fairness in executing the rule of law are viewed as critical to gaining an advantage in the money laundering war. Essentially, evil money will attract evil associations – characters, organisations and networks on an increasing scale. Left to itself, therefore, a nation could find itself encrypted in a tomb from which resurrection could prove a deathly challenge.

There is the sense in which the role of the IFC and its contribution to the life of global capital cannot be left up to onshore nations. Any recasting of IFCs' sullied image must be from the inside out, that is, by the IFC repositioning itself and taking responsibility for promoting its own self-image on a global scale and this despite continued opposition to its contribution. Political leadership is therefore believed to be of generational importance.

Not surprisingly, the "one voice" theme promulgated by the consulate officer hints at the importance of unity if the region is to be heard on the global front. Despite the historical attempts and failures to do so, one notes the role of the CFATF and ongoing efforts of regional regulators to ensure more dynamic collaboration.

Generally, there appears to be concord regarding the protection of the broader society from criminal behaviour. Despite the impression conveyed in sections of the media that client privacy appears to be subjugated to the broader shared concern to expose and penalise criminal behaviour, the belief is, in fact, offset by devising the appropriate legal systems to prosecute malicious reporting. At the end of either process, the broader society remains the beneficiary as it is insulated on both fronts. This is why it is felt society in general should be engaged more and their awareness level enhanced. Professionals such as attorneys and accountants have a particular role to play in the engagement of international business, in order to have a fighting chance at mitigating the risk of "dirty" money entering the jurisdiction. However, they must be guided by integrity to, let us say, avoid becoming part of the problem.

Conclusion

Caribbean IFC regulators are committed to ensuring the mitigation of reputational risk in their respective jurisdictions by promoting adherence to the global AML/CFT policy agenda. Amongst regulators there is an intolerance of the criminal use of the financial system, particularly as it affects the ability to attract good business. These two postulates, especially, enable the regulator to execute its primary responsibility to maintain the necessary social order that is required in the financial system.

The global policy diffusion agenda, notwithstanding its impositionary orientation, is aimed at dealing swiftly with threats to the macro-social order. However, at the national, jurisdictional level, there is more hand-holding when it comes to interacting with regulatory constituents, consistent perhaps with the relational culture present in smaller societies. Besides guarding the financial system, regional regulators also viewed their assignment as maintaining a corresponding national or societal brand. That branding consists of a strong consumer protection dynamic which, in turn, promotes an environment conducive to good business.

As agents of the state, regulatory personnel represent the fixed variable in the social order equation. Thus, their knowledge levels must be upgraded continually in order to effectively execute their role of guardians of the social order. This is so particularly because of the continuously evolving and innovative approaches adopted by criminals. Even though crime at the institutional level is somewhat mitigated through:

a   effective, group-wide risk management;
b   the international standing of regulated institutions; and
c   the reasonable expectation that institutional agents will operate with integrity,

it should be noted that corporate deviance is still possible depending on the institution's perception of its social (business) reality. Added to this is the individual's perception of his or her personal reality. Either way, a corresponding response will be evoked resulting in a conforming or deviant behaviour.

Structured reviews are an important feature of the AML policy diffusion agenda. It is a feedback mechanism aimed at monitoring policy implementation. Unfavourable reviews can create a perception that the social order has gone awry. At this juncture, a signal is sent of a potential regulatory breakdown. Across IFCs there are, indeed, gaps in the implementation of international standards. However, the general tenor of mutual evaluations executed by the CFATF would suggest that adequate efforts are in train to achieve compliance. This demonstrates the region's commitment and that of the various governments, regardless of the political parties in residence, to putting in place the mechanisms as stipulated by supra-national authorities. After all, full compliance is also a process and not simply an act.

In terms of the occurrence of money laundering, IFC jurisdictions generally represent an area of concern for US authorities, particularly in light of their geographic location as potential transshipment points for illegal drugs acquisition and disbursement. That said, the interconnectedness of nations brought about by global finance renders money laundering a universal reality. The ranking, therefore, of OECD nations alongside Caribbean and other IFCs in terms of concerns relating to potential money laundering is not surprising.

Weaknesses in the financial social order (regulatory system) may be exploited by the criminally minded and potentially spill over into the broader community. As a strong preference for the allocation and/or temporary respite of global capital, IFCs must adopt a mature approach to their financial affairs. This requires ensuring the appropriate control environment is cultivated to host capital and its various agencies. The region must raise its self-esteem to new levels such that it is able to articulate standards from a position of strength and in the process command respect from "capital visitors/tourists" (offshore business) to its respective shores. Continuing this metaphor, some "capital visitors" may have an agenda contrary to societal norms, and therefore it is understood that such undesirables should neither be sought after via marketing campaigns nor allowed to remain if found to have made it past IFC due diligence checkpoints. With this in mind, secrecy can no longer be viewed in the traditional sense; that is, if it is deemed to be undermining the social order. Legal remedies must therefore be available to extricate the broader society from the harm of deviant individuals and/or institutions.

Appropriate channels of communication must be opened to foster dialogue and co-operation among the broader global society as this is precisely how deviant elements maximise opportunities in the competition for capital. At the national level of each respective IFC, a new customer service dynamic that exceeds the colonial notion of the "welcoming society" must be cultivated and demonstrated if the region is to lure the right kind of capital. Given its premier role in the forefront of international finance, there is available to the IFC a prime opportunity to rewrite its own script, acknowledging the negative, but more-so highlighting the positive contribution of the region to financial globalisation. To come to this position as an IFC requires strong political will, resilience and leadership to make the decisions necessary for advancement.

Notes

1 For confidentiality purposes, I have redacted the names of the countries involved, related statistical tables and other information which might potentially indicate the specific jurisdiction reviewed. Instead, I present a brief overview of findings under various monikers before drawing brief conclusions.
2 See http://www.fatf-gafi.org/pages/0,3417,en_32250379_32236982_1_1_1_1_1,00.html
3 US State Department website at: http://www.state.gov/p/inl/rls/nrcrpt/index.htm
4 US State Department website at: http://www.state.gov/p/inl/rls/nrcrpt/2010/vol2/137209.htm
5 See INCSR 2010, Vol. 2, p. 30. Available at: http://www.state.gov/documents/organisation/137429.pdf

References

Durkheim, E., 1897. Reprinted 1951. *Suicide: A study of sociology*. 2nd ed. New York: The Free Press of Glencoe.
Finckenauer, M. & Voronin, Y., 2001. *The threat of Russian organised crime*. Washington: US Department of Justice.

Merton, R. K., 1938. Social structure and anomie. *American Sociological Review*, 3, pp. 672–680.

Merton, R., 1957. *Social theory and social structure*. Glencoe: Free Press.

Shelley, L., 1999. Transnational organized crime: The new authoritarianism. In: H. Friman & P. Andreas, eds. *The illicit global economy and state power*. Maryland: Rowman & Littlefield Publishers Inc., pp. 25–51.

7   Casing the joint

Prologue

Four of the seven cases earlier identified form the basis of the analysis and discussion in this chapter. The others are discussed in the next chapter. To start with, I revert to the industry transforming scandal of BCCI in the 1990s and roll into 2001 with a case that would effectively shut down an IFC's offshore industry for years to come.

Bank of Credit and Commerce International 1991

Although more than two decades have passed since the historic collapse of Bank of Credit and Commerce International (BCCI) in a $20 billion scandal, its circumstances still haunt bank regulators globally as well as law enforcement authorities. The entity's demise, which was brought about mostly through fraud to the nth degree, precipitated a string of changes to the supervision of banking entities and regulatory enforcement globally. One notable change triggered by the BCCI collapse was the enhancement of the regulatory paradigm known as "consolidated supervision", a term originating from the Basel Committee on Banking Supervision or the Cooke Committee in its early days. Consolidated supervision requires the host supervisor – that is, the national regulatory body in whose country the main/head office of the financial institution under supervision is located – to ensure it has adequate knowledge of the overall operations of the entity's other branches/subsidiaries which may be located in multiple jurisdictions. This is particularly important owing to the need to make sure there is sufficient capitalisation to undergird the level of financial risk being undertaken.

BCCI was formed in Luxembourg in 1972 by Pakistani citizen, Agha Hasan Abedi. From the beginning, the bank adopted a complex organisational structure, which made effective oversight and supervision extremely challenging. This action was deemed a deliberate exploitation of a loophole in the existing Basel Concordat at the time, which allowed for the setting up of the bank essentially using a three-parent strategy (Bench, 1991). In addition to the Luxembourg and Netherlands incorporated holding companies (BCCI Holdings SA and Credit and Commerce American Holdings NV), the entities BCCI SA Luxembourg, Credit and Commerce American Investment, BV and BCCI Overseas Ltd (incorporated in the Cayman Islands) were amongst its main subsidiaries. BCCI maintained ties to the United Arab Emirates through its Abu Dhabi shareholders whilst operating in more than a third of the world's nations at the time (Basel Committee on Banking Supervision, 2004).

Most of BCCI's banking business was conducted outside its place of legal incorporation. In fact, the bank craftily located its headquarters in *London* along with several of its offices, cleverly positioning its corporate self out of the home regulator's (Luxembourg) radar. This apart, Luxembourg did not offer deposit insurance or lender of last resort facilities to the group. These combined factors meant there was little incentive to oversee the bank on an enterprise wide scale (Herring, 2005). BCCI operated smoothly through its several London offices. However, the Bank of England's (BOE's) role, which included responsibility for the supervision of UK banks, did not extend to the group wide supervision of BCCI (Basel Committee on Banking Supervision, 2004, p. 49). This framework suited the bank perfectly, enabling it to operate in a self-directed manner and on a global scale. Compounding the situation was the fact that no one auditor company had a complete sense of the company's operations at any time. These irreconcilable variables "functioned to frustrate the full understanding of BCCI's operations by anyone" (Kerry and Brown, 1992). Moreover, it would be revealed in due course that BCCI's financial statements were falsified from the start (Basel Committee on Banking Supervision, 2004, p. 49).

In terms of initial set up, the majority of BCCI's capital was infused by the Emir of Abu Dhabi, United Arab Emirates, with a smaller portion – 25% – provided by Bank of America (BOA). There was an intended mutual benefit to the BCCI/BOA relationship (Mitchell, et al., 2001). On the one hand, BCCI would be able to convey a sense of respectability, inching its way into US markets and western business in general. BOA, on the other hand, would itself be able to access Middle East markets through Abedi's connections (Mitchell, et al., 2001).

But there was a snafu. Nobody trusted BCCI. Plus, who was the consolidated regulator? At the clearinghouse level, a breakdown in the correspondent relationship was inevitable given BCCI's ongoing lack of transparency, particularly as it related to information disclosures at the time (Mitchell et al., 2001, p. 26). The bank made quick inroads into the market, exponentially growing its client database by 800% from 19 branches at inception and $200 million in assets, to 154 branches and $4 billion by the end of 1980. It also had a voracious appetite, acquiring smaller financial institutions and consolidating their operations into other financial companies through the questionable shell company vehicle, all under the BCCI brand. There was nothing but discomfort with BCCI's activities as even the company's internal structure was out of sync with the norm: nearly 250 managers reported directly to Abedi and his CEO, Mr. Swaleh Naqvi.

With all this, American regulators felt it necessary to institute failsafe measures to ensure BCCI was unable, legally, to acquire any US banking interests. Of course, BCCI outsmarted the well-meaning Office of the Comptroller of the Currency (OCC), sneaking into the US market under the shadow of nominee companies which it used to acquire financially dishevelled US banks. These acquisitions were later merged with BCCI's branch network, leading to the burgeoning presence the bank needed to press forward with its objective to attract more western business. Also leveraged in this corporate subterfuge were prominent political, intelligence, regulatory, legislative and business professionals – retired and current. In short, having provided monetary and other favours over time to the elite and influential, chips were called in from all possible sources including the Emirates and other Middle Eastern connections. Altogether, these powerful actors erected a bridge to somewhere: enabling the market penetration process at different junctures, simultaneously. Some were embedded within circles of influence and others strategically placed on the externalities, but with no less weight. The guileful public relations agenda was skilfully whipped up through relentless frontal engagement, back-channel assignations and arm-twisting machinations until what was desired was, in fact, obtained.

But lack of regulatory oversight and secret inside dealings apart, how did BCCI pull off this high stakes horseplay with such apparent dexterity on unsuspecting depositors and creditors?

At the wholesale and retail levels, phantom loans were established on the books against actual financial inflows (deposits) that were *not* recorded. In turn, these non-loans were priced at an imaginary margin and documented as having earned substantial interest income, which boosted a trumped up bottom line (Basel Committee on Banking Supervision, 2004, p. 49). Where real lending took place, it was in disproportionately large amounts to a concentrated few, exceeding by far the best practice figure of 25% of capital to any one individual or group. The other aspect of BCCI's chicanery emanated from the treasury side and involved what Beaty et al. describe as a "planetary Ponzi scheme".[1] Classical Ponzis put incoming funds to their own use. When interest premia or other gains become due to older investors or depositors, these are paid from the newest pot of inbound monies. The mere act of not documenting or only partially recording receipt of client funds empowered BCCI to behave in a cavalier manner. This uncaptured access to client funds meant there was no accountability mechanism in place and therefore if trading activities tended towards flippancy, which they did, loss outcomes could either be buried or shielded by additional monopoly loans or, as noted, covered by real incoming deposits. This operational ploy was consistent with BCCI's calm, cool and collected criminality. Despite this mounting insolvency state, the bank continued to grow, moving into the Asian and African markets, arguing that its augmented activities were fuelled in part by the deposits of wealthy families. However, this unbridled distension proved uneasy for the regulatory community resulting in the brakes being put on any further expansion within the United Kingdom, by the BOE.

In March 1991, the accounting firm Price Waterhouse (Price) at the time was hired by the BOE to carry out an enquiry into the bank's operations. Itself, a questionable action. Apart from its role as Auditor, Price supplied consultancy and advisory services to BCCI corporate managers. Despite its own doubts as to the veracity of BCCI's financials, the apparently reputable audit firm nonetheless provided unqualified sign off over an extended period. Alongside receiving loans and other benefits coupled with inappropriate relationships with BCCI power-brokers Price's audit contract should have been cancelled due to glaring conflicts of interest. Nevertheless, a few months later the Price report codenamed "Sandstorm" was issued, citing BCCI's financial history as "difficult to reconstruct" owing to what was deemed "widespread fraud and manipulation" (Kerry and Brown, 1992, p. 54). Needless to say, the report prompted an immediate global clamp down on the bank's operations and the launching of a full investigation into its financial dealings. The end result would – mercifully – be the bank's liquidation.

From the US end of things, the Kerry Report to the Senate Committee on Foreign Relations highlighted BCCI as a "unique criminal structure and an elaborate corporate spider-web" deliberately set up by its founder Abedi to "evade regulation and government control aimed ultimately at frustrating the full understanding of its operations by anyone" (Kerry and Brown, 1992, Executive Summary, p. 4). From the get go, BCCI sought to bury its underlying operations through the manipulative use of corporate vehicles for the primary purpose of conducting illegal activity vis.:

> Unlike any ordinary bank, BCCI was from its earliest days made up of multiplying layers of entities, related to one another through an impenetrable series of holding companies, affiliates, subsidiaries, banks-within-banks, insider dealings and nominee

relationships. By fracturing corporate structure, record keeping, regulatory review, and audits, the complex BCCI family of entities created by Abedi was able to evade ordinary legal restrictions on the movement of capital and goods as a matter of daily practice and routine. In creating BCCI as a vehicle fundamentally free of government control, Abedi developed in BCCI an ideal mechanism for facilitating illicit activity by others, including such activity by officials of many of the governments whose laws BCCI was breaking.

(Kerry and Brown, 1992, Executive Summary, p. 4)

With its management setting the tone by actively engaging, supporting and promoting criminal activity, a perfect stage was set for institutional deviance. This was complemented by extensive client fraud thus cementing the overarching culture of vice. Money laundering and bribery of officials was an active and standard business tool exercised across five continents. Terrorist financing, arms and drug trafficking, trading in nuclear technologies; prostitution ring management; tax evasion, illegal immigration; illicit purchases of banks and real estate all seemed to have become key business objectives replacing the traditional goals of a regular financial institution. The report further makes the point that they were a "panoply of other financial crimes committed limited only by the imagination of its officers and customers" (Kerry and Brown, 1992, Executive Summary, p. 4, para. 3).

The instruments leveraged by BCCI to carry out its global criminal remit were not unlike those used in standard business practice, for example, the use of bank confidentiality jurisdictions, guarantees, nominee relationships, political lobbying, etc. However, when allied with the darkness of kick-backs, bribes, self-dealing and the illicit activities mentioned above, these business staples mutated to an arsenal of felonious tools. The utilisation of "straw men" also featured widely as it presented the bank with the professional face required to operate in the market place, while at the same time serving to distract from the true meaning, intent and actions of the financial institution. In the ensuing investigation, the bank was said to engage in witness intimidation, and sought the "retention of well placed insiders to discourage governmental action" (Kerry and Brown, 1992, p. 4, para. 4).

The impact of the BCCI failure across its multiple jurisdictions blew the lid off the role of the BOE and its apparent lax approach to addressing the rogue institution's uncertain operations. Indeed, fuelled by press reports and public outcry, the BOE would come in for the kind of castigation no regulator would want to experience. Some government agency, after all, had to shoulder the blame. To make matters worse, court action initiated by the BCCI's liquidator Deloitte and Touche on behalf of depositors and ongoing castigation from the press would continue to highlight the BOE in a negative light. It would be 13 long years after the case was first brought before the law courts that the BOE would be "freed" of any accountability in the failure of the BCCI. Nothing, however, could change the public's mind about its accountability in the debacle.

Bank of New York Mellon Corporation Case 1998

Founded by Alexander Hamilton, Bank of New York (BONY) opened its doors on 9 June 1784, making it one of the oldest banks in the United States. Over time, the bank would grow into a colossal financial services institution of global magnitude. At the end of 1997, BONY was enjoying its sixth successive year of record financial performance recording material improvements in net income and earnings per share ratios over the prior year.[2]

Prior to its merger with Mellon Financial Corporation on 2 July 2007, BONY found itself at the centre of a six-year investigation beginning in 1998 involving the use of its facilities in the transfer of over $7 billion from Russia under suspicious circumstances. The funds were passed through BONY offices in the United States and on to other accounts outside that country. The broader context within which the scandal took place is of significance: the movement of funds through correspondent accounts occurred at a time when the Russian economy was undergoing a historic privatisation of formerly state-owned assets. No doubt as a result of their exclusive proximity to and power over state business – not to mention the convenient lax independent oversight of the privatisation (change) process – this afforded Russian business and political incumbents an occasion to be their best corrupt and self-dealing selves.

At the centre of the movement of funds through the correspondent accounts was Russian-born Lucy Edwards, a BONY Vice President in its eastern division with authority to set up and open accounts for clients. Some of these accounts related to front companies manned by her husband, Peter Berlin, which would be used later as conduits to avoid Russian government taxes, duties and the movement of funds from various illicit sources.[3] Coincidentally, Ms. Edwards' supervisor (Natasha Kagalovsky) was also of Russian descent and even more circumstantial was that the latter's husband Konstantin Kagalovsky had connections at the level of the Kremlin and Russian business having served in both sectors.[4] In fact, exploiting his role as Russia's IMF delegate was the perfect veneer as it allowed Kagalovsky to deflect billions of IMF dollars over a three-year period to a privately owned company, Benex Worldwide Ltd. Sitting on the Benex Board as luck would have it was Peter Berlin – Ms. Edwards' spouse. The diverted, now personalised monies were intended to support Russia's transition from communist socialism to a capitalist economy.[5] Other financial institutions implicated in the transfers were Republic National Bank, a unit of Republic Bancorp, and other top European banks such as UBS Switzerland AG and Deutsche Bank AG.

Republic National Bank alerted authorities about unusually large wires coming through its accounts from Russia. Prompted by Republic's suspicious activity report, authorities were able to track and monitor remittance activity. Their observations culminated in charges of money laundering being brought against BONY.

Following the revelations of financial wrongdoing, BONY suspended Ms. Kagalovsky and fired Ms. Edwards. Ms. Edwards and her husband subsequently confessed to opening the suspect accounts at the bank, conceding they helped two Moscow banks conduct illegal operations through BONY accounts.[6] The couple later pleaded guilty to fraud charges in 2000 and were sentenced to five years' probation for their criminal involvement.[7]

For its lax oversight, weak controls and failure to follow their own policies and procedures BONY was fined $14 million. Exacerbating this matter was the fact that the bank had already been under regulatory scrutiny for deficiencies in the critical, monitoring aspect of its operations and had actually agreed to set things right.[8] However, the extent of its sincerity and commitment to do so was noticeably lacking. This was made worse in the endemic fraud which was picked up at the bank's Long Island offices and which regulators could not overlook, levying a further sanction of $24 million. No doubt the $38 million in penalties was meant to rattle the bank into a deeper remediation mode.

Citibank 1998

Appearing in the August 1998 issue of *The Banker* magazine, Citicorp, the holding company for the Citibank brand, was listed at number 21 out of 50 of the World's Top 50 banking companies, with well over $300 billion in assets. However, in February of the same year the Ranking Minority Member of the Permanent Subcommittee on Investigations of the United States Senate, Representative John Glenn, expressed concern about reports that Raul Salinas de Gotari, brother of former Mexican President, Carlos Salinas de Gotari, had allegedly been involved in laundering money out of Mexico through Citibank, to accounts in Citibank affiliates in Switzerland and the United Kingdom.[9]

An investigation was subsequently mounted by the Special Investigations Office (OSI) of the US General Accounting Office (GAO). A key objective of the exercise was to find out if there was any truth to the allegations, in particular the circumstances giving rise to the funnelling of upwards of $100 million from Mexico through Citibank entities. Also mandated by the sub-committee was an identification of the specific services provided to Salinas, and lastly the extent to which the bank's actions fell within the confines of the law.

The investigation revealed that, as a high net worth client, Salinas benefitted from the special, personalised service consistent with the private banking offering at the Citibank New York office in the period 1992–1994. Not only did Citibank's actions in fact enable the remittances to occur, but they were also instrumental in blurring the paper trail of transactions from beginning to end. In a nutshell, as a direct result of the bank's handiwork there was no telling the origin of Salinas' money or its terminus. The bank's supporting actions included overlooking reference requirements and the completion of a financial profile, a necessary document for the required comfort level for the source of one's wealth. Not that a waiver in any form had been requested in the first place, as approval for such flexibility would have been required based on the bank's Know Your Customer (KYC) rules at the time. Other findings concluded that the bank had set up offshore structures through its affiliate in Cayman, namely Trocca Private Investment Company. Trocca's principal officer and shareholder was a shell company – Tyler Ltd. Trocca's "work" was overseen by a shell company Board with shell companies performing the role of board members, namely Madeline Investment SA, Donat Investment SA and Hitchcock Investment SA, respectively. Trocca also had links to Citibank's London and Switzerland offices, where investment accounts were held (GAO/OSI, 1998, pp. 5–7).

The bank also acted in deference to Salinas, facilitating transfers between its Mexico and New York entities with the intention of concentrating monies into the New York account before onward transfer to the Cayman offshore account. Conveniently, there was no US documentation that suggested a link between Trocca (the offshore structure set up in the Cayman office) and Salinas; in particular, that the latter was in fact the individual with controlling interest in Trocca. Moreover, the fact there was no paper trail connecting Trocca and Citibank's Mexico and New York offices with Salinas is testimony to the institutional effort undertaken to keep under wraps any association with the politically exposed Salinas (GAO/OSI, 1998, p. 3).

The extent to which Citibank took care of its wealthy clients extended to quasi spouses as well. Relationship managers took complicity to a new level in allowing Mrs. Salinas to obfuscate her link with Raul by allowing her to utilise at the on-boarding stage, a portion of her maiden name.[10] That said, the report notes she had not yet been married at the time of opening her facilities with the bank (GAO/OSI, 1998, p. 4). However, this in no way minimised her proximity to power and influence and thus political exposure.

In 1995, the Salinases were both arrested for money laundering among other things; murder (Raul Salinas) and drug trafficking (Mrs. Salinas). For its client supporting efforts, the bank was paid client fees approximating $2 million. In the end, the bank conceded it violated its internal KYC policy only in so far as not preparing the required financial profile nor waiving the requirement to do so. In terms of the final outcome of its investigation, the challenge for the GAO at the time was a parallel investigation being conducted by the US Attorney's Office in the Southern District on alleged money laundering by the Salinases (GAO/OSI, 1998, p. 4). This apparently made access to information, people and other resources difficult to come by for the GAO's own investigative purposes. The GAO was therefore unable to render an opinion as to whether any laws were broken. Also based on the information presented by GAO to the OCC, the latter concluded that the bank's actions at the time "did not violate civil aspects of the US Bank Secrecy Act". The OCC further determined that private banking's KYC policies were "voluntary and not governed by law or regulation" (GAO/OSI, 1998, p. 4).

Noteworthy is that the FATF's 40 Recs. emerged in the post-1999 period, less than a year after the GAO investigation into the Salinas/Citibank case. Although furtively flying under the radar of best practice, the case is useful in so far as it shows the complicit behaviour of even top tier financial institutions and their agents in supporting the transfer and clandestine movement of funds derived from unverified, questionable sources.

First International Bank of Grenada 2001

On 28 February 2001, the Grenada Supreme Court appointed PwC LLP's Marcus A. Wide as Liquidator of the assets of First International Bank of Grenada (FIBG). The appointment came as a result of an Order sought by the Grenada Minister of Finance to wind up the bank.[11]

FIBG was granted a Class 1 offshore banking licence by Grenada regulators in October 1997. The bank later merged its limited operations with the Nauru registered Fidelity Bank, retaining the FIBG brand. The chief proponent of the entity's set up was the former Gilbert Ziegler, who subsequently became known as Van A. Brink. Brink and a number of cohorts were previously associated with Fidelity. With the integration of Fidelity and FIBG operations, the expectation was that the banks' principals could now take advantage of the full gamut of offshore financial services under a Class I licence without having to rely on other entities (banks and other intermediary companies) for administrative services (First Report of the Liquidator, March 2001, paras. 9–10).

The minimum capitalisation for an offshore bank under Grenada law at the time was $2.25 million (approximately).[12] FIBG easily met this stipulation from its cash resources made up of $500,000 – Fidelity's equity stake – alongside an "assigned precious ruby" said to value $20 million (First Report of the Liquidator, March 2001, para. 11). Through a *non-independent* source, namely Brink, the Government of Grenada and FIBG's initial auditors – the local Grenadian firm Wilson and Company – were provided with documentation which suggested that the rights of the ruby were duly assigned to FIBG. However, there was no corroborating evidence of such and hence the authenticity of title was always in serious doubt. The FBI would also weigh in on this question, noting that neither the ruby nor any interest thereof had ever been assigned to Brink or entities related to him (First Report of the Liquidator, March 2001, para. 12).

In time, the bank would also "acquire" additional "assigned" assets from venerable institutions such as the Banks of China and Taiwan, respectively, and Dai-ichi Kangyo Bank, Tokyo Mitsubishi and Union Bank of Switzerland. Together with the "ruby", these additional assets would come to be valued circa $14 billion, all within record time and touted to impress and attract would-be depositors as to FIBG's depth of business. In addition, to give the appearance of neutrality, marketing of the bank's products and services was executed on a seemingly arm's length basis through four companies going by the names of Life Offshore, Offshore Educational Institute, Granite Registry Services, and Asset Research and Development Association. Of course, all of these entities were in some form or fashion linked to FIBG (First Report of the Liquidator, March 2001, paras. 12–15).

Marketing by FIBG was also smartly effected by establishing "correspondent relationships" which provided an alternative face for the company's specious operations and the necessary distance it desired in order to appear credible. In truth, however, and once again, these correspondent entities were related to the criminal firm either directly or indirectly, with FIBG for the most part funding their operating expenses. Ultimately, whether funds were deposited directly to FIBG or via its so-called correspondent relationships, said funds remained accessible to FIBG. This was also true of the processing centres through which funds were moved to and from depositors and correspondents. The processing centres held accounts in their own name in independent financial institutions across different regions including parts of the Caribbean (St. Vincent, Nevis), Africa (Uganda), the United States (the states of Washington, Nevada and Oregon) and the Channel Isles (Jersey). The entire arrangement turned out to be just the smokescreen FIBG required to achieve its primary objective – *attract deposits and control their use* (First Report of the Liquidator, March 2001, paras. 64–76).

FIBG began to accept deposits from eligible clients some six months after acquiring initial authority from the Grenada Government. Depositors were encouraged to place funds with the bank on the basis of expected high yield returns (as much as 200%) on placements, against which they were offered certificates of deposits (CDs). The CDs were said to be fully insured (principal and interest) through an entity called the International Deposit Reinsurance Corporation (IDIC), an entity set up in Nevis – clearly an attempt at mimicking the US Federal Deposit Insurance Corporation, which under US law can only guarantee deposits of up to $100,000.

Under the so-called IDIC alternative, the bank was required to "block and lodge" sufficient of its assets with IDIC as an assurance to depositors of full repayment in the event of FIBG's failure. Depositors were further reassured of high returns by virtue of the apparent prudent trading principles adopted by FIBG, that is, only to buy where there was certainty that a corresponding security was on hand which could be sold at a higher price. It would later be determined that the bank's trading actions were entirely out of sync with its much heralded investment strategy. Of significance also, was the Board's sanctioning purchase of/investment in real estate in Grenada and Uganda; a sound recording studio, beer cooling process, cookie manufacturing and a process to reclaim gold from sand "tailings" (First Report of the Liquidator, March 2001, paras. 18–19).

Up to the point when the CDs had begun to mature, FIBG was able to provide investors with their money on a demand basis. However, as with classical Ponzis, once it became time to provide subsequent investors with their original cash plus interest, and within pre-agreed maturity terms, the fragile and fraudulent financial footing on which the bank stood could no longer sustain its dubious exploits. Its flag of deception, arrogantly hoisted over the Government and people of Grenada months before, had begun to unfurl in the wind of scepticism and investor fears of financial loss.

To its advantage, FIBG, through its principals – Brink in particular – applied the art of misrepresentation. This common feature was picked up by Wide in his investigation. Two are addressed here.

Deliberate misrepresentation of capital sources

The various elements of capital purportedly assigned to FIBG and whose value appeared on the balance sheet was aimed at giving the bank an air of strong capitalisation, in other words, a marketing gimmick. This included the idea that the supposedly valuable ruby was rightfully entrusted and indeed conveyed to FIBG. This was a fallacy (First Report of the Liquidator, March 2001, paras. 42–43).

Also called into question were 750,000 Aristocrat Endeavor Shares owned by a would-be borrower Resource Enhancement Inc. (REI), said to value up to $17.25 million at the time. Initially, the shares were assigned to FIBG by their owner in anticipation of a loan, to be secured by the shares, a standard banking practice. However, the Liquidator's investigation while indeed confirming the assignment of shares to FIBG and for the noted purpose, also determined that the intended loan was not disbursed after all. As such, the shares were assigned back to their substantive owner, REI. The Liquidator makes the point that:

> In the same way FIBG had no legitimate right or title to the ruby highlighted on its books as an asset, it was inappropriate and inaccurate for the company to represent the Aristocrat shares as an asset or fully paid up capital when at best the assigned shares appear to represent security for a potential loan that was never advanced.
> (Second Report of the Liquidator, June 2001, paras. 35–38).

Material misrepresentation of the authenticity of financial statements

Central to assessing the company's financials was the confusion deliberately created by FIBG's principals in seeking formal requests to change the entity's financial year end on at least three occasions. The impact of these deferrals was to stay the execution of any audit in the absence of a definitive period for which the assessment was to be undertaken. In addition, the Auditors:

- determined that the company's books were kept in a manner which rendered the application of generally accepted accounting principles nigh impossible;
- had significant difficulty in verifying the existence and value of asset holdings, confirming transactions, tracing trading activity and obtaining other requisite documentation germane to the audit process.

In the end, Wilson and Company resigned out of professional frustration, but relieved it had not begun the on-site portion of its review. No doubt to Brink's delight, Wilson's exit opened the door for accomplices au-fait with the bank and its principals' modus operandi. Therefore, preparing financials and also having them duly audited was suddenly not a problem after all. Particularly if the new resources employed to do so had previously had their CPA licence revoked and another jailed for fraud several years earlier (First Report of the Liquidator, March 2001, paras. 115–121)!

FIBG's much touted trading strategy was also a ruse. The Liquidator could find no evidence indicating trading of any kind had, in fact, occurred. In addition, there was clear indication the so-called depositor insurance program was without a sound financial basis and thus wholly phoney. The outcome of Wide's investigation was to therefore reaffirm what was anecdotally suspected – that FIBG was an institutional con from the start, attracting third party funds purely for the self-indulgence of its criminal associates (Second Report of the Liquidator, June 2001, paras. 7–12).

Notes

1 Beaty, J., Gwynne, S.C., Booth C., Branegan, J. & Gibson, H. BCCI: The dirtiest bank of all. *Time Magazine*, 29 July 1991.
2 Source: BONY Annual Report 1997.
3 See T. Obrien & Raymond Bonner, Banker and husband tell of role in money laundering case. *New York Times*, 17 February 2000.
4 See T. Obrien, Bank settles inquiry into money laundering. *New York Times*, 9 November 2005.
5 See M. Corey Goldman, Watching overseas funds. CNN, 1 September 1999.
6 Supra note 3.
7 See J. Sibun, Ex- BONY executive sentenced for money laundering. *Financial News*, 27 July 2006.
8 Supra note 4.
9 Source material in this specific case is drawn ostensibly from the GAO/ISO Report (GAO/ISO, 1998).
10 Having not yet been married to Mr. Salinas at the time of her introduction to Citibank Mexico by the New York office's Mexico division, Mrs. Salinas (Patricia Paulina Rios Castañon de Salinas) was introduced as Patricia Rios.
11 Details of the case have been drawn mostly from the substantive reports provided by the Liquidator under Order of the Supreme Court of Grenada. Further information is available at: https://www.pwc.com/ca/en/services/insolvency-assignments/fibg.html
12 Roughly 6 million Eastern Caribbean (EC) dollars.

References

Basel Committee on Banking Supervision, 2004. Bank failures in mature economies. *Working paper no. 13*. [Online]. Available at: http://www.bis.org/publ/bcbs_wp13.pdf [accessed 25 September 2010].
Bench, R., 1991. Power must be ceded to the central banks [Interview] (2 August 1991).
GAO/ISO, 1998. Report to the Ranking Minority Member, Permanent Subcommittee on Investigations, Committee on Governmental Affairs, US Senate. Private banking: Raul Salinas, Citibank and alleged money laundering. Washington, DC: US General Accounting Office.
Herring, J., 2005. BCCI & Barings: Bank resolutions complicated by fraud and global corporate structure. In: D. Evanoff & G. Kaufman, eds. *Systemic financial crises: Resolving large bank insolvencies*. London: World Scientific Publishing Co. Pte. Ltd, pp. 321–345.
Kerry, J. & Brown, H., 1992. *A report to the Committee on Foreign Relations*. Washington, DC: United States Senate.
Mitchell, A.et al., 2001. *The BCCI cover up*. Essex: Association for Accountancy & Business Affairs.

8 More joint pains

Prologue

I resume with three remaining cases, each fascinating in their own right. From Riggs Bank, the dearly departed doyenne of Washington DC banking we move on to unravel the malevolent Machiavellian moves of Bernie Madoff. After that, we unwittingly end up doing hard LIBOR alongside a lamazing public in the aftermath of the global financial crisis.

Riggs National Corporation and Riggs Bank (USA) 2004[1]

Headquartered in Washington DC and incorporated in Delaware, Riggs National Corporation (RNC) was a publicly traded bank holding company, which, at the close of 2003, had an asset base of $6.3 billion. The majority of these assets were held by wholly owned subsidiary, Riggs Bank (Riggs).

Riggs was solid in both the retail and corporate side of banking. The income stream from its wealth-management services was drawn from clientele across the domestic and international private banking division. The Riggs brand was also strong in investment services with several of its subsidiaries involved in this line of business. Although functioning primarily in the United States, Riggs operations extended to Europe specifically to major cities such as London and Berlin, respectively, and the offshore domains of the Bahamas and Jersey. Competitively, this external reach no doubt allowed Riggs to conduct the same type of international banking activities offered by financial institutions located in Caribbean OFCs. Riggs' location in the heart of Washington and proximity to foreign embassies and missions created a prime opportunity for the bank to monopolise a special market niche. Thus, over time, Riggs' delivery of embassy banking solutions was key to establishing a reputation as the "Presidents' bank" or alternatively the "diplomats' bank", administering accounts for more than 95% of foreign embassies and missions in the metropolitan area. For Riggs, this niche represented high revenue yields, accounting for up to 20% of deposit revenues in the years leading up to its investigation by the US Senate. Its main deposit sources were found to originate from countries in the African continent and the Caribbean (44%), the Middle East (24%), and Latin America, Portugal and Spain (17%). Only two other banks came close to competing with Riggs at the time, namely Wachovia National Bank and Congressional Bank. In referring to an OCC assessment, the Senate Report noted that Riggs' embassy client base – albeit a relatively small 7% – included relationships in countries blacklisted by the FATF (US Senate, 2004, pp. 12–14).

In terms of leadership, the Board of Directors for Riggs would often include at least one of the Allbritton family members: patriarch Joseph Allbritton, wife Barbara Allbritton or son Robert Allbritton. These family members also held the majority of shares in RNC. Additionally, the chairmanship of both entities was held by both father and son each for substantive periods. RNC and Riggs each operated a Board of Directors as well as an equal number of sub-committees including an Executive, Risk Management and Budget Committee, an Audit Committee and others focussing on core areas such as compensation, corporate governance and the companies' international operations.

This line-up of accountability groupings was boosted by the setting up of a Bank Secrecy Act and Compliance Committee, formed by each entity in response to problems identified by regulators in 2004. The objective here was to demonstrate the level of seriousness with which top management viewed the issues and its earnestness, no doubt, to resolve concerns around failure to monitor and coordinate corporate adherence to AML obligations. As it turned out, this was just a smokescreen to abate the OCC's concern at the time, but with no real commitment to change.

Riggs linked its due diligence strategy to the US State Department's conferral of the necessary diplomatic credentials on the country or individual representative. In short, the US government's approval was the institution's green-light for doing business with its foreign clients. It would later become evident that in addition to servicing the operational needs of the embassy or mission, the bank had also begun in some cases to service the personal financial needs of diplomatic personnel, their families, other government agencies, officials and individuals from the country of origin. Undisputable also was that accounts were being used for personal reasons by political leaders and their families and according to the report "in the same manner as private banking accounts" (US Senate, 2004, p. 13).

Riggs' top management was well aware of the importance of increased due diligence when it came to dealing with high-risk countries and foreign clients requiring private banking support. OCC regulations in place since the late 1980s and the Fed's 1997 guidance document for Sound Risk Management Practices Governing Private Banking Activities meant there was no excuse. Essential, simple elements such as establishing the client's source of funds, beneficial ownership and expected activity on the extended facilities were markedly absent in client documentation. Regulatory guidance also promoted the involvement of compliance officers or similar functions in deciding the extent to which certain KYC requirements could be waived. The absence of these basic elements while exposing Riggs to serious client risk mirrored the virtually permissive approach the company had adopted from square-one when dealing with its important clientele.

Even after opening an account there is still an obligation to employ the necessary systems which allow for proper monitoring and review of the account activity over time (including wires). Riggs' indifference meant there would have been an inadequate framework in place to ascertain suspicious activity, an important trigger for the involvement of law enforcement in the tracking down of potential criminals. It is no wonder then the OCC deemed Riggs' AML program "almost completely dysfunctional" (US Senate, 2004, p. 16).

Of course, the active solicitation and accommodation of high-risk clients from high-risk countries was not just part and parcel of Riggs' second-rate compliance regime, but more particular, emulated the lax governance culture spawned from the top! Why else would Riggs' officials believe they could overtly court the business of former Chilean leader Auguste Pinochet despite credible information in the public domain linking him to political murders, human rights abuses, drug trafficking and a host of other corrupt practices? Yet, despite this knowledge and much like their client-facing colleagues at Citibank some years before – who snuggled up to the politically exposed Raul Salinas – Riggs' relationship managers took their white gloved service to a new level with Pinochet. They conveniently altered account details to avoid any possible discovery of his substantial facilities that might have arisen through database sweeps. Relationship managers also supported the disguise of questionable assets and rendition of funds out of the reach of law enforcement authorities, even while knowing their client was under house-arrest and criminal proceeds pending. As a matter of fact, so in step with Pinochet's criminality were relationship managers that they went as far as permitting the use of Riggs own accounts as pass-throughs to blur transaction trails. But that was not all. Riggs' platinum service was exemplified when their reprobate first line of defence connived to provide their esteemed client with access to $2 million in cash from Chilean banks by delivering the equivalent in cashier's cheques to him while in Chile (US Senate, 2004, p. 2). Thus with the only objective to protect their client even while threatening its own – until then – apparently pristine reputation, the bank appeared cock-a-hoop in playing patronage, even if it meant resisting regulatory oversight of the accounts, overlooking numerous red flags most compliance officers would lose their job for failing to investigate; not to mention the bad press made worse by mounting legal actions instigated against Pinochet by stiffed countries at the time.

But how else were relationship managers expected to respond when faced with the contradictory roles of attracting business and simultaneously keeping an eye out for suspicious activity on the very accounts they worked hard to open? And on which their incentives were based at that? Surely duplicity was bound to emerge at some point and therefore it would have been better to delegate the monitoring element to parties not aligned to the sales process. This is where functions such as compliance and internal audit come in. Yet, although these offices were in place, they proved ineffective in addressing rampant AML breaches far less the bias of account managers (US Senate, 2004, p. 71).

The other key US Senate finding related to dealings involving representatives of the West African nation of Equatorial Guinea (EG). Over an eight-year period (from 1995), the bank was said to have opened up to sixty accounts and a dozen certificates of deposit for not only the country's government, but also numerous personal accounts for senior government officials along with their family members (US Senate, 2004, p. 37). Of note were the multiple facilities opened for the EG President himself along with his wife and children and the subsequent creation of offshore structures to conceal true ownership. In one instance, the bank accepted an amount of $13 million into the Pinochets' accounts, with "few questions asked" (US Senate, 2004, p. 37). Riggs also happily charged the EG government's oil revenues account with $35 million, ensuring the proceeds were beneficially distilled through opaque companies located offshore. A laissez-faire AML culture, alongside other internal control deficiencies made it easy for Pinochets' assigned account manager to tap into over $1 million in sovereign funds for his own benefit.

Knowing the outcome of having to let go its "premium" clients, the Board's decision to look the other way and downright obstinacy in not co-operating with its Regulator, while fiscally understandable (but above all, stupid), pointed to a kind of entitlement mentality the bank found difficult to shed, even in the face of a death blow to its reputation for conspiring with foreign politically exposed persons (PEPs).

But what of government oversight in this process and how might they have contributed to the problem? Truth be told, having "repeatedly and accurately" identified Riggs' weaknesses over at least a five-year period, the absence of regulatory enforcement was the missing link (US Senate, 2004, p. 72). In fact it was evident the OCC placed too much faith in the bank's Board and an espoused commitment to resolving the deficiencies. No doubt, the Board's word was trustworthy enough at the time to merit consistently positive OCC ratings, despite significant weaknesses noted throughout the inspections process. Still, five years is deference beyond measure. And if, institutionally, your mandate is ensuring industry compliance as part of a wider remit of safety and soundness, then passivity should never come into play. To boot, Riggs also fell under the radar of the Fed at the holding company level and also as a result of its international (foreign) business. With that, how much more enforcement power is required before the power to enforce is put into force? The US Senate report indicated a kind of professional capture promulgated unwittingly by embedding senior Examiners within the institutions for which they are responsible (US Senate, 2004, p. 86). Their ongoing engagement with the institution creates, over time – in this case 1998 through 2002 – an ideal situation in which independence could possibly be compromised through familiarity with flexibility, inchingly, becoming the norm (US Senate, 2004, p. 86). Thus, knowing full well the weight of his office, Riggs' Examiner-in-Charge (EIC) Mr. R. Ashley Lee, advised against enforcement action despite more than adequate evidence pointing to the contrary.

Additionally, by keeping material information pertaining to Pinochet, the PEP, under wraps, one-up reviews and important second opinions were deliberately impeded. Unfortunately, while a key advocate of monitoring systems for identifying and reporting suspicious activity, neither Regulator was adept at sniffing out interdicting behaviour amongst their own. For all that, there was no mistake about possible capture when, on his retirement, EIC Lee was offered and accepted the position of Executive Vice President and Chief Risk Officer with the very institution he watched over. But even this the OCC bungled, failing to prosecute on the grounds of the two-year moratorium prohibiting ex-agents from engaging with their former employer on matters which they dealt with directly or were substantially aware of just prior to moving on. Lee was therefore never challenged to remove himself from meetings involving discussion of Riggs' AML compliance issues. Neither did Lee see it professionally fit to adhere to the OCC's post-employment requirement to seek permission to attend said meetings. In fact, it may have been his familiarity with regulatory laxity which provided surplus comfort that nothing would become of his violation of the law despite a possible five-year prison term and a $50k fine per violation (US Senate, 2004, pp. 86–89).

Bernard L. Madoff and Bernard L. Madoff Investment Securities LLC (BMIS) 2008

On 11 December 2008, the SEC blew the whistle on the operations of the broker dealership and investment advisory operations administered by Bernie Madoff, when it filed an emergency action in New York's Southern District Court (Securities Exchange Commission, 2008).

The complaint charged that over an "indeterminate period of time" Madoff committed a number of fraudulent acts and that by his own admission to employees had been conducting a Ponzi scheme over the years he was in business. The complaint sought relief from the court to restrict Madoff from handling any remaining assets to which he had access as there was strong reason to believe he intended to distribute what was left to select investors, friends and family, thus creating an inequitable situation in regard to the other investors (Securities Exchange Commission, 2008).

In addition, therefore, the complaint also sought full control over monetary and other resources through the appointment of a receiver, full access to information and the prevention of the destruction of documents. Completing the SEC's formal action was the request for permanent injunction, disgorgement of ill-gotten gains and an exacting of full restitution by way of "pre-judgment interest and civil monetary penalties" against Madoff and the firms represented by him (Securities Exchange Commission, 2008, paras. 2–3).

Madoff pleaded guilty to a range of charges filed against him. These included securities fraud, money laundering, theft, embezzlement, perjury and making false filings with the SEC. In the wake of these allegations, supplemented by what he knew was glaring evidence, Madoff threw out the window any chance of a plea bargain, falling on his own sword and accepting full responsibility for his actions. His claim that the company's fraudulent foundation and activities were known only to him was consistent with one wishing to shield one's family from culpability. After all, both of Madoff's children along with his wife, brother and niece were employed at the firm in various senior level capacities. Unfortunately, the repercussions would be far-reaching. While brother Peter would be sentenced to ten years in prison, Madoff's sons Mark and Andrew lost their lives in the ensuing years with Mark committing suicide and Andrew succumbing to cancer.

Outside the formal charges, the US government also sought an additional $170 billion in forfeited assets from Madoff. In light of the long-term nature of the rip-off, this was felt to be the best estimate of the illicit proceeds thought to have flowed through the accounts.[2] However, this figure was challenged by Attorneys citing the carte blanche approach of investigators and their lack of distinction between licit and illicit funds.

Madoff's scam resonated globally, outdoing the "puny regional ambitions of Charles Ponzi [himself]" leaving a "zigzagged path of financial destruction" and establishing a "universal lesson" that "when money goes global, fraud does too" (Henriques, 2008, 2010). The scam echoed yet again in Madoff's use of IFCs and other global banking centres. In the First Interim Report provided to the Court, the Trustee responsible for liquidation proceedings, Irving H. Picard, uncovered a money trail spanning Caribbean IFCs, among them Bermuda, BVI, Cayman Islands and the Bahamas, as well and banking centres in the United Kingdom, Gibraltar, Ireland, France, Luxembourg, Switzerland and Spain (Picard, 2008). Speaking to the complexity involved in the asset forfeit and seizure processes both domestically and internationally, the report called attention to the intricate relationships which had to be unravelled, given the plethora of countries – and by extension – jurisdictional issues, funds and opaque corporate structures utilised to mar the money trail (Picard, 2008, pp. 27–28).

Madoff's rise was not necessarily of fairy tale trappings. The advisory firm he founded in 1960 was underwritten through earnings from two jobs he had held down. Assistance from a financially astute father-in-law allowed him to grow the firm whose client base did not extend beyond a small circle of friends and family.[3] Straddling both the buy and sell side of the securities market, BLMIS quoted bid and ask prices and, along the way, developed an innovative technology solution which enabled the firm to compete more effectively with the traders on the New York Stock Exchange trading floor. This technology allowed quotes to be generated efficiently and eventually became the fore-runner to the NASDAQ[4] system of operations of which Madoff became its first non-executive Chairman in 1990.[5] In the course of time he would earn a great deal of respect for philanthropy, serving on various charities and other boards over many years. In terms of the prominence of Madoff securities within the industry, the firm at one point was the largest market maker at the NASDAQ and in 2008 ranked amongst the tops firms of its kind on Wall Street.[6] According to the SEC's complaint, Madoff ran the company from a separate floor in the firm's New York offices and was often secretive and withholding whenever questions were raised about the company's activities. Moreover, he kept the firm's financial statements under lock and key (SEC Complaint, paras. 16–17).

In divulging additional details about his Ponzi scheme, Madoff confessed to hoodwinking clients from the early 1990s, although experts believed it to be closer to the firm's inception in the 1960s.[7] As it turned out, client monies were never really invested, but stowed in Madoff's business account at Chase Manhattan Bank. And in typical Ponzi style, any investment yields accruing to earlier depositors were shelled out from the principal received from new deposi-tors. Madoff admitted to engaging in false trading activities which were masked by foreign transfers and false SEC filings.[8] He told the Court his intention had always been to resume legitimate trading activity, but it proved "difficult and ultimately impossible to extricate myself and my clients from the scheme".[9] Pending liabilities had at the time reached the $50 billion mark. On the receiving end of the deception were numerous victims including individuals, charitable organisations, trust funds and hedge funds. When all was said and done, Madoff knew full well his caper would eventually be exposed.

Needless to say, the entire debacle raised questions on the efficacy of regulation and supervision by the oversight body, in this case the SEC. Why was the ruse not picked up for close to twenty years? As it turned out, questions were in fact raised about Madoff's securities on numerous occasions and over a lengthy period of time just prior to dis-closure at the public level. The SEC, upon conclusion of its investigation, exonerated its employees from inappropriate conduct with either Madoff, his family or staff, suggesting there was no untoward influence in the conduct of its examination or investigative work. This exculpation also included the fact that a former SEC senior official was romantically involved with Madoff's niece (Office of Inspector General, 2009).

The Office of Inspector General's (OIG's) real concern, however, was the SEC's fail-ure to act on plausible and detailed information presented to officials at least on eight occasions between 1992 – *just one year into the scam* based on the timeline provided by Madoff – and December 2008. The report noted that despite frequent notification from external sources:

> The SEC never properly examined or investigated Madoff's trading and never took the necessary, but basic, steps to determine if Madoff was operating a Ponzi scheme. (Office of Inspector General, 2009, p. 22)

This lethargic response may well have constituted a breach of public trust, particularly given the ultimate fallout on innocent investors.

LIBOR Rigging 2012[10]

A primary constraint of commercial banks is having the necessary liquidity available to meet daily needs. The other ongoing concern is to satisfy the broader regulatory requirement to hold cash or cash equivalents (easily convertible assets), in reserve. Unless carefully managed, the dynamism of cash inflows (deposits and loan repayments) and cash outflows (withdrawals and interest disbursements), may well impair liquidity. And the last thing a reputable financial institution would want is a prevailing view that it is somehow unable to repay funds on demand. Consequently, and partially to address this lurking shortfall, banks tend to borrow from each other on an overnight (short-term) and unsecured basis.

Globally, this interbank market spans the most creditworthy financial institutions which function across multiple currencies, business segments and jurisdictions. Anecdotally linked to the deal-making skills of Minos Zombanakis,[11] LIBOR is rooted deep within this system of interbank engagement. In 1969, the Greek-born banker was in charge of the London branch of Manufacture's Hanover (the forerunner to JP Morgan), when he was said to have craftily spread the risk involved in lending $80 million to an Iranian sovereign amongst a group of comrade financial institutions. The client's borrowing rate was set against the composite cost of taking on the risk perceived by each financial institution and the potential reward at the back end.

Although not intended as a gold standard at inception, LIBOR evolved as a natural reference point in an expanding Eurodollar market in the 1960s and onward (Schenk, 1998; McGuire, 2004). Fuelling this expansion, more or less, was the absence of regulatory restrictions such as deposit insurance and cash reserves which, in turn, meant that European banks could take advantage of a liquid position and on-lend their US funds at competitive prices (McConnell, 2013, pp. 61–62). Endemic to the expanding Eurodollar market were innovative financial products known as derivatives (swaps, options, futures, etc.), which required pricing at various short-term maturities. Thus, outside its reference rating utility for loan agreement terms, it also became possible for banks to structure derivative contracts in such a way as to virtually protect themselves from a negative payday (Hou and Skeie, 2014). LIBOR also developed into a means of assessing the extent to which institutional and other investments performed on a relative scale. In time, LIBOR-like benchmarks would become internalised within and across the world's major financial markets; and this, despite the ascendancy of the US LIBOR. The subjacent effect of multiple LIBORs was to have a common barometer by which market vibrancy on the whole could be analysed (Hou and Skeie, 2014).

This brings us square on to the circumstances enveloping the manipulation of the financial world's most critical benchmark, which unravelled in 2012. In refrain, the set of rates constituting LIBOR is based on the largest and soundest financial institutions' perceived cost of borrowing. These institutions – contributor banks as they were called – made up a specific currency panel and, by virtue of their market dominance, often overlapped multiple currencies. Each institution would supply its loan price in consideration of the longstanding, hypothetical question:

> At what rate could you borrow funds, were you to do so by asking for and then accepting interbank offers in a reasonable market size just prior to 11.00 a.m.?[12]

Various tenors or maturity periods were also factored into contributor banks' rate origination. The next step was to cauterise 25% of both the high and low contributions and use the remaining estimates to come with an average for each currency and their respective maturity periods (McConnell, 2013). This cauterisation process was executed by an independent entity which then made the final, fixed rates available to the global public by midday. The untested belief was that contributing banks would be unbiased in the representation of their true cost of funds; that proper judgement would be exercised and a true inference of their capacity for borrowing profitably, disclosed (Wheatley, 2012, p. 82). However, what actually went on behind the scenes told a different story. But, before we get there we need to understand the reality of capitalist business and how it is played out in that virtual, cosmic space, known as the financial market.

For traders to locate persons interested in their clients' business, they would need to scour the market. While not impossible, this is certainly not a wise course of action. The truth is that in the time taken up to personally match these kindred spirits, circumstances could materially change for traders, requiring a new strategy by previously interested parties. Put another way, time in such a context is not only money, but lots of money. Enter the inter-dealer broker, a key market player whose job it is to be in the know. As experts themselves, these "fast-talking middlemen, involved in every trade" as described by Vaughan and Finch (2017), could quickly bring together mutually interested counterparties for each other's benefit. In this way inter-dealer brokers were known to facilitate countess deals a day in the life of markets, between traders, and thus have tremendous insight regarding its workings (Vaughan and Finch, 2017). This is precisely the information source leveraged by bankers to come up with their own LIBOR setting rate, even though it was expected that they unilaterally derived their own price after due consideration of their risk tolerance levels vis. à vis. credit, financial and related concerns. Original intention aside, it was this very collaboration on which unsure, but still competitive bankers relied, and in which they sought a kind of solace having advanced knowledge of the direction the benchmark was likely heading. This way they could adjust their submissions in advance and make their esteemed institutions look good when the final rates were made publicly available, as was the custom. Wheatley (2012) notes the final rates disclosure as imaginably casting aspersions on the bank's credit worthiness. For example, high contributor rates (costs of borrowing) may indicate financial stress which, though giving a much-needed boost to the bottom-line through interest income, also signalled to the discerning investor or customer that liquidity may be a challenge and hence their funds may be at risk. With this in mind, an incentive was created for contributing banks to understate their submissions (Wheatley, 2012, p. 79).

Vaughan and Finch (2017) note this heavy reliance on broker knowledge as unwittingly elevating this group to uncontested influence in the market, so that although not having a formal role in the LIBOR-setting process, brokers were in actuality a cornerstone in the LIBOR architecture. More insightful investment bank traders figured out that their interest rate-dependent positions could be directly impacted by these intermediaries and so double tapped the apparently inconspicuous inter-dealer broker target by: (a) encouraging broker contacts to understate or, if necessary overstate their predictions when bank representatives made their inevitable calls; and (b) offsetting these agents' personal risk by offering a sizeable kickback for their "sacrifices". In the event of push-back by a specific broker, the negative incentive was to threaten to take one's business (of subterfuge) elsewhere. Thus, with apparently unfettered power to, in effect, shape LIBOR's outcomes, marauding bankers had found a sure-fire way "to tilt part of the planet's financial infrastructure" (Vaughan and Finch, 2017). And tilt it did, when, in the midst of the financial crisis, LIBOR appeared to remain consistently and strangely low even when other similar indices were trending consistently upward (Hou and Skeie, 2014).

The disparity, when combined with a groundswell of gossip of LIBOR rigging, triggered investigations by both US and UK authorities. As it turned out, the US Commodity Futures Trading Commission (CFTC) revealed deep manipulation by agents of top banks in the years just prior to, during and immediately following the global financial crisis. Rather than submit rates which reflected the true cost of borrowing from each other, banks colluded to submit rates that would actually benefit traders' positions (McBride et al., 2016). That senior managers were either tacitly aware or themselves tangibly involved in the unsophisticated sophistry, spoke of a vibrant culture of dirty dealing among panel banks, including Barclays, Citibank, Deutsche Bank, Lloyds Banking Group, Rabobank and UBS.

All in the hundreds of millions of dollars price range it was all the CFTC could do to serve up humongous civil penalties to what were clearly trust-deficient institutions whose agents overlooked that the basis of their business was, ironically, trust. In settlement for charges of manipulation, attempted manipulation and falsifying LIBOR reports and other benchmark interest rates, Barclays agreed to pay $200 million (US CFTC, 2012a), Citigoup $175 million (US CFTC, 2016), Deutsche Bank $800 million (US CFTC, 2015), Lloyds Banking Group $105 million (US CFTC, 2014), Rabobank $475 million (US CFTC, 2013) and UBS $700 million (US CFTC, 2012b). Surely the unprecedented level of sanctions was also meant to deter high flying wannabees from future roguish behaviour. In fact, one of the human decimals found to be recurring in this sum of all "fares" was former master trader Tom Hayes. His was a set of skills which profited former employers UBS and Citigroup. In August 2015, Hayes was found guilty of market rigging and sentenced to 14 years in prison, later reduced to 11.

But what of the role of regulators – in this case, the BOE – and sitting politicians at the time of this debacle? Could it be that these parties had *absolutely* no knowledge of LIBOR's rampant manipulation by the City's top banks and their executives especially at a juncture of such globally visible and systemic turmoil in financial markets? Or were there – all things considered – deliberate machinations to influence the critical benchmark at the highest levels, political and regulatory, to counter even greater blowback from the crisis? The absence to date of a formal inquiry into regulatory involvement of LIBOR's fixing jacks up further, unresolved speculation over the vexing issue of abuse of power by institutional agents and the proverbial weak controls which continue to give life to its perpetuation. The apparent emergence of a recording,[13] obtained by the British Broadcasting Corporation, featuring a discussion between top bankers in relation to regulatory pressure to influence LIBOR, would do little to move law enforcement's needle in the direction of an investigation.

Notes

1 This information is drawn from the US Senate Report, which was released in conjunction with the Permanent Subcommittee on Investigation's Hearing involving Riggs Bank on 15 July 2004 (US Senate, 2004).
2 *Bernard L. Madoff ordered to forfeit over $170 billion; Government settles claims of Ruth Madoff against forfeited property.* FBI New York Field Office. US Attorney's Office. Southern District of New York. June 2009.
3 The Madoff files: Bernie's billions. *The Independent*, 29 January 2009.
4 National Association of Securities Dealers and Quotes.
5 Ex NASDAQ Chair arrested for securities fraud. *CNN Money*, 11 December 2008.
6 Investors remain amazed over Madoff's sudden downfall. *USA Today*, 15 December 2008.
7 Full details regarding Madoff's statement to the New York Southern District Court may be found at http://www.justice.gov/usao/nys/madoff/madoffhearing031209.pdf
8 Supra note 7.
9 Supra note 7.

10 The discussion of LIBOR and the events surrounding the scandal are based on how LIBOR was administered through the British Banking Association prior to its wholesale transition to the Intercontinental Exchange Benchmark Administration Ltd. on 31 January 2014. For further information, see: http://www.theice.com/iba.jhtml
11 A Greek banker spills on the early days of the LIBOR and his first deal with the Shah of Iran. *Reuters*, 8 August 2012.
12 See: http://www.bbatrent.com/explained/the-basics
13 LIBOR rate rigging: Chancellor urged to call inquiry into Bank of England allegations. *The Guardian*, 16 April 2017.

References

Henriques, D., 2010. Article on file with the author. The New York Times.
Henriques, D. B., 2008. Madoff fraud rippled around the world. [Online]. Available at: www.nytimes.com/2008/12/21/business/worldbusiness/21iht-madoff.4.18852346.html [accessed 26 September 2010].
Hou, D. & Skeie, D., 2014. *LIBOR: Origins, economics, crisis, scandal and reform.* New York: Federal Reserve Bank of New York.
McGuire, P., 2004. A shift in London's eurodollar market. *BIS Quarterly Review*, September, pp. 67–78.
McBride, J., Alessi, C., Sergei, M. A. & Sergei, M. A., 2016. Understanding the LIBOR scandal [Online]. Available at: https://www.cfr.org/backgrounder/understanding-libor-scandal [accessed 8 April 2018].
McConnell, P., 2013. Systemic operational risk: The LIBOR manipulation scandal. *Journal of Operational Risk*, 8(3), pp. 59–99.
Office of Inspector General, 2009. Report of investigation. New York: US Securities and Exchange Commission.
Picard, I., 2008. Trustee's first interim report. New York: Baker & Hostetler LLP.
Schenk, C., 1998. The origins of the Eurodollar market: 1955–1963. *Explorations in Economic History*, 35, pp. 221–238.
Securities Exchange Commission, 2008. SEC Complaint. New York: United States District Court Southern District of New York.
US CFTC, 2012a. CFTC Release #6289. Washington, DC: US Commodities Futures Trading Association.
US CFTC, 2012b. Release #6472. Washington, DC: US Commodities and Futures Trading Commission.
US CFTC, 2013. Release #6752. Washington, DC: US Commodities Futures and Trading Commission.
US CFTC, 2014. Release #6966. Washington, DC: US Commodities Futures and Trading Commission.
US CFTC, 2015. Release #7159. Washington, DC: US Commodities and Futures Trading Commission.
US CFTC, 2016. Release #7372. Washington, DC: US Commodities and Futures Trading Commission.
US Senate, 2004. Report by the Minority Staff, Permanent Subcommittee on Investigations, Committee on Governmental Affairs, US Senate. Money laundering and foreign corruption: Enforcement and effectiveness of the Patriot Act. Case study involving Riggs Bank. Washington, DC: US Senate.
Vaughan, L. & Finch, G., 2017. Libor scandal: The bankers who fixed the world's most important numbers [Online]. Available at: https://www.theguardian.com/business/2017/jan/18/libor-scandal-the-bankers-who-fixed-the-worlds-most-important-number [accessed 8 April 2017].
Wheatley, M., 2012. The Wheatley review of LIBOR: Final report. London: Her Majesty's Treasury.

9 Whodunit and other tales of the bored

Prologue

As this work draws to a close, I know we are all interested in finding out who the culprits were, although it should be somewhat evident at this stage; how they did what they did and got away with it, at least up to a certain point; and what motivated their actions in the first place. Also, where should final accountability lie, in the circumstances?

Uncovering the plot

An analysis of Table 9.1 indicates there are recurrent themes across several cases. For example lax AML procedures characterised the operations of BONY, Citibank and Riggs. Each entity had compliance mechanisms in place as prescribed by international standards and certainly by Bank Secrecy Act requirements. However, there was a failure on the part of these entities represented by their human agents, to *follow* protocols. BONY, in particular, was required to report the suspicious transactions observed to be flowing out of Russia in light of the elevated volume of transactions and the high-risk country from which they originated. Citi's failure was rooted in its apparent lack of knowledge about its client's monetary source(s), particularly since that client Augusto Pinochet, by virtue of his political function as leader of a nation and questionable involvement in human rights abuses, fell into a high-risk category. Riggs, too, failed to secure sufficient knowledge of its customer. Its inability to produce complete customer files covering basic information such as the clients' background and source of wealth was a demonstrated violation of its own rules. While violating internal protocols is not illegal, it does speak to the institution's attitude towards order and a potential to be laissez-faire with procedures. FATF Recs. 5–6 speak of the requirement to conduct due diligence such that a financial institution is comfortable with the potential client's bona fides, especially where they fall into PEP category. By failing to adhere to these protocols, there was no telling who the client truly was, which means the institution ran the risk of infiltration by criminal elements.

BONY's, Citi's and Riggs' failure to abide by internal protocols was compounded by *inadequate oversight* by management of these entities. Needless to say, lack of effective oversight is a phenomenon which can be reflected all the way up the line as far as the Board, spilling into and creating a lax culture or attitude towards risk management. In these cases, risk mitigation does not appear to have been taken seriously even at the level of the Board. For example, while Riggs had implemented governance mechanisms in the form of several management committees which were said to have met regularly, this did

Table 9.1 Analysis of money laundering/fraud cases vs. Merton's modes of adaptation

Name of money laundering/ fraud case	Category codes										Merton's modes of adaptation		
	Employee collusion with client	Regulatory collusion with bank	Independent action by employee	Independent action by client	Institutional deviance	Lack of regulatory oversight	Lack of management oversight	Risk taking culture	Lax AML procedures	Failure to follow procedures	Goals	Means	Behaviour
BCCI	Y	N	N	N	Y	Y	N/A	Y	N/A	N/A	Y	N	Innovation
BONY	Y	N	Y	N	N	N	Y	Y	Y	Y	Y	Y	Conformity
Citibank	Y	N	N	N	Y	N	Y	Y	Y	Y	Y	N	Innovation
FIBG	N	Y	N	N	Y	Y	N/A	Y	N/A	N/A	Y	N	Innovation
RIGGS	Y	Y	N	N	Y	Y	N/A	Y	Y	Y	Y	N	Innovation
Madoff/BMIS	N	N	Y	N	Y	Y	N/A	Y	N/A	N/A	Y	N	Innovation
LIBOR	N/A	Y	Y	N/A	Y	Y	Y	Y	N/A	Y	Y	N	Innovation
Frequency Y	4	3	3	0	6	5	3	7	3	4	7	1	
Frequency N	2	4	4	6	1	2	0	0	0	0	0	6	
N/A	1	0	0	1	0	0	4	0	4	3	0	0	

not seem to make any difference to the entity's failings. The implication here is that oversight committees were either unaware of what their responsibilities were or, simply unproductive in doing their job. It could also mean the set up was merely a smokescreen to convey an impression of governance in order to keep regulators at bay. The appearance of complicit behaviour between Pinochet and the bank certainly conveys this specific notion. Findings suggested, for example, that the active pursuit, solicitation and concealment of accounts of questionable clients were all undertaken with the express knowledge of Riggs top management. By virtue of their own professional conduct (or lack of), this leadership group set the tone of client engagement and by default institutionalised deviant behaviour as an acceptable mode and hence, value, in the organisation.

With BONY, on the other hand, while there was definitely collusion with the client (the manager's husband), this appeared to have been limited to the manager responsible for the accounts, although that person did, in fact, hold a senior level role. This, therefore, may have been an issue of weak supervision of staff. This also appeared to be the case with Citibank.

In the absence of tangible evidence, *regulatory malaise* in enforcing accountability measures against Riggs could have been related to its prominence in the industry given its worthy clientele. It may also have been a *misplaced confidence* in senior management to correct the noted deficiencies. Other reasons for the excess flexibility afforded Riggs by the OCC will never be known. That said, the other sticking point not to be overlooked was the violation of federal law by the EIC in deciding to transition to a senior level role within the firm he supervised during what was supposed to be sort of a cooling-off period to avoid any semblance of a conflict of interest. Not enforcing this rule, clearly aimed at maintaining an important perception of transparency, only made OCC laxity look worse. It certainly makes you wonder if the EIC did all to maintain his independence throughout the examination process or if he leveraged his positional power to broker a deal for the senior level role he ultimately obtained.

The plot thickens

Let us turn now to the other cases, which amongst them also carry recurring themes. In the case of FIBG it is clear this entity was never interested in building a reputation but, rather, in the short-term gain of attracting easy money to fulfil its malevolent intentions. The bank was constructed on the premise of fraud and took full advantage of a small island nation's zeal for foreign capital, unfamiliarity with the vagaries of offshore finance and, at the time, lax regulatory standards. This aside, the entity still fell far, far short of the premise of evil on which BCCI was configured. BCCI's business was concocted on a systemic scale, involving the complicit behaviour of governments, business and political elites, supra-national espionage agencies, organised crime syndicates, terrorists and a possible litany of other collusive human and institutional agents.

In our assessment, BCCI and FIBG in particular are un-rated in some areas in light of these entities' established *foundation* of supreme corporate deception. In short, it was never either's intention to conform to the socially accepted standards established by the institutional collective: AML policies, procedures and control systems; effective management oversight (except, of course, to sanction deviant behaviour) and the like.

Both the FIBG and Madoff cases are similar in so far as they involved their principals' diverting investor funds for personal use and making interest payments on earlier investments with incoming funds. The ruse evoked in investors a level of comfort that their money was being put to good use and for their benefit. To be therefore delighted to roll over their funds upon maturity went without saying. Of course, they were likely oblivious to the fact that their decision to reinvest actually exacerbated the rip-off. Ultimately, in order to make peaceful use of the proceeds of this crime, Madoff's optimal action would have been to create a safe cyber distance between the funds' legitimate derivation and their eventual, criminal use.

The distinction in these two cases, however, appears to lie in the premise; for whereas FIBG was set up to defraud at the outset, the Madoff calamity – by the principal's own admission – began in the early 1990s. Thus, with his company BMIS in existence from the 1960s, we are left to believe (uneasy though it is) that, in the intervening 31 years, the business was operating in a manner consistent with industry standards and expectations. Probably not; but assuming it was, what could have accounted for this paradigm shift from good business conduct to a level of financial deviance unmatched thus far in history and, furthermore, by an individual of such apparent probity and enviable professional status? According to Madoff, there was every intention of resuming proper business dealings but the entire scenario got out of hand and subsequently became unmanageable.[1] But why stray from the collective norm in the first place? Or better yet, was the collective norm (of the securities industry) in fact an embedded hot bed of deviance yet to be unearthed?

According to a 5 March 2009 *Financial Times* report by Joanna Chung and Brooke Masters, virtually every week following the uncovering of the Madoff and Stanford scams, there was at least one new Ponzi scheme charge from the Department of Justice, SEC or the CFTC vis:

> In the past month alone, at least 12 complaints involving "Ponzis" or other similar scams, have been filed, including a CFTC complaint filed on Thursday alleging that a Texas man bilked 250 investors of $10.9m … the sheer number of schemes under investigation and their geographic spread – literally from Alaska to Florida and with a whole raft of overseas investors as well – dwarf what was uncovered in any recent recession.

The evil alternative

To help us comprehend why the entities under study engaged in corporate misbehaviour, albeit in various ways, and why certain of them chose to endanger their reputation and ongoing viability as business institutions, we need to reinsert at this juncture Merton's (1938) adaptive behaviour model. Of the modes of behaviour discussed in this book – namely, conformity, innovation, ritualism and rebellion – we would agree that neither entity *simultaneously* embraced the culturally acceptable goals of an organisation along with the *means* of achieving them. Even if they did so at the outset of operations, we must seek to identify potential reasons as to why the deviation occurred as in, for instance, the Madoff case. That said, what could be considered an organisation's goals and the culturally accepted means of achieving them?

Under capitalism, profit making (wealth accumulation) is deemed the ultimate and commonly accepted aim or goal of the firm. The means by which these goals are achieved are historical and evidentiary. For example, at the level of government facilitation, we note that in order for firms to function within their competitive space, they require access to the markets of their choice and focus. Appropriate laws and regulations must, therefore, be established to promote fair competition and rules of behaviour acceptable to the wider community. Financing opportunities should also be created to secure essential capital. In addition, the very important national educational framework must be constructed and implemented to enable firms to draw on the human resource base crucial to executing institutional goals. At the level of the firm itself, goals related to market share and financial aims such as projected increases in sales revenue, income, earnings per share or other shareholder enhancing measurements, all constitute potential and indeed acceptable goals of a firm operating in a broader industry of firms. Among the acceptable ways to attain goals are:

- efficient and effective operational, tactical and strategic engagement;
- erudite financial management;
- effective marketing and product development;
- customer service excellence;
- ongoing research and development efforts; and
- maximising prevailing opportunities as they emerge.

Undergirding all the above is the even more noteworthy expectation that business firms will conduct themselves out of an ethical centre, follow the law pertaining to their operations where in existence and generally act in ways that promotes trust, especially where the handling of public funds is concerned. Where a firm chooses to operate outside these collective expectations, it immediately sets itself up for non-conformist conduct. And because of the aberrant features of such conduct, the perpetrating entity makes itself conspicuous to the economic collective.

In each of the cases analysed in this book, there were material variations from the means, while institutional prosperity (a culturally accepted goal) remained of high value. The pressures on these organisations to deliver successful outcomes lead to Merton's innovative mode of adaptation. In the cases reviewed, the conduct of actors fell under the radar of what was acceptable. The actions included:

- turning a blind corporate eye to suspicious financial activity;
- embracing deposits from questionable sources without proper due diligence;
- deliberately seeking out the custom of corrupt politicians;
- manipulating systems to conceal the true (illegal) nature of funds;
- engaging in collusive conduct;
- tricking investors;
- lying to regulators; and
- myriad other nefarious actions

Arguably, these actions may be regarded as an inevitable response to the strain associated with attempting to satiate, an otherwise insatiable institutional appetite for capital.

This brings to the fore again, the "receding goals" concept espoused by Durkheim (1951). Essentially, he suggests that in the business contest one's aim is at a perpetually moving target and, as such, it is likely never to be hit. By application, a financial institution may come within striking distance of its profit or other prescribed goal. It may even meet the goal. But inherent in achieving the goal is the seed or desire for another, higher goal. Thus the cycle of accumulation is triggered again. The competition gets fiercer; greater risks are undertaken, as previous highly valued self-regulatory restraints are now thrown off to be able to access greater possibilities. New innovations are imagined, complete with novel language and impressive discourse. This is all geared towards luring wealth from nervous, yet financially ambitious client hands, to the colossal bosoms of Madoffic-like "experts". In such an intense atmospheric setting, regulatory breakdowns are inevitable and, indeed, may be a relief! Only then may the collective be able to come to terms with the resident evil and so undertake the pursuit of a new and better way.

From Table 9.1 it is evident that where the innovative mode of adaptation is present, institutional means did not always retain their important governance role. It would seem that what constitutes the collective order which Durkheim (1951) speaks of is not easily applied within the four walls of an institution. Unless, of course, there is a conjoining of expectations with actions. Truth is, in order for the collective order to have a chance at regulating a firm's behaviour, a permeating tone mirroring expectations must be exalted by a person or group of persons with the legitimacy to establish intended standards. Naturally, deviating tendencies would be culturally abhorred. Such a role falls squarely on the shoulders of leadership. An engaged board of directors, supported by a strong executive team and led by an ethical CEO, is the best starting point. What is expected by these groups must be lived by them in order for the correct regulative force to emerge and take root within the institution. Only then could the notion of institutional means be even considered as the plumb-line which will superfluously expose unacceptable behaviour.

Double agents

This is a good segue to the function of agents in executing the expectations of their principals and helps us to look at the agency theory from another perspective. The fact that an institution, acting through its agents can either exploit, compromise or ignore standards and, instead, embrace illegal means to achieve goals, would indicate that perhaps conforming behaviour over the long term is subjugated to the decisions and/or actions taken by these agents. How else could standards suddenly lose their value as the compass of order and somehow become a stumbling block in the race for capital accumulation rather than a reference point for good choices? Standards are valuable, yes, but are merely a benchmark or expectation. They have no soul. An agent's right to choose is always able to trounce standards. Yet, paradoxically, standards are meant to influence agents into defaulting to them as the better and preferred alternative in the face of choices or impending decisions, if only for the *sake* of order.

This is why what I refer to as "the Judas wild card" will inevitably emerge from time to time. It is a narcissistic defiance of accepted protocols by an agent (or agents) making choices on the basis of personal interest at the expense of the collective advantage. Such a position is evident across the majority of the cases and was particularly deadly to:

a   BCCI which, though globally liquidated decades ago, remains an issue in some law courts across the world;
b   Riggs, which was sold off for a cost well below its book value;
c   FIBG, whose license was revoked, but left its small island host embarrassed in matters pertaining to offshore finance; and
d   Madoff/BMIS whose assets were garnished/sold off by the state and an all-points bulletin placed on his remaining global wealth.

These entities' premier and/or senior leader(s) condoned unethical behaviour by themselves engaging in illicit corporate practices. By creating the internal environment for deviance by the tone they set and the behaviour exhibited, line staff would naturally be at serious risk of non-conformist behaviour as well.

The matter of regulatory failure contributing to the breakdown in the social order is another element which is captivating to say the least. It is one which also forces us to consider an even broader application of agent-principal intercourse. In the Riggs Bank matter, the optics suggest some kind of collusion between the federal Examiner and Riggs senior management. As a representative of government, the former was obligated to act for the good of the principal (public). Instead, he appeared to have leveraged the power inherent in his agency role, opting to put himself first. In the matter of FIBG, anecdotal information also suggested an unhealthy liaison between FIBG principals and oversight authorities. In such circumstances, the only viable outcome is the financial harm to unsuspecting, honest depositors and equally trusting members of the public.

In the Madoff matter, however, we note a materially different occurrence, but with the same disastrous outcome. While there was a proven absence of collusion with company officials, there was a tangible presence of *inaction* and *costly reticence* to act on the part of the SEC. Outside the investigative bungling, there was the issue of the personal, professional power and status Madoff enjoyed, such that SEC officials, inexperienced though they were, believed him incapable of acting with such calculated deviance (Office of Inspector General, 2009). What bears this out is the tenor of the several complaints made to regulators. For example, the first grumbling alleged that an unregistered company (Madoff's) was actually promoting 100% safe investments. Really? No risk whatsoever? Ever? Surely in the absence of facts, the gut speaks; which is perhaps why the SEC was said to have had suspicions the said company was operating a Ponzi scheme. It also admitted learning in the course of its investigation that all of the investments were not only placed entirely through Madoff himself, but also that consistent returns were claimed to have been achieved for numerous years without a single loss (Office of Inspector General, 2009). This complaint, the first of eight, should have been enough to call in the cavalry. After all, was it not the seed of a classic Ponzi? Yet, by OIG accounts there was neither corresponding response from the SEC nor, by implication, any attempt on the SEC's part to execute institutional responsibility to protect the public interest in general and that of depositors in particular. I argue that Blau's (1964) view on exchange and power was at work in the social exchange which took place between Madoff and the regulatory side of the securities industry.

While this should not be considered as the main reason for the regulatory failures in this case, it certainly can be regarded as a contributing factor vis: it was over several years that Madoff developed his enviable Wall Street reputation. His contribution to the development of the NASDAQ system; his chairmanship of the NASD and other prominent leadership roles; involvement in charitable and developmental organisations in addition to his apparently successful business operations, altogether accentuated the fact that over a concrete period, he had visibly given a lot to the growth and development of the industry. His was a celebrated name, made more prominent through connections to the political elite and other local and global power brokers. It is these very social exchanges which appeared to have given Madoff relational power over the young, inexperienced and poorly trained Examiners, resulting in elementary operational and investigative failings. It is the same relational power exercised over the mature, who could not fathom this man, of such repute, as a mere low life fraudster. What I am proposing here is that regulatory actors perhaps felt they owed Madoff for his good deeds (favours), particularly in relation to the business he dominated. A kind of regulatory capture, this may have been the constraint the powers that be had to work through before bringing themselves to enforcing legal action.

Gatekeeper role aside, regulators should not think themselves exempt from competitive strains. In the wake of the LIBOR rigging scandal, the gossip on Canary Wharf was the political pressure brought to bear on contributor banks to lowball the benchmark. To date, there has been no formal enquiry to determine whether or not this happened. Nonetheless, let us for discussion purposes assume it did.

As we have seen, a primary drawing card for doing business in a jurisdiction is the perception of stability. This feature is significant to market players, especially those in major global financial hubs. For a regulator, though, jurisdictional stability irrespective of geographic location takes on a different tone. I would assert that stability is to the regulator what profitability or prosperity is to business. Hence, in the event stability comes under threat due to competitive strains – as it did in the wake of the 2008 financial crisis – regulators are also faced with making certain choices. Under pressure, these choices may fall outside normative expectations of the broader collective. With no real regulation around LIBOR at the time, the apparent (and, I hasten to say, unproven) regulatory tampering with LIBOR would have fallen into the Merton (1938) adaptive mode of innovation. The broader society's acceptable means of fixing LIBOR was quite simply for contributing banks to be honest in its configuration. In terms of the regulator, it was not to be involved in its fixing at all.

Second line of defence

At the outset of this book, I described what I believed were the risk(s) facing IFCs doing business in the contemporary world of finance. At this juncture, I pause to bring to the fore the idea of compliance risk within the organisation even as I moot the question, where was the compliance function in all this? To help resolve this concern, we need go no further than the insight provided by the Basel Committee, vis:

> the risk of legal or regulatory sanctions, material financial loss, or loss to reputation a bank may suffer as a result of its failure to comply with laws, regulations, rules, related self-regulatory organization standards, and codes of conduct applicable to its banking activities.
>
> (Basel Committee on Banking Supervision, 2005)

Rounding off the equation intrinsic to this definition, in my opinion, is the veiled, yet critical, governance variable. In the simplest of terms, that poor risk management when combined with compliance failures, point to the weak governance or oversight dynamic within the company. It may also be proposed that compliance failures are, arguably, the outworking of issues with risk management and weak governance. The other correlation we can assert is the idea that heightened risk outcomes are likely in the face of compliance failures and weak governance. These interactions are visually portrayed in Figures 9.1–9.3.

Applied to the money laundering harm confronting financial institutions (a compliance risk), we note how these GRC^2 variables interacted across a number of the cases. In particular, BONY, Citibank and Riggs all had some form of AML policies and procedures in place, no doubt to inhibit the use of their respective conversion and transfer mechanisms as conduits for laundering money. Riggs appeared to back its efforts in this

Figure 9.1 GRC interaction – Risk outcome

Figure 9.2 GRC interaction – Quality of oversight

Figure 9.3 GRC interaction – Organisational dysfunction

regard with oversight committees, even if for showboating purposes. Accountability systems were also likely in place at BONY and Citi, given their international standing. No such claim of a compliance program can be made, certainly in the cases of the criminal corporations BCCI and FIBG. In the Madoff mire, compliance did not appear to matter given the deep rooted deceit upon which any program in place at the time may have been established in the first place.

Nonetheless, modern-day best practice specifically dictates an empowered second line of defence in the form of a compliance function. Ideally independent from the business, that is, from the front-line – or first line of defence – and with a direct reporting line to the Board or sub-committee thereof, compliance oversees the implementation of the broader compliance risk strategy and in so doing assumes an important control functionality. That said, depending on the business model in question, compliance may, in fact, be embedded within daily operations as a quality assurance check in an effort to address control weaknesses in short order, thus pre-empting their exposure by the third and last line of defence – the audit function. The blatant compliance failures at work in the noted firms suggest this philosophical perspective may have been far from the minds of individuals involved in the incidents at the time.

Compliance officer – agent triple X

Earlier, I highlighted the frailty of banking in view of its early formation on the premise of trust. I also spoke of how trust is subject to perception, whether intentionally or unintentionally shaped. In addition, I expressed the idea of the "intimacy" between the regulator and the jurisdiction they regulate. Of course this all occurs outside the bounds of the financial institution itself. However, there is an important linkage to be made between the work of governing actors *within* the institution and that of governing actors without. In other words frailty can be defended at both internal (micro) and external (macro) levels. Its common denominator is good governance practices. Its common outcome? A good jurisdictional reputation.

Good governance after all has a face. It looks like something. In the context of the financial services sector, good governance has to do, in part, with creating and maintaining an enabling environment for both business and the consumer alike. Such an environment is driven by public (government) policy which is then delivered through an appropriately configured legal, regulatory and supervisory framework. At the institutional level, good governance is mirrored, for example, in a financial company's adherence to regulatory restrictions with regard to concentrated lending, maintaining capital adequacy, promoting asset quality and robust know your customer principles.

The face of good governance is also reflected in the expectation of the broader collective (society). It is expected, for example, that financial services firms would make good on their promise to have depositors' funds available to them as contractually agreed; that clients would be treated fairly; that firms would act ethically despite competitive strains; and that managers would carry out their duties responsibly and with due care. Good governance is also exhibited in the quality of management's interface with its Board, shareholders and other key stakeholders.

It is within this domain of engagement that the work of the compliance officer, though executed in the milieu of the firm, carries macro consequences. What do I mean? By keeping the Board of Directors abreast of pending regulatory change, the compliance officer not only supports effective corporate planning, but also promotes ownership of the change at the highest level. This, in turn, enables a more fluid assimilation process within the business. In terms of checks and balances, these are required to ensure operational integrity. However, such protocols may only be configured against a policy setting which accurately reflects legal requirements, related guidelines or, in their absence, international best practice. In this regard, the compliance professional's role in policy development cannot be discounted. In fact, without a clear understanding of what new laws/guidelines mean for the firm's operations, their translation into guiding principles or policies may be off the mark, potentially affecting the entity's regulatory risk profile and skewing risk measurements at the macro level.

If ongoing training is the central medium for preparing staff for new regulatory realities, then monitoring and reporting have the added advantage of promoting accountability of action among employees. The outcome of monitoring is of significance to oversight bodies. Board interface is also necessary to convey the status of internal controls as it relates to primary concerns such as conflicts of interest, insider trading, market abuse, bribery, corruption, money laundering and fraud prevention, to name a few. Unmanaged, these elements can bring into question the organisation's reputation and credibility, unsettle its customers and potentially undermine profitability. Without doubt, Boards need to be aware of these kinds of risk.

As discussed in Chapter 4, the ultimate end of compliance is order. Achieving such a state within a financial institution transcends the firm itself in that it contains or restricts prospective harm to the society, given the systemic environment of banking. Outside the areas mentioned in this section, another means of accomplishing intended order is perhaps the most important one. This involves building, over time, an appropriate, enterprise-wide, culture of compliance; one which (among other things) values doing the right thing, following the rules while exercising the flexibility necessary from time to time (to avoid bureaucracy); and promotes the right attitudes indispensable to achieving this outcome. As noted elsewhere in this work, an institution's Board and top management are the best purveyors of expected institutional behaviour. The compliance function must work with these parties to assure these goals are attained.

Doing the right thing is accomplished out of an ethical, almost moral posture and is an expectation of the broader society. For compliance officers this "bridge of conscience" type of role is not inconsistent with the moral dimension professionals in general are deemed to bring to bear in the execution of their responsibilities (Sama and Shoaf, 2008).

The eclectic mix of these various functions makes for a master agent of formidable skill, trust and reliability. It is no wonder why in many jurisdictions compliance officers are held to a higher standard, reflected in personal legal liability for failing to do their job. Undoubtedly, this is influenced by the reality that the work of these professionals renders them important allies in financial sector governance.

But will the compliance function on its own be able to stem the tide of bank failures and other corporate misdeeds going forward? Of course not! The last thing this professional and similar officers need is a messianic complex. Based on the "receding goals" concept espoused by Durkheim (1951) and the thoughts of Merton (1938) in relation to the disjunction between goals and means, the compliance function will continue to be fleshed out in a capitalist system of risk-taking and wealth accumulation where shifting goal posts do not allow for satiation of desires but the igniting of new ones, just before the earlier aspirations are achieved. However, by proactively working with the Board and top management to influence organisational culture, backed by supporting controls and strong risk management, the work of the compliance officer would, over time, create added value to the organisation and the community it is meant to serve.

Notes

1 Full details regarding Madoff's statement to the New York Southern District Court may be found at: http://www.justice.gov/usao/nys/madoff/madoffhearing031209.pdf
2 Governance, risk management and compliance.

References

Basel Committee on Banking Supervision, 2005. *Compliance and the compliance function in banks.* Basel: Bank for International Settlements.

Blau, P., 1964. *Theory and exchange in social life.* New York: John Wiley and Sons Inc.

Durkheim, E., 1897. Reprinted 1951. *Suicide: A study of sociology.* 2nd ed. New York: The Free Press of Glencoe.

Merton, R. K., 1938. Social structure and anomie. *American Sociological Review*, 3, pp. 672–680.

Office of Inspector General, 2009. *Report of investigation.* New York: US Securities and Exchange Commission.

Sama, L. & Shoaf, V., 2008. Ethical leadership for the professions: Fostering a moral community. *Journal of Business Ethics*, 78(1), pp. 39–46.

10 Island risk exposure (IRIE) mitigation

Epilogue

"Irie" is a state of being. A conviction that everything is and will be okay despite what may be going on around you. Irie is a state of peace. The word was originally coined by the Rastafarian sect in Jamaica during the rise of this indigenous group in the 1930s. It is a term further brought to life in the Jamaican artistic culture, particularly in the home-grown reggae music genre pioneered and popularised by the legendary Bob Marley. Irie is now a familiar term to Caribbean island nations and is also a staple idiom among the Diaspora across North America and the United Kingdom.

I capitalise the IRIE nomenclature and apply it to the state of peace, above the global fray, which IFCs can attain despite the never-ending bombardment against their qualifications to function within the sacred offshore space. By placing these threats within a risk management framework and systematically working towards their mitigation at a trinary level – jurisdictional, institutional and personal – the governance of evil money may be disbursed across wider accountabilities thus standing a better chance of yielding good results. Consequently, Table 10.1 is my first shot at creating the IRIE Matrix. No doubt, it will require amendments from time to time even as more thought is applied to solving the areas of risk highlighted. Also, it is likely the mitigation actions noted are already in place, which means Caribbean IFCs are well ahead in their risk management efforts in the offshore domain and merely need to affirm themselves and consolidate. Conversely, the Matrix offers guidance in the absence of such efforts or where enhancements are needed.

What brought me here?

As to whether evil money is a real or perceived threat to IFCs is the question I considered in this book. I also explored whether compliance regimes, the key mitigating tool deployed by global policy-makers, were enough to address the issue. Such a focus I thought to be not only pertinent but also timely, given the intense focus accorded these centres in the last few decades.

In light of the interaction of politics (power), economics (livelihood) and sociology (personal impact) in crafting this work, it was superfluous to situate this endeavour in international political economy discourse. To boot, its proximity to the legal and psychological spheres made for an undeniable multidisciplinary approach to investigating the matter at hand.

Table 10.1 IRIE Mitigation Matrix

	Island compliance risk dynamics				Island compliance risk mitigation processes			
Risk name	**Risk description**	**Jurisdiction risk**	**ODDS**	**Mitigation measures**	**Residual risk**	**Monitoring systems**	**Freq.**	**Stewardship**
(1) Evil money risk.	The risk of IFC jurisdictions being used as vehicles to conceal and move illicit funds; or to finance terrorism and proliferation.	Political; Economic; Social.	High.	Implement deterrence mechanisms: (1) Develop legal and regulatory framework which absorbs FATF's 40 Recs.; (2) Actively prosecute perpetrators; (3) Promote non-cash instruments as viable commercial alternative.	Medium.	National risk assessments. Trend analysis reviews. Robust regulatory surveillance and supervision. Peer reviews.	As required.	Authorised government body/bodies.
(2) Reputational risk (Jurisdiction).	The direct hit to the integrity of IFCs on account of their negative portrayal by competing, external forces and jurisdictions' (internal) failure to enforce their laws on an even-handed basis.	Political; Economic; Social.	High.	Deploy three lines of defence model: (1) Threat impact assessment (operational level); (2) Threat control actions (tactical level); (3) Threat reduction measures (strategic level).	Medium.	Report to oversight ministry.	Annual.	Independent oversight entity.
(3) Reputational risk (Institution).	The direct hit to the integrity of a financial institution on account of stakeholder perception of inaccessibility to funds due to incursions by or institution's association with criminal elements.	Political; Economic; Social.	High.	(1) Ensure good governance practices in general; (2) Implement robust AML/CFT compliance regime; (3) Ensure AML/CFT awareness levels are high across the organisation; (4) Implement robust board reporting mechanism.	Medium.	Ongoing scanning of external environment at all media points. Institute client feedback portals enabling ongoing engagement between financial institution and client.	Ongoing.	Senior management.
(4) Intervention risk.	The risk of intrusion into island governance polities by industrial states due to espied weaknesses in these islands' legal/regulatory frameworks against evil money.	Political.	High.	Ensure strong jurisdictional oversight through: (1) robust vetting of market entrants; (2) systematic risk-based monitoring and supervision of constituents; (3) early warning signal identification and management.	Medium.	Report to oversight ministry.	Annual.	Independent oversight entity.
(5) Non-state actor risk.	The risk of intervention into island governance polities by international quasi-state agencies, intermediaries, MNCs, influential NGOs, and super-powerful individuals.	Political.	High.	(1) Develop a "forward engagement" strategy with non-state actors; (2) Factor ratings and other pertinent observations into governance processes ensuring they are given adequate attention in bringing about their resolution where possible.	Medium.	Report to oversight ministry.	Annual.	Foreign Affairs Ministry or similar.

(Continued)

Island compliance risk dynamics				Island compliance risk mitigation processes			
(6) Margin-alisation risk.	The risk of exclusion from the social, economic and political engagement of the global community of nations and access to the mutual benefits that are to be derived from said engagement.	Political; Economic; Social.	High.	Manage reputational risk at item (2) above.	Medium.	As required.	Foreign Affairs Ministry or similar.
(7) Regulatory laxity risk.	The failure of regulators to act expeditiously in implementing the necessary reforms and otherwise exercising their responsibility in the governance of evil money.	Political; Economic.	High.	Deploy an anticipatory governance model parallel to the customary reactive strategy often necessary to respond to public outcry.	Medium.	As required.	Regulatory board sub-committee.
(8) Bank supervisory risk.	The failure to execute effective monitoring and supervisory capabilities sufficient to proactively identify and solve emerging institutional or systemic issues.	Political; Economic; Social.	Medium.	(1) Deploy enhanced recruitment strategy, ensuring adequate staffing of agency; (2) Strengthen review process by ensuring only properly configured, competent examination teams are deployed; (3) Maintain impartiality when dealing with regulated entities regardless of institutional prominence or that of their leaders; (4) Encourage agency staff to avoid/disclose conflicts of interest; (5) Implement declaration of assets model for senior staff; (6) Follow through on anomalous activity and act swiftly when evidence points to wrongdoing; (7) Invest heavily in IT resources.	Low.	Annual.	Regulatory board sub-committee.
(9) Forum shopping risk.	The failure to create a robust regional regulatory environment which deters investor island hopping in pursuit of relaxed standards and cheaper regulatory costs.	Economic.	High.	(1) Empower regional representative bodies to establish minimum (tax) standards; (2) Promote and seek out bilateral agreements with like-minded jurisdictions; (3) Deploy information sharing mechanisms to allow for effective regional cross-checks at due diligence stage.	Low.	Ongoing.	Designated national oversight entity.

Peer review system to confirm consistency of implementation and best practice. Periodic review of effectiveness of regional alert systems.

Quality assurance testing by compliance type function. Internal/external audits. Periodic peer reviews.

Empower independent Board sub-committee of responsible regulatory body to oversee implementation of requirements.

Discussions with/updates by stakeholders.

	Island compliance risk dynamics			Island compliance risk mitigation processes			
(10) Cultural risk.	The risk of non-actualisation of IFC potential as a result of insularity, competitiveness and lack of trust bred within in a historical context of oppression.	Social.	High.	Low.	Review travel and other statistics at ports of entry/exit. Review island trading actions for compliance with prevailing treaty arrangements.	Annual.	Designated regional entity.
(11) Principal risk.	The risk of institutional deviance (sanctioned and propagated by the Board and/or top management) in the face of intense competition.	Economic; Social.	Medium.	Low.	At regulatory level: (1) Robust due diligence (pre-approval stage); (2) Ongoing monitoring and regulatory supervision (post-approval stage). At institutional level: (1) Implement non-executive Chairperson role; (2) Select and empower independent and non-executive directors in ratios higher than or matching executive directors.	Annual.	Jurisdiction's regulator.
(12) Operational risk.	The risk of loss resulting from inadequate or failed internal processes, people and systems or, from external events. (Adapted in part from Basel Committee.)	Economic; Social.	Medium.	Low.	(1) Ensure AML policies and procedures are clear and understood by all stakeholders; (2) Ensure risk screening and assessment procedures are effectively deployed at the front line; (3) Implement second line of defence tier (compliance/similar function) which oversees and tests compliance with policies and procedures; (4) Promote regime of regular staff training.	Quarterly.	Senior management.

(Continued)

	Island compliance risk dynamics			Island compliance risk mitigation processes			
(13) Agency risk.	The risk of independent (rogue) or collusive action by institutional agents *against* their principals.	Social.	High.	(1) Enforce rule of law in general; (2) Introduce/enforce anti-corruption legislation or similar; (3) Develop robust control environment within the organisation, e.g. separation of duties and delegated authority with adequate oversight; (4) Ensure transparent HR practices and policies governing promotion and advancement on merit are in place, underscored by fair disciplinary processes; (5) Implement competitive salaries and benefits framework; (6) Define clearly, risk tolerance levels within a broader culture which promotes behaviours consistent with organisational and societal values.	Medium.	Code of conduct/ethics sign off by incumbents. Supervisory engagement of charges. Monitoring of high risk front-line and senior staff. Effective performance appraisal process. Mark to market reviews of salaries and benefits.	Ongoing.	External consultant; Internal audit or similar.
(14) De-risking risk.	The curtailment or reduction in correspondent banking relationships with Caribbean/IFCs due to revised cost-benefit calibrations and the perceived long term viability of high risk market portfolios within an expanding risk universe.	Economic; Social.	High.	(1) Stratify IFC based financial institutions according to criteria appealing to correspondent banks (e.g. capital and asset strength, international standing, high compliance standards etc. (2) Route international transactions of indigenous IFC-based financial institutions through Central Bank or similar portal; (3) Determine extent to which financial technology option(s) may be engaged.	Medium.	Report to oversight entity.	Annual.	Designated oversight entity.

For example, the diffusion of global AML policies with the expectation that they are implemented, failing which sanctions may be applied across defaulting sovereign nations, speaks to the political nature of the issue. The fact that capital is at the heart of the debate with risk to emerging economies in the face of its sudden outward transfer, not to mention the risk of infestation of markets by illicit capital itself, all reflect the economics dialectic underpinning the discussion. International standards would be unable to reach their domestic target unless, of course, they are neatly plaited into the braids of local laws and regulations. And this is how independent legal frameworks are impacted. In addition, because it is people – agents – who, ultimately, are required to exercise certain behaviours, or motivations towards certain behaviours to assure compliance, the point is made clear that there is also a psychological character to the debate. In the final analysis, these branches are all part of a larger social tree, whose roots go deep down for purposes of continued growth, sustenance and maintenance of a broader collective order.

In terms of my analytical framework, functional theory was my baseline and allowed for the integration of the views of Durkheim (1951), Merton (1938) and Blau (1964). That said, being hinged to an environment in which rules must be applied on a daily basis, I cultivated the view that rather than a stringent approach, sufficient elasticity should be built into regulatory governance processes to account for and deal with system failures, negative bureaucratic influences, abuse of rights and the like. These elements I believe potentially hinder social flow as it relates to problem solving and the identification of better ways of doing things.

I designed this work against the belief that just one means of information gathering would be insufficient if I wanted a fuller understanding of what I was dealing with. Helpful, therefore, was a varied approach to gathering information. What also served me in good stead was maintaining eyeshot of additional considerations. For example, unlocking the source of tensions between onshore and offshore was a question I found intriguing. Also, with the idea of money laundering hailed in prevailing discourse as a challenge to states, it made me wonder if, indeed, the threat was exclusive to the offshore space. So, what constituted money laundering, what were its precipitating factors and association with other deviant activities such as organised crime and corruption, were of tremendous concern to me. The other attention-grabbing issue was what appeared to be a risk-taking culture amongst financial institutions and by extension their agents. What was it about capitalism itself that appeared to incite risk-taking even when the legal consequences were clear? Also, how did contemporary state acquiescence to external derived dictates square with traditional state sovereignty nodes and the requirements to maintain age old respect for client privacy? Lastly, I looked to the jurisdiction's gate-keeper – the regulators – to understand what their work entailed; what made them tick, that is, their underlying motivation for doing their job and what was expected of constituents.

Evil money risk: governing the threat

Prevailing discourse suggests – sometimes overtly, other times subtly – that money laundering is relatively easy to engage, if not rampant in the Caribbean IFC, when it clearly is not. The concealment process endemic to the laundering of funds is such that illicit monies could have been laundered well before entering offshore space. The IFC is, by and large, a critical player in the architecture of global finance. Its systems can be co-opted by criminal elements to support their activities, but is this not true of all locations which house or facilitate the movement of capital? Financial globalisation carries within its traits the tendency to do both good and bad, as it is with most areas of life. Education may be both applied to the cause of human development and, at the same time, employed as a tool of creativity aimed at unearthing new forms of crime.

Financial globalisation is that phenomenon which has catapulted small island jurisdictions into the limelight of borderless money. As criminal networks and organisations also have access to the potential inherent in the global financial system, they are also able to access, dole out, exchange, market and otherwise make capital available to would-be purchasers. Indeed, criminals will leverage the vastness of the financial markets and their high-tech transfer mechanisms simply because it provides them with just the camouflage needed for concealment and the handling of ill-gotten gain. To this end, there can be no discounting controls as being essential for human interaction.

However, the controls here are not simply based on operational inputs residing in the risk management framework of an organisation. Rather, they are based on a socio-legal interface which stipulates, shapes and enforces modes of behaviour, the chief aim of which is stability or order of a collective, the collective being the broader grouping (e.g. nation) or sub-grouping (e.g. institution, school, family, team), as the case may be.

As major players in the global capital league, IFCs are exposed to possible incursions of evil money particularly at the layering stage; that money laundering phase where financial transfer mechanisms are engaged to create an important distance between the original criminal derivation of funds and their intended subsequent use. It was mooted by the court-appointed trustee in the Madoff case that fraudulent proceeds had been tracked to certain IFCs. However, a noticeable fact is that onshore nations such as the United Kingdom, France and Spain as well as other European jurisdictions, including Switzerland, Ireland, Luxembourg and Gibraltar, were also identified as connected to the fraud. In short, that investor funds had been laundered in these jurisdiction as well. Furthermore, the US State Department's INCSRs, while identifying the IFCs of Bahamas and the Cayman Islands as jurisdictions of primary concern for money laundering, also specified all of the OECD countries and, indeed, the larger industrial nations as of primary concern. The notion of money laundering being exclusive to Caribbean IFCs is absurd to say the least.

Relieving congestion

Capital accumulation is at the nexus of onshore and offshore rivalry. It is a certainty not unlike that which exists amongst competitors. Essentially, one party is of the view it has the right to do all in its power to maximise opportunities for its people in light of the apparent lack of other utilitarian resources to do so. This concept must certainly be true for all countries in the world. The other faction's perspective is that the quest for capital should not come at the expense of the acquisition of illicit funds whose original source resulted in some measure of social dislocation or pain to an individual or people group. Restitution must be made to disparaged parties such that the system is regarded as fair and just. Thus, asset seizure and recovery must be deemed primary features in any compliance regime.

In addition, all efforts should be made to discourage this type of capital accretion through, first and foremost, political will. Not only must an unequivocal message be sent concerning an IFC's stance against criminal money as noted by the foreign consulate (and this despite the region's yearning for capital), but also the appropriate *behaviours* should be modelled by leaders in terms of an overt position against corruption and the establishment of a personal covenant to act in the interest of the public, as its agent. Thus the tendency to accept bribes, kickbacks, deliberate engagement in conflicts of interest and the myriad types of fraud typical of compromised governments, although likely to still emerge, are at least circumvented – at the outset – by one's internal motivation or posture, to act in a manner that is not detrimental to the reputation of the country. In short, apart from regulatory forces external to the individual, there needs be a concurrent self-regulatory mooring which governs individual actions, choices and decisions. To be successful, that kind of bearing must be supported by a legal dynamic which demands transparency and accountability of actors, through sanctions. Such penalties must be seen to be enforced if regulatory legitimacy is to be maintained (Tyler 2006).

What is not articulated though is the increasingly large slice of capital, being carved off by IFCs from the previously delectable fiscal pie enjoyed by onshore nations. The fact that IFCs can continue to appeal to prominent institutional and personal investors would suggest there is a prevailing interest in what IFCs have to offer global business, despite the hits to their reputation through blacklisting and media derision. That said, the long-lived perception fed by folklore and artistic licence will continue to have its impact. In that regard, IFCs should dig in for the long haul while embracing externally imposed reform measures. Their image of locations of intrigue, mystique, concealment and the object of fable remains so dominant in the psyche of onshore nations that these historical pictures continue to resonate, thereby shaping popular belief. This often leads to unfair and often inaccurate judgements. It is acknowledged that weak regulation, inadequate laws and monitoring and supervision in the past had characterised certain jurisdictions of the Caribbean. Nevertheless, it is evident that negative conclusions are still being formed despite these locales' continuing acceptance and adherence to international money laundering and other standards through exponential legal and regulatory reform and improved monitoring and supervision. These historical pictures seem to be randomly stored in the memory of certain onshore states and at an opportune time accessed, regurgitated and manipulated by dominant news vehicles, entertainment and other casual yet potent forms of avenues such as popular movie culture spurred by the Hollywood dynamic. For the IFC, therefore, the battle is not so much about offshore finance as an alternative foreign exchange earnings stream as it is about the geographical locations from which these services are delivered. Remember similar services are delivered by major capitols of the world and also certain states on the US mainland. In addition, therefore, to exceeding and not merely meeting international expectations, media strategies must be developed to help re-script the region's persona as wild, untameable and in need of external regulation to control behaviour. This is not something to be left to external powers. Rather, there must be a deliberate, systematic effort on the part of national leaders to counter these negative images from all possible angles. The OECD's invitation to nations interested in refining an inclusive framework addressing base erosion and profit shifting may be a useful global forum where IFCs could begin and, indeed, continue to re-script their graven image. The highly ranked IFCs of Cayman and BVI have embraced this opportunity especially, and have earned their seat at the table.

Agency risk management

The cases analysed in this book do not necessarily include third parties acting independently to criminally outwit the financial institution. But those on which I settled have demonstrated the potential for money laundering and, indeed, the reality of it happening when aided and abetted from within the four walls of the organisation. As demonstrated, for subsequent laundering to occur, a predicate act of fraud or other omission either through individual action or at the institutional (governance) level itself, is likely to have taken place. In a nutshell, independent action by:

a   the employee; or
b   collusive action between the employee and client; or
c   collusion between the institution (board/top management) and client,

can combine to breach the protective shield enabled by AML regulatory rules and other internal compliance standards. Ultimately, institutional leaders and their representatives can take certain actions for various reasons and leverage their agency function to knowingly facilitate the abuse of institutional mechanisms such that money is laundered. Against this Judas factor, regulation that is extrinsic to the actors involved may prove insufficient to curb deviant internal tendencies. In that sense, a *purely* regulatory fix should not be expected to solve the problem of money laundering in the long run.

Regulatory processes can no longer be divorced from the broader civil society. This latter group (schools, churches, synagogues, mosques, charitable organisations and other non-governmental organisations) must be engaged to promote strong values of personal virtue and moral excellences as critical to a functioning society. In time, these elements will spill into organisations stimulating further the development of good business practices at both the level of the institution and the individual.

At the heart of the actions which spur agents to undermine their principals, is the notion of perception. Yes, that word yet again! It starts with an image of reality that may or may not be true. But its avatar is real enough to provoke a tangible response. In that sense, corporate and other institutional agents would be more attracted to crime where they perceived blockage or other hindrances to their goals. This is why it is important that opportunities to achieve and excel are made available and a suitable societal and/or global framework created for this to occur. Having said that, we should be under no illusions that this scaffolding would be sufficient to curtail deviance. As the driving force of capitalism, the relentless pursuit of wealth by firms and people alike has, in its wake, generated such intense competition as to spawn non-conformist modes of behaviours. These are manifested in various forms such as self-dealing, corruption, organised crime and other types of roguish conduct. Performance pressures on employees to deliver upwardly trending often unrealistic targets could well force them into the innovative mode of behaviour, thereby deviating from the collective expectation of how goals are to be achieved.

Even outside the independent, rogue behaviour of an agent is the reprehensible conduct of institutional leaders. Although diabolical, their quest to enhance shareholder value and maintain an upper hand over competing fellow institutions is not inconsistent with what we now recognise as Durkheim's (1951) "receding goal" paradigm. Based on this principle, there is never a point at which the craving for money ceases. The shifting of the goal post just when you are about to score is testimony to this notion. The tendency, therefore, to self-indulge is thus, unending, and strengthens my position that a purely regulatory fix will *not* solve the problem.

Jurisdictional risk management

Against the dominance of the financial globalisation hybrid and its insidious nature, how can the IFC survive? One thing is clear: there must be, at minimum, concerted effort to follow international requirements and other regulatory dictates as part of a responsibility to the global community of nations. Money laundering is, after all, a problem common to all jurisdictions. From a reputational perspective compliance is non-negotiable. While this is already the raison d'être adopted by IFC regulators, it is a stance which must continue to be promoted and cascaded down to the level of institutional agents that a higher level of service and commitment are critical to exercising supervisory and regulatory responsibilities. Strong jurisdictional oversight, rigorous due diligence both at the on-boarding stage of new market entrants and at the level of monitoring and supervision post-approval, are essential mitigating activities. The risk of intervention is also similarly deactivated when these measures are undertaken, as is regulatory laxity. Also, the notion of forum shopping, which sees potential investors knocking about for the best price and more relaxed standards, is also offset by effective regulatory insertions. In the end, the potential for marginalisation or exclusion from the global community of nations for non-compliance is offset.

In terms of the laxity component, if we isolate, for example, the Madoff case, we note how regulatory passivity led to severe financial loss for many persons. For a US regulator to demonstrate such a level of bungling in the contemporary setting of tight regulation is, to say the least, highly embarrassing. However, it emphasises my point that long-term regulatory compliance depends in part on the commitment of institutional and public agents to act in concert with the expectations of their principals. Note, too, that the authorities in Grenada also dropped the ball with regard to FIBG. However, it is now a part of the historical record as to which of these two jurisdictions suffered the most from their respective fall-outs. Although considered the most lethal investor fraud to date, costing investors countless billions, the US securities industry and economy was massive enough to absorb the regulatory failure and this in spite of the competing downturn in the economy. Not so with Grenada. The subsequent harm to that nation's reputation was a death knell to the industry, resulting in a political decision to literally shut down its offshore finance offerings for the ensuing years. Its impending resurrection has also been discouraged by external observers. What has unfolded here is the certainty that for regulation to be effective it must be supported by effective supervision. Mitigation actions for supervisory risk are also captured in the IRIE Matrix.

To say that co-operation amongst IFCs is crucial if risks pertaining to the governance of evil money are to be mitigated goes without saying. At the level of government, task forces need to be configured. These may be drawn from relevant and impacted ministries, the international business and academic community as well as civil society, So too, at the regional level, with a reporting line to the governments involved. As it relates to Caribbean IFCs in particular, regional integration entities such as Caricom may be engaged in this process. Of course, the erstwhile cultural risk born out of a colonial past and which has continued to hinder efforts at working together will also need a mitigation strategy. This is also included in the IRIE Matrix.

In the end, successful governance of the problem of evil money requires unprecedented levels of cross-border engagement and a greater degree of sovereign openness. The truth is that autonomous national actions would be wholly insufficient to counter the global challenge posed by money laundering. The problem far outstrips any one nation's capacity. For small IFCs in particular, sovereignty claims are difficult to hold fast in such an environment, that is, a context of virtual money markets and the seamless movement of capital, some of which will be illicit, across jurisdictions. What makes it harder are G20 empowered, non-state actors who are able to exert conformance pressures on presiding governments, often at risk to the jurisdictions they govern. Given these complexities, interaction with non-state actors is no longer avoidable. It is better to face up to this reality and embrace this change dynamic once and for all. This means factoring in observations, ratings and other potential negative comments, assertions, written or otherwise, with a view to systematically manage out their impact.

Fuerth (2009) speaks of the notion of *forward engagement* to address such transcendent matters impacting the state. Also promulgated is the idea of *anticipatory governance*, which brings to life in the present, those distant weak signals, with a view of putting in place measures to offset their pending impact. It is these kinds of engagements which I believe IFCs operating in the offshore space need to embrace and for which future research is necessary to affirm their applicability.

References

Blau, P., 1964. *Theory and exchange in social life*. New York: John Wiley and Sons Inc.

Durkheim, E., 1897. Reprinted 1951. *Suicide: A study of sociology*. 2nd ed. New York: The Free Press of Glencoe.

Fuerth, L., 2009. Foresight and anticipatory governance. *Foresight*, 2(4), pp. 14–32.

Merton, R. K., 1938. Social structure and anomie. *American Sociological Review*, 3, pp. 672–680.

Tyler, T., 2006. *Why people obey the law*. Princeton: Princeton University Press.

Index

accountability 60; collective 75–6; groupings 105; mechanism 96; systems 46
adaptation, modes of 55
Adoboli, Kweku 18
affirmative motivations 52
agency risk management 133–4
agent-principal intercourse 120
agent-principal theory 44
ALB *see* attorney at law/businessman (ALB)
Alldridge, P. 16
AML *see* anti-money laundering (AML)
analytical framework 131
Andreas, P. 17, 62
anomie 54–6; articulation of 76; Durkheim's theory of 54; theory of 54
anticipatory governance 136
Antigua 84
anti-money laundering (AML) 15, 16, 54, 64, 106; effectiveness of 79; physical proximity of 81; policies 16, 131; policy diffusion 65; procedures 114; purpose of 87; risk mitigation efforts 80
anti-money laundering policy diffusion 15
appropriate laws 117–18
arms smuggling 42
artistic licence 62–3
Ashley Lee, R. 107
asset management 9
attorney at law/businessman (ALB) 85
authenticity of financial statements 102–3
autonomy 3

Bahamas 62, 84
balance of power 30
bank failures 3
banking: business 52, 63; business of 2; elements of 34; original configuration of 12; outcomes 19; privacy 19
banking system 27, 34; criminals 15; environment of 124; open market operations in 11
Bank of Credit and Commerce International (BCCI) 1, 94–8, 116; banking business 94–5; failure of 97; financial history 96; illicit activity 97; lack of transparency 95
Bank of New York Mellon Corporation 1998 (BONY) 66
Bank Secrecy Act requirements 114
bank solvency 11–12
Barbados 85
Barbuda 84
base erosion and profit shifting (BEPS) mitigation 1
Basel Capital Accord of 1998 29
Basel Committee 121
Basel Core Principles of Banking Supervision 65
BCCI *see* Bank of Credit and Commerce International (BCCI)
behaviour: modes of 77; nepotistic 61; neutralising mode of 61; non-conforming 78
Bernard L. Madoff and Bernard L. Madoff Investment Securities LLC (BLMIS) 67, 107–9
bilateral diplomatic relations 4
biological needs in individuals 76
Blau, P. 61; exchange theory 62; views of 131
BLMIS *see* Bernard L. Madoff and Bernard L. Madoff Investment Securities LLC (BLMIS)
board interface 124
borderless money: acts of transnationals 27–30; legitimacy and legality 26–7; mirror formations 23–5; original planting 22; pressure points to OFCs 25–6; state autonomy and structural powers 26; statehood model 30; words and power 23
borrowers 11
Bowles, R. 44, 45
branding, significance of 52
Bravo jurisdiction 79
Bravo regulators 71–5
bribery of officials 97
bribes 44
Brown, Gordon 7
Buffet, Warren 66
bureaucracy 89

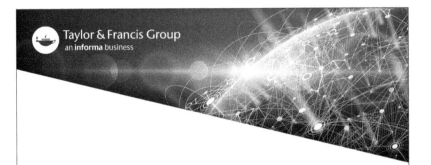